1

The Books of the New Testament

by Leighton Pullan

Contents

CHAPTER I THE NEW TESTAMENT

[Sidenote: Its Name.]

After the gift of the Holy Spirit Himself, we may justly reckon the New Testament as the most precious gift which our Lord Jesus Christ has given since His Ascension to those who believe on His Name. The word "testament," which is in Latin *testamentum*, corresponds with our word "covenant," and the phrase "New Testament" signifies the record of that new covenant in which God bound man to Himself by the death of His Son. The truth that this was a new covenant, distinct from the covenant which God made with Abraham, was taught by our Lord when He instituted the memorial of His death and said, "This cup is the new covenant in My Blood." We do not know precisely at what date the Christians began to call this record "the New Testament," but we do know that they used this name before A.D. 200.

[Sidenote: Its Language.]

In the time of our Lord the popular language of Palestine was Aramaic, a language which was akin to Hebrew and borrowed some words from Hebrew. Hebrew was known by learned people, but the language which the Son of God learned from His blessed mother and His foster father was Aramaic, and He spoke the Galilean dialect of that language. From a few words preserved in the Gospels, it is plain that the gospel was first preached in that tongue. In the 7th century after Christ, the Mohammedan conquerors, who spoke Arabic, began to supplant Aramaic by Arabic, and this is now the ordinary language of Palestine. As many people who spoke Aramaic were at one time heathen, both the Jews and the Christians adopted the habit of calling their language *Syriac* rather than Aramaic. The great centre of Christian Syriac literature was Edessa, and in the eastern part of the Roman Empire Syriac was the most important and most elegant language next to Greek. It is still used in the Church services of many Oriental Christians, and it is spoken in ordinary conversation in parts of North Mesopotamia and Kurdistan. Further west it is only spoken in a few villages of Anti-Libanus. In the course of this book it will be necessary to refer occasionally to the Aramaic language.

It is highly probable that some of the earliest Christian writings were in Aramaic, but all the books of the New Testament which we now possess are in Greek. The Greek language was known by many people in Palestine, and it was splendidly fitted to be the medium of God's revelation. It was widely known among the civilized nations of the time, and it is so rich and expressive that religious ideas are better conveyed in Greek than in almost any other tongue. Whereas it was essential that the gospel should be preached first in Aramaic, it was equally essential that it should be written in Greek, for the benefit of people who did not live in Palestine or who lived there as strangers.

[Sidenote: The Canon.]

The New Testament Scriptures consist of twenty-seven different books, written by nine different authors. Each book has some special characteristics corresponding with the mind of the writer and the circumstances under which it was written. Yet these books exhibit a manifest unity of purpose and doctrine. Under many differences of dialect and expression there is an internal unity such as we do not find in any secular literature, and this unity is due to inspiration. The whole collection of books is called the CANON of the New Testament. This Greek word "canon" originally meant a straight rod, such as could be used for ruling or measuring, then it was employed to signify a rule or law, and finally it meant a list or catalogue. As applied to the New Testament, the word "canon" means the books which fit the Church's rule of faith, and which themselves become a rule that measures forgeries and finds them wanting. The Church set these genuine books apart as having their origin in inspiration which came from God. They were all either written by the apostles or by men who were trained by the apostles, and thus they contain a unique account of the sayings of the Lord Jesus and the teaching of those who received their commission from Him. They are therefore documents to which the Church can refer, as a final court of appeal, in all questions of faith and conduct.

It was only by degrees that the Church realized the importance of placing all these twenty-seven books in the canon. This was finally done in the western Churches of Christendom in A.D. 382, by a Council held at Rome.[1]

The disciples first endeavoured to collect the sayings of our Lord and the record of His life. Thus the four Gospels constitute the first layer of the New Testament canon. The canon of our four Gospels existed by A.D. 150, as is shown by Hermas and Justin Martyr.

The next layer of the canon consists of the thirteen Epistles of St. Paul and the Acts. To these the Epistle to the Hebrews was generally attached in the east, though not in the west. This layer of the canon was universally recognized towards the close of the 2nd century, and perhaps some years earlier, for the books composing it were used and quoted throughout the 2nd century.

The third layer of the canon gained its place more slowly. It consists
of what are called the "Catholic Epistles," viz. those of St. James,
St. Peter, St. John, and St. Jude, together with the Revelation or
Apocalypse of St. John.

A crowd of works circulated among the Christians of the and century, including some forged Gospels and Apocalypses, the Epistle of St. Clement, Bishop of Rome, written about A.D. 95, and the allegory known as the *Shepherd* of Hermas, written about A.D. 140. Several of these works appear to have enjoyed a popularity in excess of that which attached to some of the books now included in the canon. Nevertheless they were rejected when they were examined. It was not merely a wonderful intellectual feat on the part of the Church to have sifted out this mass of literature; it was an action in which the Christian cannot fail to see the hand of God.

One question remains to be asked after drawing this small sketch of the history of the canon. Why is it that for several generations the canon of the New Testament varied in different countries, containing fewer books in one place than in another? Two reasons may be given: (i.) Certain books at first enjoyed only a local popularity; thus "Hebrews was saved by the value set upon it by the scholars of Alexandria, and the Epistle of St. James by the attachment of certain Churches in the East." (ii.) The books of the New Testament, when translated into other languages, were not all translated together. The Gospels were naturally translated first, as containing the words of our Lord. The other books followed gradually. Interesting information is given us with regard to the latter fact by the *Doctrine of Addai*, a Syriac book of which the present form dates from about A.D. 400, but which appears to describe the condition of the Syrian Church in the 3rd century. The writings of *Aphraates*, a Syrian writer, A.D. 338, supplement this information. We find from these books that about A.D. 160 the Syrian Christians possessed a translation of the Gospels. Early in the 3rd century they used a harmony of the Gospels with Acts and the Epistles of St. Paul. In the 4th century they used also the Epistle to the Hebrews. It is fairly evident, from the *Doctrine of Addai*, that only the Old Testament and the Gospels were at first used by the Syrian Christians, and that St. Paul's Epistles and Acts arrived later. And as late as A.D. 338 they knew nothing of the Catholic Epistles and Revelation, though these books were well known by the Christians who spoke Greek and Latin.

[Sidenote: Ancient Versions.]

The most ancient versions or translations of the New Testament were in those three great languages spoken by people who touched the borders of the districts where Greek was spoken. These were Latin, Syriac, and the Coptic language spoken by the Egyptians. It seems probable that a large part of the New Testament was translated into these languages within about a hundred years after the time of the apostles. The oldest version in any language closely akin to English was that made by Ulphilas, the celebrated bishop of the Goths, who translated the Bible from Greek into Gothic about A.D. 350. There is a most beautiful manuscript of this version preserved at Upsala, in Sweden. The Goths were then settled in the country between the Danube and the Dnieper. As late as the 17th century their language was still spoken in part of the south of Russia. A carefully revised translation of the Latin Bible was made by St. Jerome between A.D. 382 and 404, and this version came to be used by the Church throughout the west of Europe.

[Sidenote: English Versions.]

The Gospel of St. John and perhaps the other Gospels were translated by the patient historian and monk, the Venerable Bede, who was buried at Durham in A.D. 731. Parts of the Bible, especially the Psalms, were soon fairly well known through translations. King Alfred was translating the Psalms when he died, in A.D. 901; and soon after A.D. 1000, Archbishop Aelfric translated large portions of the Bible. As the language of England gradually changed, new versions of the Psalms were made, and most of the Bible was known in a version made before 1360. But perhaps there was no complete version of the Bible in English until the time of John Wyclif (1380). Wyclif translated most of the New Testament of this version, and a priest named Hereford translated the Old Testament. Wyclif held various opinions which the Church of England at that time condemned, and some of which she still rightly condemns. The result was that in 1412 Archbishop Arundel denounced Wyclif's version, but it seems to have been revised and to have come into common use. All these versions or partial versions in the English language were made from the Latin. But after the Turks captured Constantinople from the Greeks in 1453, a number of learned Greeks fled for refuge to the west of Europe. The result was that Greek books began to be studied again, and the New Testament began to be read once more in the original language. Three important editions were printed in 1514, 1516, and 1550 respectively. The first was printed under the direction of the Spanish Cardinal Ximenes, but owing to various causes was not published until 1522. The edition of 1516 was printed under the direction of the great Dutch scholar Erasmus. That of 1550 is important as being substantially the "received text" which has appeared in the ordinary Greek Testaments printed in England until the present day, and as being the foundation of our English Authorised Version. This "received text" was printed by Robert Estienne (or Stephanus), a great printer of Paris. About the same time a desire for a reformation of abuses in the Church caused a deeper interest to be taken in the Word of God. The first English translation of the New Testament shows a desire for a reformation of a somewhat extreme kind. It was the version of *William Tyndale*, which was printed at Worms in Germany, in 1525. In 1534 the Convocation or Church Parliament of England made a petition to King Henry VIII. to allow a better version to be made. The work of translation was interrupted by an order to have an English Bible in every church. As the Church version was not completed, a version made in 1535 by *Miles Coverdale* had to be used instead. Two other versions, also somewhat inferior, appeared in 1537 and 1539, and then a slightly improved version called the *Great Bible* appeared in April, 1539. It is also called Cranmer's Bible, because Archbishop Cranmer wrote a preface to the second edition. Three other important versions were published before the end of the 16th century. The Calvinists, who were the predecessors of the modern Presbyterians, published a New Testament at Geneva in 1557, followed by the whole Bible in 1560. The English bishops published what is called the *Bishops' Bible* in 1568, and the Roman Catholics published an English New Testament at Rheims in France, in 1582. We cannot fail to be impressed by the eager desire felt at that time by the people of Great Britain, of all religious parties, to study the Holy Scriptures, a desire to which these various translations bear witness.

All previous English versions were thrown into the shade by the brilliant *Authorised Version*, which was commenced in 1604 and published in 1611. Its beauty and accuracy are so great that even the Presbyterians, both in England and Scotland, gradually gave up the use of their Genevan Bible in favour of this translation. But since 1611 hundreds of manuscripts have been discovered and examined. "Textual criticism," by which an endeavour is made to discover the precise words written by the writers of the New Testament, where discrepancies exist in the manuscripts, has become a science. Many results of this criticism have been embodied in the *Revised Version*, published in 1881. The English of the *Revised Version* is not so musical as that of the *Authorised Version*, and it seems probable that a deeper knowledge of the ancient versions will before long enable us to advance even beyond the verbal accuracy attained in 1881. But at the same time we know that both our modern English versions give us a noble and trustworthy interpretation of the Greek. And criticism has made it certain that the earliest Greek manuscripts are essentially the same as the original books written by the apostles and their companions. The manuscripts are almost utterly free from wilful corruptions. And concerning the small variations which they contain, we can fitly quote the words of a fine old English scholar, Bentley: "Even put them into the hands of a knave or a fool, and yet with the most sinistrous and absurd choice, he shall not extinguish the light of any one chapter, nor so disguise Christianity but that every feature of it will still be the same."

For the sake of space the works of the evangelists are often referred to in an abbreviated form; *e.g.* "Matt." has been written for "the Gospel according to St. Matthew," and "Mark" for "the Gospel according to St. Mark." But when the writers themselves are mentioned, their names are usually given in full, with the title which Christian reverence has bestowed upon these "holy men of old."

[1] See Mr. C. H. Turner, *Journal of Theological Studies*, July, 1900.

CHAPTER II THE GOSPELS

[Sidenote: Their Name.]

The modern English word "Gospel" is derived from the Anglo-Saxon word *Godspell*, which means "God story," the story about the life of God in human flesh. It does not, therefore, exactly correspond with the Greek name *euaggelion*, which means "good tidings." In the earliest times the Greek name meant the good tidings proclaimed by our Lord about the Kingdom of God which He had come to establish. And, as our Lord Himself rules over this kingdom, the tidings about the kingdom included tidings about Himself. So Christ Himself says, "for My sake and the gospel's" (Mark viii. 35). After the Ascension of our Lord and the disappearance of His visible presence, the *euaggelion* came to mean the good tidings about Christ, rather than the good tidings brought by Christ (see 1 Cor. ix. 14 and 2 Cor. iv. 4). So St. Paul generally means by *euaggelion* the good news, coming from God, of salvation freely given to man through Christ. When he speaks of "My gospel" (Rom. ii. 16), he means "my explanation of the gospel;" and when he says, "I had been intrusted with the gospel of the uncircumcision" (Gal. ii. 7), he means that he had been appointed by God to preach the good tidings to the Gentiles, with special emphasis on the points most necessary for their instruction.

The word *euaggellon*, in the sense of a written gospel, is first found in the ancient Christian manual called the *Didaché*, or *Teaching of the Twelve Apostles*, in ch. xv.: "Reprove one another, not in anger but in peace, as ye have it in the gospel." This book was probably composed about A.D. 100. The word seems to have been still more definitely applied to a written account of the life of Christ in the time of the great heretic Marcion, A.D. 140. The plural word *euaggelia*, signifying the Four Gospels, is first found in a writing of Justin Martyr,[1] about A.D. 152. It is important to notice that he also calls them "Memoirs of the Apostles," and that he refers to them collectively as "the Gospel," inasmuch as they were, in reference to their distinctive value as records of Christ, one book.

[Sidenote: Their Genuineness.]

The first three Gospels do not contain the name of the writers in any connection which can be used to prove conclusively that they were written by the men whose names they bear. On the other hand, the fourth Gospel in a concluding passage (John xxi. 24) contains an obvious claim to have been written by that intimate friend of Jesus to whom the Church has always attributed it. But the titles, "according to Matthew," "according to Mark," "according to Luke," rest on excellent authority. And they imply that each book contains the good news brought by Christ and recorded in the teaching of the evangelist specified. These titles must, *at the very least*, signify that the Christians who first gave these titles to these books, meant that each Gospel was connected with one particular person who lived in the apostolic age, and that it contained nothing contrary to what that person taught. The titles, taken by themselves, are therefore compatible with the theory that the first three Gospels were perhaps written by friends or disciples of the men whose names they bear. But we shall afterwards see that there is overwhelming evidence to show that the connection between each book and the specified person is much closer than that theory would suggest.

Speaking of the four Gospels generally, we may first observe that it is impossible to place any one of them as late as A.D. 100, and that the first three Gospels must have been written long before that date. This is shown by the internal evidence, of which proof will be given in detail in the chapters dealing with the separate Gospels. The external evidence of the use of all the four Gospels by Christians, and to some extent by non-Christians, supports the internal evidence. Let us begin by noting facts which are part of undoubted history, and then work back to facts of earlier date. It is now undisputed that between the years 170 and 200 after Christ our four Gospels were known and regarded as genuine products of the apostolic age. St. Irenaeus, who became Bishop of Lyons in France in A.D. 177, and was the pupil of Polycarp, who had actually been a disciple of St. John, uses and quotes the four Gospels. He shows that various semi-Christian sects appeal severally to one of the four Gospels as supporting their peculiar views, but that the Christian Church accepts all four. He lays great stress on the fact that the teaching of the Church has always been the same, and he was personally acquainted with the state of Christianity in Asia Minor, Rome, and France. His evidence must therefore be considered as carrying great weight. Equally important is the evidence of Tatian. This remarkable Syrian wrote a harmony of the Gospels near A.D. 160. Allusions to this harmony, called the *Diatessaron*, were known to exist in several ancient writers, but until recently it was strenuously maintained by sceptical writers that there was not sufficient evidence to prove that the Diatessaron was composed of our present Gospels. It was suggested that it might have been drawn from other Gospels more or less resembling those which we now possess. This idea has now been dispelled. A great Syrian father, Ephraim, who died in 373, wrote a commentary on the Diatessaron. This was preserved in an Armenian translation which was made known to the world in 1876. The discovery proved that the Diatessaron had been drawn from our four Gospels. In 1886 an Arabic version of the Diatessaron itself was found, and it proved conclusively that Tatian's Diatessaron was simply a combination of our four canonical Gospels. About the same date as Tatian, a famous Gnostic writer named Heracleon wrote commentaries on Luke and John, and it can also be shown that he was acquainted with Matt. There can therefore be no doubt that all our four Gospels were well known by A.D. 170.

Between A.D. 130 and 170 our Gospels were also in use. The most important evidence is furnished by Justin Martyr, who was born near Samaria, and lectured in Rome about A.D. 152. He says "the apostles handed down in the Memoirs made by them, which are called Gospels;" he shows that these Memoirs were used in Christian worship, and he says that "they were compiled by Christ's apostles and those who companied with them." This exactly agrees with the fact that the first and the fourth of our Gospels are attributed by the tradition of the Church to apostles, while the second and the third are attributed to companions of the apostles. The quotations which Justin makes show that these Memoirs were our four Gospels. It has been thought that Justin perhaps used some apocryphal Gospel in addition to our Gospels, but there is no sufficient proof of this. We may explain that he uses the term "Memoirs" in order to make himself intelligible to non-Christian readers who would not understand the word "Gospel."

The *Shepherd* of Hermas, which was written at Rome, probably about A.D. 140, but perhaps earlier, uses expressions which imply an acquaintance with all our Gospels, though none of them are directly quoted. Moreover, the *Shepherd*, in depicting the Christian Church as seated on a bench with four feet, probably refers to the four Gospels. This would be in agreement with the allegorical style of the book, and it gains support from the language of Origen and Irenaeus.

The testimony rendered to the authenticity of the Gospels by the heretics who flourished between A.D. 130 and 170 is of importance. At the beginning of this period, Basilides, the great Gnostic of Alexandria, who tried to replace Christianity by a semi-Christian Pantheism, appears to have used Matt., Luke, and John. The fact that they contain nothing which really supports his peculiar tenets, forms an argument which shows that the genuineness of these documents was then too well established for it to be worth his while to dispute it. Marcion, whose teaching was half Gnostic and half Catholic, endeavoured to revive what he imagined to be the Christianity of St. Paul, whom he regarded as the only true apostle. He believed that Judaism was the work of an inferior god, and he therefore rejected the whole of the Old Testament, and retained only the Gospel written by St. Luke, the friend of St. Paul, and ten of St. Paul's Epistles. Modern writers have sometimes urged that Marcion's list of New Testament books proves that all other parts of the New Testament were regarded as doubtful about A.D. 140. But it is quite evident that Marcion, unlike those Gnostics who adapted uncongenial books to their own systems by means of allegorical explanations, cut out the books and verses which would not correspond with his own dogma. In spite of his pretended fidelity to St. Paul, he mutilated not only St. Luke's Gospel, but even the Epistle to the Galatians. So whereas it is certain that he used our Luke, there is no indication to show that he did not admit that the other Gospels were really the work of the writers whose names they bear.

In the period between A.D. 98, when the death of St. John probably took place, and A.D. 130, we find several signs of acquaintance with the Gospels. About A.D. 130, Papias, Bishop of Hierapolis, wrote a book called *Expositions of the Oracles of the Lord*. It may be regarded as almost certain that the word "Oracles" signifies written Gospels, just as in the New Testament the word signifies the written documents of the Old Testament. He mentions Gospels written by St. Matthew and St. Mark, and we know from Eusebius that he made use of 1 John. It is deeply to be regretted that we only have a few remaining fragments of the writings of this early bishop, who was acquainted with men who knew our Lord's disciples. In the letters of St. Ignatius, the martyred Bishop of Antioch, A.D. 110, we find signs of acquaintance with Matt. and John. The Epistle written by St. Polycarp to the Philippians soon after the death of St. Ignatius contains quotations from Matt. and Luke, and the quotations in it from 1 John almost certainly imply the authenticity of St. John's Gospel, as it is impossible to attribute the Epistles to any writer except the writer of the Gospel. The *Didaché*, about A.D. 100, shows acquaintance with Matt. and Luke, and contains early Eucharistic prayers of which the language closely resembles the language of St. John. The Epistle of Barnabas, probably about A.D. 98, contains what is probably the oldest remaining quotation from a book of the New Testament. It says, "It is written, Many called, but few chosen," which appears

9

to be a quotation from Matt. xxii. 14. The Epistle of St. Clement of Rome, written to the Christians of Corinth about A.D. 95, is full of the phraseology of St. Paul's Epistles, but contains nothing that can be called a direct quotation from our Gospels. But it does contain what are possibly traces of the first three Gospels, though these passages are perhaps quoted from an oral Gospel employed in the instruction of catechumens.

We must conclude that, considering what a large amount of early Christian literature has perished, the external evidence for the authenticity of our Gospels is remarkably strong. They are genuine writings of the apostolic age, and were received by men whose lifetime overlapped the lifetime of some of the apostles. In the early Christian literature which remains, there is much which lends support to the authenticity of the Gospels, and nothing which injures a belief in that authenticity. And there are strong reasons for thinking that in the early Christian literature which has perished, there was much which would have made a belief in their authenticity quite inevitable.

It would be an aid to modern study if we could be certain when and where the four Gospels were put together in one canon. In the 4th and 5th centuries it was believed by some Christians that the collection had been made at Ephesus by St. John himself, and that he had prefixed the names of the writers to the Gospels when he published his own Gospel. It is at present impossible to discover how far this supposed fact is legendary or not, but modern criticism has done something to corroborate the idea that the Gospels were really collected first in Asia Minor, and if St. John did not make the collection himself, it was probably made by his disciples soon after his death.

[Sidenote: Their Diversity.]

If we compare the four Gospels together, it is as plain as daylight that there is a marked difference between the first three Gospels on the one hand and the fourth Gospel on the other hand. The first three Gospels are usually called the *Synoptic Gospels*, because they give us one *synopsis* or common view of our Lord's work. To a great extent they record the same events and the same discourses, and in many passages they express themselves in almost identical words. The account which they give of our Lord's work is mostly confined to His ministry in Galilee, the birthplace of our religion, and it includes only one visit to Jerusalem. But St. John's Gospel differs widely in language from the other Gospels, and also gives an account of no less than five visits to Jerusalem, and chiefly describes the scenes connected with our Lord's ministry in Judaea. Whereas our first three Gospels can be appropriately printed in three parallel columns, the greater part of St. John's Gospel cannot be appropriately placed by the side of the other three. Another most important difference is that St. John's Gospel is marked by a tone and teaching which are seldom to be found in the Synoptic Gospels. The difference was well expressed by Clement of Alexandria, who calls the Synoptic Gospels *bodily* and St. John's Gospel *spiritual*; and by Theodore of Mopsuestia, who says that St. John declared that "doubtless it was not right to omit the facts told with regard to the sojourn of Christ in the flesh, but neither was it right to omit the words relating to His Divinity." For the Synoptic Gospels relate the outward events connected with our Lord's ministry, while St. John records the discourses and works which reveal our Lord's heavenly origin and divine authority. Again, the Synoptic Gospels report Christ's addresses to simple Galilean people, addresses consisting largely of *parables*; while St. John reports discourses, frequently expressed in the language of *allegory*, and uttered to the Jews of Jerusalem or to His own intimate disciples.

[Sidenote: The Synoptic problem.]

The Synoptic problem consists in the difficulties raised by the fact that the Synoptic Gospels show both a remarkable similarity and a remarkable dissimilarity. It is just because the similarity is often so astonishing that we find it all the more difficult to explain the dissimilarity when it exists. A study of the Synoptic problem is valuable for the Christian student, inasmuch as it directs our attention to the sources employed by the evangelists, and thus leads us nearer to the actual events connected with the rise of Christianity.

The RESEMBLANCES between the Synoptic Gospels may be observed in the following points:—

(a) *A common plan.*—The general view of the course of events is almost identical. St. Matthew and St. Luke give separate accounts of the infancy of our Lord, but they then join with St. Mark in their account of St. John the Baptist, the baptism and temptation of Christ, and the beginning of His ministry. Later all three direct their attention mainly to Christ's work in Galilee, while St. John describes much that took place in Judaea and Samaria. They pass rapidly over some considerable space of time until they come to the last week of His life, where all three give a detailed account.

(b) *A common selection of facts.*—By far the larger number of both events and discourses are found in all three Gospels. If anything is recorded in Mark it is generally to be found in Matt. and Luke, and almost always in either Matt. or Luke. If the whole number of incidents in the Synoptic Gospels be reckoned as eighty-eight, the distribution of the incidents shared by at least two Gospels is as follows:—

In all three Gospels 42
In Mark and Matt. 12
In Mark and Luke 5
In Matt. and Luke 12

If we add the above together, we realize that seventy-one incidents out of a total of eighty-eight are to be found in more than one Gospel. Of the remaining seventeen incidents, three are peculiar to Mark, five to Matt., and nine to Luke.

(c) *Similar groups of incidents.*—Not only is there a common selection of facts, but detached events which happened at different times are sometimes grouped together in the same way in all of the Synoptic Gospels or in two of the three. Thus in all three we find together the cure of the paralytic, the call of Levi, and the question of fasting (Matt. ix. 1-17; Mark ii. 1-22; Luke v. 17-39); so also the plucking of the ears of corn and the cure of the withered hand—events separated by at least a week (Matt. xii. 1-21; Mark ii. 23-iii. 6; Luke vi. 1-11). Thus also the death of John the Baptist is introduced both in Matt. xiv. 3 and in Mark vi. 17 to explain the fear felt by Herod Antipas that he had risen from the dead. In fact, when a parallel passage is found in all three Synoptic Gospels, it is never immediately followed in *both* Matt. and Luke by a whole separate incident which is not in Mark.[2] There is a general tendency in Matt. and Luke to narrate the same facts as Mark in the order of Mark. And therefore it is difficult to think that the original basis of the Synoptic Gospels, whether written or unwritten, did not coincide closely with Mark in the order of events.

(d) *Similarity of language.*—The Synoptic Gospels often agree verbally. And this agreement is not merely found in the reports of the sayings of our Lord, but even in the narrative of events. It extends even to rare Greek words and phrases. The clauses are often remarkably similar. Sometimes quotations from the Old Testament are found in two or three Gospels with the same variations from the original. Matt. iii. 3, Mark i. 3, and Luke iii. 4 have the same quotation from Isa. xl. 3, in which they agree in every word, although at the end they depart in the same way from both the Hebrew and the Greek version of the Old Testament, for they put "His paths" instead of "the paths of our God." Another interesting instance is to be found in Matt. xxvi. 47, Mark xiv. 43, and Luke xxii. 47, where all three evangelists, apparently without any necessity, explain that Judas was one of the twelve. Again in Matt. xxiv. 15, 16, and Mark xiii. 14, we have the note or parenthesis "let him that readeth understand," which one evangelist seems to have copied from the other.

The DIFFERENCES between the Synoptic Gospels may be observed in the following facts:—

(a) *Facts peculiar to one or two Gospels.*—There is a wide difference between the account of the birth and infancy of our Lord given in Matt. and that given in Luke. In Matt. we have recorded an angelic communication to St. Joseph concerning the future birth of Jesus. In Luke, an earlier and fuller annunciation to St. Mary is recorded. In Matt. the story of the infancy is centred at Bethlehem, in Luke at Nazareth. The accounts given of the appearances of our Lord after the Resurrection record different events. In Matt. and Mark Galilee is the scene of His appearances, in Luke the scene is laid in Jerusalem and its neighbourhood. There is not the least reason for regarding these accounts as contradictory, but there is reason for inquiring why the different writers selected different appearances.

(b) *Different accounts of the same facts.*—The three distinct incidents of the temptation of our Lord are recorded in a different order in Matt. and Luke, and the temptation is recorded without these incidents in Mark. St. Luke's version of the Beatitudes is reduced in number, and is followed by corresponding denunciations. In Mark x. 46 and Matt. x. 29 we have the cure of Bartimaeus on the departure from Jericho, in Luke xviii. 35, xix. 1 at the entrance of the city. In Matt. viii. 28 there are two demoniacs, while in Mark v. 2 and Luke viii. 27, which seem to narrate the same event, only one demoniac is mentioned. All the Synoptic Gospels give slightly different accounts of the inscription on the cross, and the words spoken by the centurion at the death of Jesus vary in Luke from the words in Matt. and Mark.

(c) Differences in the order of words and sentences.—Although Matt. and Luke do not combine against Mark in narrating a whole incident in an order different from Mark, it is important to notice that there are some cases in which Matt. and Mark agree against Luke, or Mark and Luke agree against Matt. And we must not omit a significant instance where Matt. and Luke agree against Mark in the order of *part* of an incident. In Matt. iii. 11, 12 and Luke iii. 16, "I indeed baptize you with water," etc., comes *before*, in Mark i. 7, 8 it comes *after*, the description of Jesus as "He that is mightier than I." No doubt one author who copies another may often omit something stated by the first author. But, surely, he is not very likely to invert the order of the materials before him, especially when no obvious purpose can be served by such an inversion. Another instance of inversion is this: in Mark ix. 12, 13 the rejection of the Son of Man is mentioned by our Lord *between* two statements of His about Ehas, in Matt. xvii. 12 it is mentioned *after* both statements. Such inversions would naturally take place in the case of oral transmission of the sacred story, but they would be less likely in the case of one writer copying another.

(d) *Verbal differences.*—Striking verbal differences occur even when the general resemblance is most close. In Matt. ix. 1-17, Mark ii. 1-22, Luke v. 17-39, there are verbal changes even where the sentences closely coincide. Other instances might be quoted. All three evangelists have a style of their own, and show a marked preference for particular idioms and words. In narrating the sayings of our Lord, they narrate them with some verbal differences, and in the case of the history of His ministry, they narrate it with numerous verbal differences. It is therefore evident that St. Matthew and St. Luke, if they used St. Mark's work, felt themselves at liberty to deal with it very freely.

The above brief account of the chief resemblances and differences between the first three Gospels is an attempt to give a fair though condensed statement of certain facts which appeal with different force to different minds. "How came these Gospels to be so alike and yet so different?" This is the "Synoptic problem," and great divergence of opinion exists as to the solution.

[Sidenote: Possible solutions.]

The most important views propounded to solve the problem are—

(1) Both St. Matthew and St. Luke copied the Gospel of St. Mark, while not omitting to make use of other documents. In the case of St. Luke, his acquaintance with earlier written stories about our Lord is rendered indisputable by his own statement. Sometimes it has been thought that St. Luke made use of the Gospel according to St. Matthew as well as the Gospel according to St. Mark. This theory is most appropriately called the *theory of the mutual dependence of the documents*.

(2) The three Synoptic Gospels put down in writing different, but closely similar forms of an oral tradition concerning the teaching of our Lord. It is thought that the statements made by the apostles about Christ were repeated by them and occasionally added to, and treasured up in faithful memories. The idea of a *literary* connection between the Gospels is dismissed, and it is held that the methods of teaching employed among the Jews, and the probable existence of a school of trained catechists, will account sufficiently for the fixed form of the tradition. According to this hypothesis the differences between the Synoptic Gospels are to be explained by the necessity of teaching different aspects of the truth among different classes of inquirers, and by the fluctuating memories of the teachers. This theory is known as the *oral theory*.[3]

(3) The three Synoptic Gospels are based upon one original Gospel written in the Aramaic language. A large number of verbal variations can thus be accounted for. They might have sprung from different renderings of the same Aramaic original, and various passages derived from oral tradition might have been added to the original Gospel when it was translated. It has been held by some that there was at least an Aramaic document behind Mark, if there was not an Aramaic original employed by all the Synoptics. The different forms of this hypothesis can be described as the *theory of an Aramaic original*.

It is now generally believed that the three evangelists did not employ one original Aramaic Gospel. The agreement between the Greek words of the Synoptic Gospels is too close to be explained by the use of an Aramaic original. The real controversy, therefore, lies between the scholars who support theory (1) or theory (2).

[Sidenote: Probable conclusions.]

On the whole, it appears that a general agreement is being arrived at. It is becoming evident that the theory of the mutual dependence of the documents and the oral theory are *both* partly true, and that neither of them can be held in an extreme form. In the first place, the resemblances between the first three Gospels make it extremely probable that St. Matthew and St. Luke employed the work of St. Mark. In England, Germany, and France the opinion of scholars seems steadily tending towards this conclusion. The chief reasons for it are undoubtedly that (i.) the order of facts in Mark is the *normal order* of the whole narrative of the Synoptists, and (ii.) in the main, the language of Mark explains the verbal agreements between Matt. and Luke. Therefore among the probable conclusions with regard to the Synoptic problem we must reckon the fact that *Mark is earlier than Matt. and Luke, and was employed in the composition of them both*. This is the first important conclusion.

But we must also allow room for the influence of oral tradition.

We have already noticed many differences between the Synoptists, all of which more or less suggest that the Gospels are largely based on oral tradition. We may now mention a few other facts which point in the same direction. There are cases in which Matt. or Luke has a more decided appearance of originality than Mark. These cases include words, phrases, and even sections. For instance, Matt. employs several times the phrase "the Father who is in heaven," a phrase which our Lord must certainly have used, but which in Mark only occurs once (xi. 25). Mark i. 40-45, ii. 1-12, iii. 1-6, x. 35, appear less original than the parallel passages in the other Synoptic Gospels. Moreover, there are statements in Matt. of a striking kind, which are not at all likely to have been invented, but which are entirely absent from Mark. We may notice the texts, "Go not into any way of the Gentiles, and enter not into any city of the Samaritans; but go rather to the lost sheep of the house of Israel" (Matt. x. 5, 6); and again, "I was not sent but unto the lost sheep of the house of Israel" (Matt. xv. 24). In both cases the context has a parallel in Mark, but the verses in question do not occur in those parallels.

Also there are certain passages to be found in Mark which are in neither Luke nor Matt. If we believe that the Gospels are largely based on oral tradition, it is easy to account for the absence of a passage in one or two of the three Synoptic Gospels. An incident which was remembered in one place might be forgotten in another. But if we exclude the influence of oral tradition, there are only two solutions of the problem raised by these passages. Either (a) St. Matthew and St. Luke were ignorant of them, because they were added to Mark later than the date when they used Mark; or (b) they knew them and omitted them. In other words, we have to ask, Did they use an original form of the second Gospel, a form to which German scholars apply the name *Ur-Marcus* and French scholars apply the name *Proto-Marc*, or did they omit passages in Mark which suggested difficulties or appeared unnecessary? The main argument against the existence of a Proto-Mark is that neither Papias nor any known Father of the Church preserves the least recollection of it. It has simply been invented to account for the difficulties of the Synoptic problem. If, on the other hand, St. Matthew and St. Luke deliberately abbreviated or altered the narrative of St. Mark, we must naturally inquire why they did so. The authors who maintain that they did alter the material which lay before them, account for some of the changes as having been made from a mere desire to abbreviate, or to remove a few verses which might prove "hard sayings" to Jewish or Gentile Christians respectively. Some think that other passages in Mark were emitted because St. Matthew and St. Luke considered them to be derogatory to our Lord's power or the character of His apostles. For instance, St. Matthew omits the rebuke administered to the apostles in Mark viii. 17, 18, and he does not mention our Lord's use of spittle as a means of healing. He also in ch. xiii. 55 represents the Jews as calling our Lord "the carpenter's son," whereas in Mark vi. 3 they call Him "the carpenter."

This latter line of argument is often hazardous and occasionally profane. And in special reference to the points just described, we may remark that St. Matthew in ch. xiv. 28-33 does not hesitate to record the weakness of even St. Peter's faith; and that St. John, although he gives the greatest prominence to the majesty of our Lord, does in ch. ix. 6 record His use of spittle in healing. And if St. Matthew thought it irreverent to record the fact that the Jews called Jesus "the carpenter," he might have naturally shrunk far more from saying, as he does, that they named Him "the carpenter's son," a title which might seem to imply an ignoring of His miraculous birth.

It seems, therefore, that we must be content to acknowledge that we cannot always determine the reasons which influenced St. Matthew and St. Luke, but we can say that in some cases they were probably influenced by the mere desire to abbreviate, and that they were also influenced by the forms which the oral teaching of the Gospel had assumed. We may also regard it as almost certain that St. Luke sometimes altered words in St. Mark's narrative simply because he preferred a more elegant and less homely form of Greek. The textual criticism of the oldest manuscripts of the New Testament also points to the fact that for a few generations, when reminiscences of our Lord and His apostles were still handed down, writers occasionally tried to make room for these reminiscences when they copied the books of the New Testament. A famous instance of this is John vii. 53-viii.

11, which was almost certainly not written by St. John, and is almost certainly a genuine story which the apostle knew, and which Christians afterwards inserted in his Gospel. We believe, then, that *all the Synoptic Gospels are influenced by oral tradition.* This is the second important conclusion.

Thirdly, it seems that *Matt. and Luke, and perhaps Mark, made use of written collections of Logia, or sayings of our Lord.* Evidence of one such collection comes to us on the high authority of Papias. He says—

Matthew then composed the Logia in the Hebrew tongue, and every one interpreted them as he was able.

An equally important statement which Papias makes with regard to the composition of Mark, is made on the authority of John the Presbyter who had been a personal follower of the Lord and was an elder contemporary of Papias. It is at least possible that Papias derived his information about Matt. from the same authority. It is almost inconceivable that between the time of Papias and that of Irenaeus, whose life probably overlapped that of Papias, the name of Matthew became wrongly affixed to our first Gospel. We may therefore regard it as certain that in our first Gospel is contained the book of sayings, which St. Matthew himself wrote. In our third Gospel we find that St. Luke has inserted much information with regard to our Lord's teaching which is apparently derived from a version of the Logia. The order of the sayings is more original in Luke than in Matt. The reason for this assertion is the following:—

The two evangelists arrange the sayings of our Lord differently. In more than two-thirds of the instances in which they seem to employ some collection of *Logia*, they place their materials in a different setting. It has often been remarked that St. Matthew places the discourses of our Lord together in large blocks, while St. Luke records them separately, and in many cases records the circumstances which led up to them. Instances of this are—The Lord's Prayer (Matt. vi. 9-13 and Luke xi. 1-4); the treasure and the heart (Matt. vi. 19-21 and Luke xii. 33, 34); God and Mammon (Matt. vi. 24 and Luke xvi. 13). It would therefore seem plain that either one evangelist or the other altered the places of these discourses. Examination makes it equally plain that the alteration was made in Matt. Much of Matt. is arranged in numerical forms, and this is especially true of those passages which are not derived from Mark. The numbers 5, 10, and 7 are used as helps to memory. Thus in Matt. we find *five* chapters (called by the Jews "Pereqs") of the sayings of our Lord, ending respectively at vii. 28; xi. 1; xiii. 53, xix. 1; xxvi. 1. The number five was a favourite number with the Jews in such cases; thus we have five books of the Pentateuch, five books of the Psalms, the five *Megilloth* or festival volumes, and the five parts of the *Pirqe Aboth*. In chs. viii. and ix. we have a collection of *ten* miracles, in spite of the fact that three of these miracles are placed elsewhere by St. Mark and St. Luke. The petitions of the Lord's Prayer are arranged as seven, there are *seven* parables in ch. xiii., *seven* woes in ch. xxiii., and the genealogy of our Lord is arranged in three *fourteens*. As these numerical arrangements are specially characteristic of Matt., and certainly appear to be caused by a desire to aid oral repetition, we are led to the conclusion that the Logia are to be found in a less artificial and therefore earlier form in Luke. We are also led once more to the conclusion that though we cannot say that the whole of Matt. owes its form to oral teaching, yet many sections of it are moulded by oral teaching.

It must lastly be noted that although the collection of Logia employed in Luke contained much material which is also found in Matt., the parallel passages vary considerably in style and language. Examination of these passages seldom enables us to prove what expressions were specially characteristic of the Logia. But we can assert with a fair amount of confidence that the version, or versions, of the Logia so employed, had a simple and Hebraic style; and that whereas Luke has kept the order of the Logia better than Matt., the latter preserves the style more faithfully.

In addition to Mark and collections of the Logia, St. Matthew and St. Luke employed other sources now unknown to us. The narratives of the infancy and the Resurrection are independent, and are so different that they point both to the fact that the two evangelists were here employing different sources, and that each was unacquainted with the Gospel written by the other. Also, St. Luke's account of our Lord's ministry in Peraea and elsewhere, contained in ix. 51-xix. 28, is peculiar to his Gospel.

[Sidenote: The relation of St. John's Gospel to the Synoptic Gospels.]

The difference between the theological tone of St. John's Gospel and that which we find in the Synoptists is mentioned in our account of the separate Gospels. Besides this difference of tone, there is a decided difference in the march of the events which are recorded and some difference in the narrative of passages which are parallel. The first rough impression which we gather from the Synoptists is that our Lord did not visit Jerusalem until shortly before the Crucifixion. Matthew and Mark refer to one Passover only for which Jesus comes to Jerusalem. The scene of His ministry is Galilee. On the other hand, the centre of interest in John is not Galilee, but Jerusalem and Judaea. But a minute examination proves that the narrative of St. John fits that of the Synoptists in a remarkable manner. In the first place, the Synoptists give us hints of our Lord's earlier visits to Judaea and Jerusalem. In Luke iv. 44 (see margin R.V.) we find Him preaching in the synagogues of Judaea (cf. Acts x. 37). In Luke v. 17 the presence in Galilee of Pharisees from *Jerusalem* is a testimony to the impression which Christ had produced in the holy city. Both Matt. (xxiii. 37) and Luke (xiii. 34) record the lament of our Lord, "O *Jerusalem*, . . . how *often* would I," etc. So from John iv. 3, 43 we learn of our Lord returning to *Galilee* after His first visit to Jerusalem. This second journey into Galilee recorded by St. John brings us to a point corresponding with the early days of the ministry in Galilee described by the Synoptists. In John vi.-vii. 9 we have narratives connected with *Galilee*, and this section belongs to an interval of time between the approach of Passover in March A.D. 28 and the feast of Tabernacles in September A.D. 28. Of this period the Synoptists give a much fuller account.

The question of the length of our Lord's ministry is thus intimately connected with that of the scene of His ministry. St. John marks the length of our Lord's ministry, not by ordinary chronology, but by the mention of various Jewish feasts. The dates of these feasts show that His ministry lasted two years and a half. The absence of dates in the Synoptists has led to the opinion that they represent our Lord's ministry as only extending over one year. This opinion may be summarily dismissed. The mention of ripe corn in Mark ii. 23, and green grass in vi. 39, implies two spring-times before the last Passover. It is impossible to compress the teaching which the Synoptic Gospels relate into the period of one year, and they show a hostility towards Christ on the part of the ruling classes in Jerusalem which could not have sufficiently fermented in the space of a few months. We may also notice that there is a close agreement between the Synoptists and St. John with regard to the points on which the conflict between Christ and the Jews turned (cf. Matt. xvi. 1-4, Mark viii. 11-13, Luke xi. 16, 29-32, with John ii. 18). The Jews specially charged Him with being possessed by a devil (cf. Matt. xii. 24, Mark iii. 22, Luke xi. 15, with John viii. 48 and x. 19), and also with breaking the sabbath (cf. Matt. xii. 9, Mark iii. 1, Luke vi. 6, xiii. 10, with John v. 10, vii. 22, ix. 14).

The dates of two important incidents have been the subjects of much discussion. A cleansing of the temple by our Lord is related by the Synoptists at the close of our Lord's ministry (Mark xi. 15). John ii. 14 places a cleansing of the temple at the very beginning of our Lord's ministry. If we have to choose between one record and the other, we should perhaps be inclined to say that the narrative in John is the more probable. But there is no good reason for making such a choice. No one who is at all familiar with the history of the abuses which took place in some mediaeval churches would find a difficulty in believing that the temple needed a second cleansing by our Lord. The first cleansing is the natural outcome of His righteous indignation in beholding for the first time the holiest place in the world given up to common traffic, the second cleansing is appropriate in Him who had then openly proclaimed His divine authority and Messiahship.

The day of our Lord's death is a date about which there is an apparent discrepancy between the Synoptists and St. John. The discrepancy has been elevated into momentous importance by the sceptics of the last sixty years, and has been employed as one of the most formidable arguments against the authenticity of St. John's Gospel. The argument employed by these critics is as follows:—(1) The Synoptic Gospels contain the original apostolic tradition, and they agree in stating that Jesus celebrated the ordinary Jewish passover on the evening between the 14th and 15th of the month Nisan; they therefore represent the crucifixion as taking place on the 15th, after the passover had been eaten. (2) The fourth Gospel places the Last Supper on the evening between the 13th and the 14th of Nisan. It therefore represents the crucifixion as taking place on the 14th, and tacitly denies that Christ ate the usual Jewish passover. (3) The Churches of the province of Asia, which were founded by St. John, were accustomed in the 2nd century to keep their passover on the 14th of Nisan, and declared that they derived their custom from St. John. They consequently believed that Christ died on the 15th, and that He ate the usual Jewish Passover. (4) Therefore the fourth Gospel was not written by St. John, but by a forger who wished to emphasize the break between Judaism and Christianity.

This argument can be turned with fatal force against the critics who made it. It is no doubt true that St. John by numerous indications (xiii. 1; xviii. 28; xix. 14, 31) implies that the Last Supper was eaten the day before the usual passover, and that Christ died on Nisan 14. But the usage of the Christians of the Asiatic Churches in the 2nd century absolutely corroborates these indications. These Churches when they celebrated the passover were not celebrating the anniversary of the Last Supper, but the anniversary of the death of Christ, the true Paschal Lamb. By doing this on Nisan 14, they showed that they believed that Christ died on that day, and there is particularly strong evidence of a belief among the early Christians that our Lord did die on Nisan 14. Moreover, although the account of the Synoptists is not free from ambiguity, it bears many testimonies to St. John's chronology. They record as happening on the day of Christ's death several actions which the Jewish law did not permit on a feast day such as Nisan 15, and which must presumably have taken place on Nisan 14. The Synoptists make the Sanhedrim say that they will not arrest Jesus "on the feast day," the guards and St. Peter carry arms, the trial is held, Simon the Cyrenian comes from work, Joseph of Arimathaea buys a linen cloth, the holy women prepare spices, all of which works would have been forbidden on Nisan 15. Finally, the day is itself called the "preparation," a name which would not be given to Nisan 15. The conclusion is irresistible. It is that our Lord died on Nisan 14, that St. John is correct, and that the Synoptists in most of the passages concerned corroborate St. John. The only real difficulty is raised by Mark xiv. 12 (cf. Matt. xxvi. 17; Luke xxii. 7), which seems to imply that the Paschal lamb was sacrificed on the day before Christ died. If so, this verse implies that Christ died on Nisan 15. But we must observe that not one of the Synoptists says that the disciples ate a lamb at the Last Supper, and also that, for all ceremonial purposes, the day for killing the lamb began on the evening of Nisan 13. It is therefore doubtful whether there is even as much as one verbal contradiction on this point between the Synoptists and St. John.

The omission of events which are of importance in the Synoptic Gospels is a striking feature in St. John's Gospel. But these instances of omission can be more reasonably explained by the hypothesis that the author was content to omit facts with which the Christians around him were well acquainted, than by the hypothesis that he was a spiritualistic writer of the 2nd century who wished to make his Gospel fit some fanciful theory of his own. In fact, the latter hypothesis has proved a signal failure. The critics who say that the writer omitted the story of our Lord's painful temptation as incompatible with the majesty of the Divine Word, may be asked why the writer gives no fuller account of the glorious transfiguration than the hint in i. 14. Those who say that sentimental superstition induced the writer to omit the agony the garden, may be asked why the writer records the weariness of Christ at Samaria and His tears at the grave, of Lazarus. There are gaps in the evangelist's narrative, but we cannot argue that the Gospel is therefore a forgery. The evangelist is acquainted with the Ascension (vi. 62), though he does not record it; and he knows that Nazareth was the early home of Christ (i. 46), though he does not narrate the story of the sacred infancy. The Gospel of St. John is none the less genuine for being of the nature of a treatise, intended to bring certain aspects of the life of our Lord to bear upon the intellectual life of Ephesus. Much has been made of the fact that he says nothing of the institution of the Eucharist. Nor does he record the command of Jesus to baptize. Are we to suppose that a writer who has told us how "the Word was made flesh" so shrank from believing material things to be connected with a spiritual efficacy that he rejected the sacraments? Is it not more probable that among people who were perfectly familiar with both Baptism and the Eucharist he preferred to tell what Christ had said about being born again (iii.), and about the assimilation of His life by the believer (vi.)? This seems to us more reasonable. The fourth Gospel, though it has a character and purpose of its own, and might even have been written if there had been no other Gospel, yet was intended to supplement either the Synoptic Gospels or else a body of teaching corresponding with that contained in those Gospels.

The facts which St. John records in common with the Synoptists before the Last Supper, the Passion, and the Resurrection are—the Baptism of John (i. 26), the Feeding of the 5000 (vi. 10), the Walking on the Sea (vi. 19), the Anointing at Bethany, with the action of Judas (xii. 1), the Triumphal Entry into Jerusalem (xii. 12). Even in connection with these incidents St. John gives his additional details, and therefore the character of his work is here, as elsewhere, both independent and supplemental.

It remains to ask whether any words used by St. John seem to show that he borrowed expressions from the Synoptic Gospels.

The following passages may be noticed: John v. 8 f. (Mark ii. 11 f.), vi. 7, 10, 19 f. (Mark vi. 37, 40, 49 f.), xii. 3, 5, 7 f. (Mark xiv. 3-6), xiii. 21 (Mark xiv. 18), xviii. 18, 17 (Mark xiv. 54, 69), xviii. 22 (Mark xiv. 65). For the quotation from Zechariah in xii. 15, cf. Matt. xxi. 5. The words of our Lord in John xv. 18-xvi. 2 have been compared with those in Matt. x. 17-22. Sometimes John has more points of contact with Luke than with the other Synoptists; *e.g.* there is the journey of Christ to Galilee before the death of John the Baptist, the fact that the scourging of Christ by Pilate was intended to restrain the Jews from demanding His death, and the visit of St. Peter to the sepulchre. It has been thought that John xii. 3 is based upon Luke vii. 38. The anointing of our Lord's *feet* in both is certainly remarkable. Sometimes John agrees with Matt. and Mark and not Luke, as in recording the binding of Jesus, the crown of thorns, the purple robe, and the custom of releasing a malefactor at the feast. Such coincidences between John and the Synoptic Gospels are so slight and disconnected that it seems doubtful whether the former uses any material drawn from the latter. Nevertheless, the story contained in the Synoptic Gospels, though not quoted, is presupposed. A good instance is in John vi. 5, where St. John does not stop to explain that the hour was late and the people therefore hungry.

[1] *Apol.* i. 66.

[2] The longest instance of a passage in Matt. and Luke being parallel in these Gospels and without a parallel in Mark is the short passage, Matt. iii. 7-10, Luke iii. 7-9.

[3] This theory was first clearly expounded in 1818 by Gieseler, a celebrated German Protestant Church historian. It has been more popular in England than in Germany.

CHAPTER III THE GOSPEL ACCORDING TO ST. MATTHEW

[Sidenote: The Author.]

St. Matthew is one of the least known of the Apostles. He was first called Levi the son of Alphaeus, and was a "publican" or collector of customs at Capernaum. At the call of Jesus, "he forsook all, and rose up and followed Him." He then made a great feast, to which he invited his old companions, no doubt that they too might come under the influence of the Lord. After the appointment of the twelve Apostles, he was put in the second of the three groups of Apostles. The New Testament gives us no further information concerning him. An early tradition narrates that the Apostles remained at Jerusalem until twelve years after the Ascension, and certainly St. Paul does not seem to have found any of the Apostles at Jerusalem when he was there in A.D. 56 (Acts xxi. 17). According to Clement of Alexandria, A.D. 190, St. Matthew led a rigorously ascetic life, such as is also recorded of St. James. Nothing certain is known of his missionary labours. Parthia, Ethiopia, and India were believed in the 4th and 5th centuries to have been visited by St. Matthew. We learn from Clement of Alexandria that he did not suffer martyrdom.[1] The fact that he disappears almost completely from the realm of history is an additional reason for believing the tradition which connects our first Gospel with his name. A false tradition would have probably connected it with one of the more favourite figures of early Christian story.

It is repeatedly asserted by the Fathers that St. Matthew wrote his Gospel in *Hebrew*, which may either mean the sacred language of the synagogues, or the popular language of Palestine which we now call Aramaic. It should, however, be remembered that Papias, our earliest authority, describes St. Matthew's composition by the word *Logia*, which seems to point to a list of sacred sayings or "oracles" of our Lord, rather than to a historical narrative. About A.D. 125, Papias writes: "Matthew then composed the Logia in the Hebrew tongue, and every one interpreted them as he was able." [2] About A.D. 185, St. Irenaeus writes: "Matthew published a Gospel among the Hebrews in their own dialect." [3] Origen and Eusebius make similar statements. St. Jerome, in A.D. 392, writes: "Matthew, also called Levi, who from being a publican became an apostle, first wrote a Gospel of Christ in Judaea, and in Hebrew letters and words for the benefit of those of the circumcision who believed. Who afterwards translated it into Greek is not quite certain." [4] We naturally inquire what became of this Hebrew Gospel?

St. Jerome, in A.D. 392, believed that he had found it. He says that it was still preserved at Caesarea, and that the Nazarenes, a Jewish Christian sect of Palestine, allowed him to transcribe a copy of it at Beroea (now Aleppo). In A.D. 398, he says that he had translated this Gospel into Greek and Latin. It is known that it was used by the Nazarenes and by the Ebionites, a Jewish sect which admitted that Jesus was the Messiah, but denied that He was divine. Lastly, we find St. Epiphanius, about the same time as St. Jerome, describing the Hebrew "Gospel according to the Hebrews" as the Gospel written by St. Matthew.

So at the end of the 4th century it was generally believed that the Gospel used by the Nazarenes, and ordinarily known as "the Gospel according to the Hebrews," was the original Hebrew version of Matt. The opinion arose from the two simple facts that it was known that (1) St. Matthew originally wrote in Hebrew, and that (2) the Nazarenes possessed *a* Gospel in Hebrew. The conclusion was natural, but it was false. Clement of Alexandria and Origen, who quote the Gospel according to the Hebrews, do not represent it as the work of St. Matthew. St. Jerome himself felt doubts. When he first discovered the Hebrew Gospel, he felt the enthusiasm of a critic who has made an important find. He believed that he had discovered the original Gospel. He afterwards became more cautious. His later allusions to the Gospel say that "it is called by most the original Matthew," [5] and that it is "the Gospel according to the Apostles or, *as most suppose*, according to Matthew." [6] In fact, this Hebrew Gospel, which bore sometimes the title of "the Hebrews," sometimes "the Apostles," sometimes "St. Matthew," was not the Hebrew original of our present Matthew, nor could it have been written by an Apostle. The fragments of it which now remain come from two versions. Both versions show traces of a mixed Jewish and Gnostic heresy, and are plainly apocryphal. The Holy Spirit is called the "mother" of Jesus, and represented as transporting Him by a hair of His head to Mount Tabor, and our Lord is represented as handing His grave-clothes to the servant of the high-priest as soon as He was risen from the dead. The Gospel certainly seems not only to be a forgery, but to betray a knowledge both of our Greek Gospel according to St. Matthew and that according to St. John.[7] We are obliged to conclude that it throws no light on the origin of our Matt., and that the original Hebrew Matt. was lost at an early date.

On the other hand, it is certain that our Greek Matt. was regarded as authentic in the 2nd century, and it is plain that it records the sayings of Christ with peculiar fulness.

We must now return to what was stated in our previous chapter when dealing with the Synoptic problem. We there saw that there is a great mass of common material in all three Synoptic Gospels, and saw that Mark was probably used as a groundwork for Matt. and Luke. We therefore are led to the conclusion that the Gospel according to St. Matthew is a combination of a Greek version of St. Matthew's original Hebrew Logia—St. Matthew possibly wrote a Greek version of it as well as the Hebrew—with the Gospel written by St. Mark. The combination was apparently made either by the apostle himself, or by a disciple of the apostle as the result of his directions. The Catholic Jewish Christians, knowing that the Gospel contained St. Matthew's own Logia, and that the rest of the Gospel was in accordance with his teaching as delivered to them, called it "the Gospel according to Matthew." The less orthodox Jewish Christians, as we have seen, invented a Gospel of their own.

A little help is given us by the internal evidence afforded by Matt. The author appears to be writing for Greek-speaking converts from Judaism, who need to have Hebrew words interpreted to them. Thus he interprets "Immanuel" (i. 23), "Golgotha" (xxvii. 33), and the words of our Lord on the cross (xxvii. 46). The numerous quotations from the Old Testament have for a long time exercised the ingenuity of scholars, who have believed that they enable us to determine how the Gospel was written. On the whole these quotations suggest two conclusions: (1) That the evangelist knew both Greek and Aramaic, (2) that the Gospel is not a mere translation from the Aramaic or Hebrew. Roughly speaking, the quotations which St. Matthew has in common with the other Synoptists are from the Greek (Septuagint) version of the Old Testament, while those which are peculiar to his Gospel show that the Hebrew has been consulted. Altogether the quotations number 45. Of these there are 11 which are texts quoted by the evangelist himself to illustrate the Messianic work of our Lord, and 9 of the 11 seem to imply a knowledge of Hebrew. They are i. 23; ii. 15, iv. 15-16, viii. 17, xii. 18-21; xiii. 14-15; xiii. 35b; xxi. 5; xxvii. 9, 10. The other 34 texts comprise the quotations which are made in the discourses of our Lord, and they are sometimes called context-quotations or cyclic quotations, as coming in the cycle of discourses. Perhaps 6 or 7 of these 34 texts imply a knowledge of the Hebrew. But it is certain that this class of quotations is far nearer to the Septuagint than the other class. This conclusion remains good in spite of the fact that even the Messianic quotations show the influence of the Septuagint, *e.g.* in i. 23 the writer uses the Septuagint, inasmuch as the Greek word translated "virgin" *necessarily* implies the unique condition of the mother of our Lord, whereas the corresponding Hebrew word does not *necessarily* imply the same condition. Now, it is plain that if the Gospel had been translated from the Hebrew, the context-quotations would probably have been as near to the Hebrew as the quotations made by the evangelist himself. This is not the case. The quotations in Matt. show that the writer knew Hebrew but wrote in Greek, and based part of his work on a Greek document.

The fact that the Gospel was written in Greek does not prove that it was not written in Palestine. It has been urged that it cannot have been written in Palestine, because in ix. 26, 31 we find Palestine called "*that* land," but the phrase may refer only to a part of Palestine, and therefore can hardly be urged as proving anything. It is well known that educated persons in Palestine were acquainted with Greek, although the majority spoke Aramaic. The two languages existed side by side, very much as Welsh and English exist side by side in North Wales. If the Gospel was not written in Palestine, it was probably written in South Syria.

[Sidenote: Date.]

The date must be shortly before A.D. 70. A favourite argument of modern sceptics is that it contains a reference (xxii. 7) to the burning of Jerusalem by the Romans in A.D. 70, and therefore must have been written after that event. The argument rests upon the assumption that our Lord could not have foreseen the event predicted—an assumption which no Christian can accept. Even the favoured servants of God in later ages have sometimes possessed the gift of prophecy. Savonarola certainly foretold the fall of Rome, which took place in A.D. 1527, and the prophecy was printed long before the event seemed credible. Much more might the Son of God have foretold the fall of that city which had so signally neglected His summons. Such expressions as "the holy city," "the holy place," "the city of the great King," suggest that when the Gospel was written it had not yet become the home of "the abomination of desolation." And a far stronger proof is afforded by the caution of the writer in xxiv. 15, "let him that readeth understand." This is an editorial note inserted by the evangelist, as by St. Mark, before our Lord's warning to flee from Judaea. We learn from the early historians of the Church that the Jewish Christians took warning from this statement to flee from Judaea to Peraea before the Romans invested the holy city in A.D. 70. Now, it would have been absurd for the evangelist to insert this note after the Roman forces had begun the siege, as absurd as it would have been to warn the Parisians to flee to England after Paris had been surrounded by the Prussians in 1870, or to warn the English to leave Ladysmith in 1900 after it was surrounded by the Boers. Another and final proof that the Gospel was written before A.D. 70 is given by the form in which the evangelist has recorded our Lord's prophecy of the end of the world (the so-called "eschatological discourse" in chs. xxiv.-xxv.). The prophecy of the destruction of Jerusalem and that of the last coming of the Lord are placed side by side with no perceptible break. Ch. xxiv. 29-31 refers to the last coming of Christ, whereas the verses which immediately precede it refer to the destruction of Jerusalem, and so do vers. 32-34. It is impossible to resist the conclusion that the evangelist believed that the judgment upon Jerusalem would be immediately followed by the last judgment of the world. He knows that our Lord foretold both, and both events loom large in his mind. As a traveller in a valley sees before him two great mountains which appear close to one another, though really separated by many miles, so the evangelist sees these two events together. After the fall of Jerusalem he would almost certainly have made a definite break between the two subjects.

[Sidenote: Literary Style.]

We have already noticed in ch. ii. the fondness for numerical arrangement, which is a marked characteristic of the style of this Gospel. There are other proofs of the fact that this Gospel is more Hebrew in tone than the others. In the other Gospels we find the expression "the kingdom of God," but here we find it called "the kingdom of heaven," an instance of the peculiarly Jewish reverence which shrank from uttering the name of God. There are a few Aramaic words found in this Gospel—*raca* (v. 22), *gehenna* (v. 22), *mammon* (vi. 24); and we should add the peculiar use of "righteousness" in vi. 1, where the word is used in the sense of "alms" in accordance with a Jewish idiom. But the Greek phrases are often neat and clear-cut. They sometimes seem to imply a play upon words, *e.g.* in vi. 16 and xxiv. 30. This is another indication that the Gospel, as it stands, was first written in Greek. The Greek is smoother than that of St. Mark, though not so vivid. The evangelist writes with a joyous interest in his work. The historical parts of it are full of beauty, but he uses them mainly as a framework for the discourses of Jesus, which he preserves with loving fidelity.

In St. Matthew's Gospel the Old Testament is frequently quoted, that the reader may see that Jesus is the realization of the hopes of the Jewish prophets. With set purpose the fair picture of the Servant of Jehovah drawn by Isaiah is placed in the middle of the Gospel (xii. 18-21), that we may recognize it as the true portrait of Christ. Close to it on either side the blasphemies of the Pharisees are skilfully depicted as a foil to His divine beauty. We have already noticed the bearing of these quotations on the origin of the Gospel, but we must speak further of their bearing on the evangelist's view of the Old Testament. His Messianic quotations are introduced by such phrases as "that it might be fulfilled which was spoken by the prophet," or, "then was fulfilled," etc. The tendency of modern scepticism to ridicule the supernatural element in prophecy has caused some writers to depreciate this method of quotation. And we find even a thoughtful Roman Catholic writer speaking of it as "giving the impression that the supple and living story of the life of Jesus is only a chain of debts which fall due, and fulfilments which cannot be avoided." [8] In particular, it has been alleged that the Greek word translated "that," or "in order that," and prefixed to these quotations, implies this fatalistic necessity. But this particular argument is mistaken. In later Greek the use of the word was vaguer than it had been formerly.[9] It cannot be narrowed down so as to prove that the evangelist thought that events in the Old Testament only took place in order to be types which the Son of God constrained Himself to fulfil. And, speaking more generally, we may say that the evangelist shows an exquisite taste in his selection of Messianic quotations. Convinced that Jesus sums up the history of Israel, he does not hesitate to quote passages in the Old Testament, whether they directly refer to the Messianic King, or only call up some picture which has a counterpart in the life of Christ.

Thus the quotations in i. 23 and ii. 6 directly refer to one who is the expected King, that in viii. 17 to one who is the ideal martyred Servant, that in ii. 15 to Israel conceived of as the peculiar child of God and so a type of Christ. In ii. 23 the evangelist finds in the name of *Nazareth* an echo of the ancient Messianic title *Netzer* (a branch). In ii. 18 we see that the tomb of Rachel near Bethlehem reminds him of the mothers of Israel weeping over the death of their children at the hands of the Babylonians; and as Jeremiah poetically conceived of Rachel weeping with the mothers of his own day, so St. Matthew conceives of her as finding her crowning sorrow in the massacre of the Holy Innocents.

Three other quotations deserve special notice: (1) That in xxvii. 9, which the evangelist quotes from "Jeremiah." It is often said that this is a mere mistake for Zechariah. But it is a quotation combined, according to the Jewish method known as the Charaz, or "string of pearls," from Zech. xi. 12 and Jer. xix. 1, 2, 6, the valley of the son of Hinnom being regarded as typical of "the field of blood." (2) That in xxvii. 34, from Ps. lxix. 21. It is said that the evangelist, in order to make our Lord's action correspond with the words of the Psalmist, makes Him drink "gall" instead of "myrrh" (Mark xv. 23), and thus represents the soldiers as cruelly giving Him a nauseating draught instead of a draught to dull His pain. The argument will hardly hold good, for the Greek word translated "gall" can also signify a stupefying drug, and thus Matt. and Mark agree. (3) That in xxi. 2-7, where our Lord is represented as making use of both an ass and a colt for His triumphal entry into Jerusalem. The other Synoptists mention a colt only, and it is supposed that the evangelist altered his narrative of the fact in order to make it agree with a too literal interpretation of Zech. ix. 9. It must be admitted that the account in Mark and Luke has an air of greater probability, and it has the support of the brief account in John. But there is not a decisive contradiction between Matt. and the other Gospels, and it is therefore unreasonable to pass an unfavourable verdict on any of them. The story in Matt. cannot be discredited as containing an apocryphal miracle, and the mere fact that it is so independent of the other Gospels suggests that it is really primitive.

[Sidenote: Character and Contents.]

The chief characteristic of this Gospel is the representation of Jesus as *the Messiah* in whom was fulfilled the Law and the prophets. It was probably placed first in the New Testament because this Messianic doctrine is the point of union between the old covenant and the new. St. Matthew's representation of the Messiah is the result of very careful reflection, and it shows that the evangelist wrote in a spirit which was philosophical and in one sense controversial. He is philosophic because he is not a mere annalist. He groups incidents and discourses together in a manner which brings out their significance as illustrating the Messiahship of Jesus and the majestic forward movement of the kingdom of God. He is in one sense controversial because he wishes his picture of Christ to correct that false idea of the Messiah and His reign which was ruining the Jewish people. The best kind of controversy is that which is intent upon explaining the truth rather than eager to expose and ridicule what is false. So the evangelist presents to his readers Jesus as the Lord's Anointed with inspired powers of persuasion. The manner in which he records our Lord's urgent warnings against going after false Jewish Messiahs at the time when the destruction of Jerusalem should draw near, is a witness to the depth of his convictions. Like the author of the Epistle to the Hebrews, who wrote shortly before him, he cannot endure the thought of any waverers or deserters. The Jewish Christian must be loyal to Jesus, even although the invasion of the holy land by Gentiles may sorely tempt him to throw in his lot with his patriotic but unbelieving kinsmen.

The very first verse suggests the nature of the Gospel—"The book of the generation" (*i.e.* the genealogical tree) "of Jesus Christ, the son of David, the son of Abraham." This "book" includes the first 17 verses of the Gospel.

While St. Luke traces the genealogy of our Lord back to Adam, the head of the human race, St. Matthew desires to show that our Lord, *as the son of Abraham*, is the child of promise in whom all the families of the earth shall be blessed, and, *as the son of David*, is heir to the kingdom of spiritual Israel. The genealogy is partly based on that of the Greek version of 1 Chron. i.-iii., and is intended to teach certain special truths. It is arranged so as to be a kind of summary of the history of the people of God, each group of 14 names ending with a crisis. Jesus is the flower and fulfilment of that history. It furnishes a reply to Jewish critics. They would say that Jesus could not be Messiah unless Joseph, his supposed father, was descended from David. St. Matthew shows that St. Joseph was of Davidic descent. Again, the Jews would say that in any case the Messiah would not be likely to be connected with a humble carpenter and his folk. The evangelist's reply is that David himself was descended from comparatively undistinguished men and from women who were despised. Thus St. Matthew meets both points raised by the Jews.

Of recent years another criticism has been passed on this pedigree of our Lord. A copy of the Old Syriac version of the Gospels, discovered at Sinai and published in 1894, says that Joseph begat Jesus, and in this way denies that Jesus was born of a pure virgin. Some writers who wish to believe that our Lord was brought into the world in the same manner as ourselves, have said that this Syriac version represents what was actually the fact. There is, however, no reason for believing anything of the kind. There is no ground for the notion that the Syriac genealogy was taken from a primitive Jewish register. It is merely a translation of the Greek, probably from some Western Greek manuscript which had "Joseph begat Jesus." When the evangelist wrote the genealogy, he can only have meant that Joseph was by Jewish law regarded as the father of Jesus; for his whole narrative of our Lord's infancy assumes that He was born of a virgin mother. The truth that our Lord was born miraculously is asserted by St. Luke as well as by St. Matthew. It is assumed by St. Paul, when he argues that the second Adam was free from the taint of sin which affected the rest of the first Adam's descendants. It was also cherished from the earliest times in every part of the Christian world where the teaching of the apostles was retained, and was only denied by a few heretics who had openly rejected the teaching of the New Testament on other subjects.

Connected with the representation of Jesus as the Messiah is the record of His continual teaching about the "kingdom of heaven." The "kingdom of heaven" or "kingdom of God" signifies the reign and influence of God. The meaning of it is best expressed by the words in the Lord's Prayer: "Thy kingdom come. Thy will be done, as in heaven, so on earth" (Matt. vi. 10). The second petition explains the first. The kingdom comes in proportion as the righteous will of our loving Father is done among men. The kingdom therefore includes the influence of God in the heart of the believer, or in great movements in the world, or in the organization and growth of His *Church* (xvi. 18; xviii. 17). The kingdom has both a present and a future aspect. In xii. 28 our Lord says to His hearers that it "is come upon you," and in xxi. 31 He speaks of people who were entering into it at the time. But the night before He died He spoke of it as still future (xxvi. 29). It is plain that He taught that it was already present, though its consummation is yet to come. The kingdom is spiritual, "not of this world," it is universal, for though the Jews were "the sons of the kingdom" (viii. 12) by privilege, it is free to others. The worst sinner might come in (xxi. 31), if he came with repentance, humility, and purity of heart. The teaching of Christ with regard to the kingdom was based upon an idea of God's personal rule, which runs through nearly all the Old Testament, beginning with the Books of Samuel and revealing itself in Isaiah, Jeremiah, and Daniel. But our Lord's teaching is original and distinctive. And it is more distant from the popular Jewish idea of a Hebrew counterpart to the Roman empire than the east is distant from the west.

Nowhere else is our Lord shown to have given such an unmistakable sanction to the Law. It is here only that we read, "Think not that I came to destroy the Law, or the prophets: I came not to destroy, but to fulfil" (v. 17).[10] Here, too, we find an allusion to the observance of the sabbath *after* the Ascension (xxiv. 20), a temporary prohibition of preaching to the Gentiles and Samaritans (x. 5), and the statement of our Lord, "I was not sent but unto the lost sheep of the house of Israel" (xv. 24). Most remarkable of all is the direction to obey the scribes and Pharisees (xxiii. 3). On the other hand, there is a rigorous denunciation of the rabbinical additions to the Jewish Law. Mercy is preferable to sacrifice (xii. 7), the Son of man is Lord of the sabbath (xii. 8), moral defilement does not come from a failure to observe ceremonial (xv. 11), the kingdom will be transferred to a more faithful nation (xxi. 43), even the strangers from the east and the west (viii. 11), the Gospel will be for all people (xxiv. 14), and the scribes and Pharisees are specially denounced (xxiii. 13).

It has been said that there is an absolute opposition between these two classes of sayings; that either Jesus contradicted Himself, or the evangelist drew from one source which was of a Judaizing character, and from

21

another source which taught St. Paul's principle of justification by faith *versus* justification by the Law. But the same divine paradox of truth which we find in Matt. runs through most of the New Testament, and is found plainly in St. Paul. In the Epistle where he exposes the failure of contemporary Judaism most remorselessly, he asserts that "we establish the Law." The true inner meaning of the divine revelation granted in the Old Testament *is* fulfilled in Christ. Not only so, but Christ Himself was "the servant of the circumcision," living "under the Law." The limits which He imposed upon His own ministry (xv. 24) and that of His apostles (x. 5) were entirely fitting until Christ at His resurrection laid aside all that was peculiarly Jewish with its limits and humiliations.

ANALYSIS[11]

The infancy of our Lord: i. 1-ii. 23.—Genealogy from Abraham, announcement to Joseph, birth, visit of Magi, flight into Egypt, massacre of innocents, settlement at Nazareth.

A.

Winter A.D. 26 till after Pentecost 27.

The preparation for the ministry: iii. 1-iv. 11.—

The ministry of John the Baptist and the baptism of Jesus, the threefold temptation.

B.

Pentecost A.D. 27 till before Passover 28.

The preaching of the kingdom of God by Jesus in Galilee: iv. 12-xiii. 58.—The call of the four fishermen, Jesus preaches and heals (iv.). The Sermon on the Mount—Jesus fulfils the law, the deeper teaching concerning the commandments (v.). False and true almsgiving, prayer and fasting, worldliness, trust in God (vi.). Censoriousness, discrimination in teaching, encouragements to prayer, false prophets, the two houses (vii.). The ministry at Capernaum and by the lake is illustrated by the record of many works of *Messianic healing power* (viii.-ix.), the apostles are chosen and receive a charge (x.), and the ministry is illustrated by words and parables of *Messianic wisdom* (xi.-xiii.). We find a growing hostility on the part of the scribes and Pharisees (ix. 11; ix. 34; xii. 2, xii. 14; xii. 24). Jesus returns to Nazareth (xiii. 53-58).

[Perplexity of Herod and death of John the Baptist, xiv. 1-12.]

C.

Passover A.D. 28 till before Tabernacles 28.

Climax of missionary work in Galilee: xiv. 13-xviii. 35.—Christ feeds the 5000, walks on the sea, heals the sick in Gennesaret (xiv.). Christ now labours chiefly in the dominions of Herod Philip, the journeys are more plainly marked in Mark. Teaching about defilement, the Canaanite woman, Christ feeds the 4000 (xv.).

Leaven of the Pharisees and Sadducees, Peter's confession of Christ, Christ's first prediction of His death (xvi.). Transfiguration, lunatic boy cured, second prediction of death, the shekel in the fish's mouth (xvii.). Treatment of children, Christ saving lost sheep, forgiveness (xviii.).

D.

Tabernacles, September A.D. 28 until early 29.

The ministry in Peraea; xix. i-xx. 34.—Christ forbids divorce, He blesses children, the rich young man, the difficulties of the rich (xix.). Parable of the labourers, Christ's third prediction of His death, the request of the mother of Zebedee's children, the two blind men of Jericho (xx.).

E.

Passover A.D. 29.

Last days at Jerusalem, and afterwards: xxi. 1-xxviii. 20.—Entry into Jerusalem, the cleansing of the temple, the withered fig tree, Christ challenged, parable of the vineyard (xxi.). The marriage feast, three questions to entrap Christ, His question (xxii.). On not seeking chief places, denunciation of scribes and Pharisees, lament over Jerusalem (xxiii.).

Predictions of destruction of temple, siege of Jerusalem, the second coming (xxiv.), three discourses on the judgment (xxv.).

The Council discuss how they may arrest Jesus, the woman with the ointment, Judas' bargain, the Passover, Gethsemane, the betrayal, the trial before Caiaphas, Peter's denial (xxvi.). Jesus delivered to Pilate, Judas' suicide, Jesus tried by Pilate, Jesus and Barabbas, the mockery, crucifixion, burial by Joseph of Arimathaea, guard granted by Pilate (xxvii.).

The women at the sepulchre, the angel, Jesus meets them, the guard bribed, Jesus meets the eleven in Galilee, His commission to baptize and teach (xxviii.).

Note on the Date of Matthew.—Irenaeus, apparently following Papias, says, "Matthew published a written Gospel among the Hebrews in their own dialect, Peter and Paul preaching the Gospel at Rome" (*Adv. Haer.* iii. 1). This would fix the date of the Hebrew Matt. about A.D. 63, if it was the intention of Irenaeus to give chronological information in this sentence. But the context makes it more probable that this is not the case, and that he simply wished to make it clear that the teaching of the four chief apostles, Peter and Paul, Matthew and John, has come down to us in writing. That of Matthew and John survives in their Gospels, that of Peter and Paul, though they wrote no Gospels, survives in Mark and Luke. Eusebius, in his *Chronicle* dates the composition in A.D. 41. This he probably does in order to make it fit with the supposed departure of the apostles from Jerusalem after twelve years from the Crucifixion. His statement is very improbable. At any rate our Greek Matt. must have been written after Mark. The frequent quotations from it in primitive literature from the Epistle of Barnabas and the *Didaché* onwards, bear witness both to its early date and its high authority. Internal evidence points to the same conclusion. In addition to what is said above (p. 38), we may note some passages likely to perplex the reader. Such are ii. 23, "the ass *and the colt*" in xxi. 7, the "three days and *three nights* in the belly of the whale" mentioned as typical of Christ's rest in the tomb (xii. 40), the absence of all reference to the *burning* of the temple in xxiv. 2, the reference to Zachariah the son of Barachiah (xxiii. 35; contrast 2 Chron. xxiv. 20). Such verses would probably have been altered if the Gospel had not gained an authoritative position at a very early date.

[1] Strom. iv. 9.

[2] Eusebius, *H. E.* iii. 39.

[3] *Adv. Haer.* iii. 1.

[4] *De Vir, Ill.* 3.

[5] *In Matt.* xii. 13.

[6] *Con. Pelag.* iii. 1.

[7] So Prof. Armitage Robinson, *Expositor*, March, 1897.

[8] Batiffol, *Six Leçons sur les Evangiles*, p. 48.

[9] Burton, *Syntax of the Moods and Tenses of New Testament Greek*, pp. 92-95.

[10] In this Gospel only is sin called "lawlessness."

[11] These analyses of the Gospels are not complete, but are arranged with the hope that the readers, by studying all the four, may gain a clearer conception of the life of our Lord.

CHAPTER IV THE GOSPEL ACCORDING TO ST. MARK

[Sidenote: The Author.]

John Mark was the son of a Mary who was an influential member of the Church at Jerusalem, as the Church met in her house (Acts xii. 12). He was a cousin of Barnabas (Col. iv. 10), who had been a man of some property. It has been thought that Mark was the "young man" referred to in the account given by this Gospel of the arrest of Jesus in the garden. To others the incident would probably have appeared insignificant. He lived at Jerusalem during the famine in A.D. 45, and Barnabas took him to Antioch on returning thither from Jerusalem at that time. He accompanied St. Paul and St. Barnabas on St. Paul's first missionary journey, and laboured with them at Salamis in Cyprus. It is possible that Acts xiii. 5 means that John Mark had been a "minister" of the synagogue at Salamis. At any rate, the Greek can be so interpreted. After crossing from Paphos to the mainland of Asia Minor, the missionaries arrived at Perga. Here St. Paul made the great resolve to extend the gospel beyond the Taurus mountains. St. Mark determined to leave him. Perhaps he was not prepared for so magnificent an undertaking as a "work" which included the conversion of the Gentiles (Acts xiv. 27), or for the substitution of the leadership of St. Paul for that of St. Barnabas.

St. Mark returned to Jerusalem, and was again at Antioch about the time of St. Paul's rebuke of St. Peter. Possibly St. Mark followed the example of most of the Jewish Christians at Antioch in inducing St. Peter and St. Barnabas to withdraw from fellowship with the Gentile converts. Whether he did so or not, it is certain that St. Paul refused to take St. Mark with him on his second missionary journey, A.D. 49. St. Barnabas then went home to Cyprus with St. Mark. We hear no more of the future evangelist until A.D. 60, when we find that he is with St. Paul in Rome, and completely reconciled to him. He is the apostle's "fellow-worker" and his "comfort" (Col. iv. 11; Philem. 24). About four years later, St. Paul, in writing shortly before his martyrdom to Timothy, requests him to come to Rome by the shortest route, and to take up Mark on the way, "for he is useful to me for ministering" (2 Tim. iv. 11). The last notice that we have of St. Mark in the New Testament illustrates how complete a harmony had been effected between the expansive theology of St. Paul and the once cramped policy of St. Peter and St. Mark. In his First Epistle St. Peter refers to "Mark, my son," and his words make it certain that the two friends were then together at Babylon, *i.e.* Rome.

In the 4th century it was widely believed that St. Mark was the founder of Christianity in Alexandria, and the first bishop of the see which was afterwards ruled by St. Athanasius and St. Cyril. It is important to notice that this tradition appears first in Eusebius, and is not mentioned in the extant works of Clement and Origen, the great luminaries of the early Alexandrian Church. But it seems to be too well supported by the great writers of the 4th century for us to regard it as a fabrication. If the tale is true, St. Mark must have brought Christianity to Alexandria either after the death of St. Peter about A.D. 65, or about A.D. 55, in the interval between his separation from St. Paul and his stay with him at Rome.

The early Fathers, so far as their testimony remains, are unanimous in ascribing this Gospel to St. Mark, and they are equally unanimous in tracing the work of St. Mark to the influence of St. Peter. Justin Martyr speaks of the "Memoirs of Peter" when referring to a statement which we find in Mark iii. 17. Papias closely associates the two saints in his account of the Gospel, and gives us his information on the authority of John the Presbyter, who was a disciple of the Lord. Irenaeus, Clement of Alexandria, Tertullian, and Origen say practically the same thing. This evidence is overwhelming, and it is uncontradicted by any early authority. The statement of Papias is as follows: "And the elder said this also: Mark, having become the interpreter of Peter, wrote down accurately everything that he remembered of the things that were either said or done by Christ; but, however, not in order. For neither did he hear the Lord, nor did he follow Him; but afterwards, as I said, he attended Peter, who adapted his instructions to the needs of his hearers, but had no design of giving a connected account of the Lord's words. So then Mark committed no error in thus writing down certain things as he remembered them; for he made it his special care not to omit anything that he heard, or to set down any false statement therein." [1] By calling St. Mark an *interpreter*, Papias perhaps means that he translated statements made in Aramaic into Greek, which was the language most used by the Christians of Rome until the 3rd century after Christ. By saying that St. Mark wrote *not in order*, Papias probably means that the Gospel is not a systematic history of all our Lord's ministry, or an orderly arrangement of subjects placed together with a view to instruction like those in Matthew. So far as we are able to test them, the facts are related chronologically in the great majority of cases.

Papias does not tell us when St. Mark wrote his Gospel. Irenaeus writes: "Matthew also published a written Gospel among the Hebrews in their own dialect, Peter and Paul preaching the Gospel at Rome, and laying the foundations of the Church. After their departure, Mark, the disciple and interpreter of Peter, delivered to us in writing the things that had been preached by Peter." [2] St. Peter and St. Paul probably died not later than A.D. 65. Eusebius quotes from Clement of Alexandria "that Peter having publicly preached the word at Rome, and having spoken the Gospel by the Spirit, many present exhorted Mark to write the things which had been spoken, since he had long accompanied Peter, and remembered what he had said; and that when he had composed the Gospel, he delivered it to them who had asked it of him, which when Peter knew, he neither forbad nor encouraged it." [3] Clement is here relying upon "the presbyters of old," and the antiquity of the tradition is proved by the fact that it does not claim St. Peter's direct sanction for the Gospel. Both Irenaeus and Clement were probably born about A.D. 130, or earlier. Irenaeus was acquainted with Rome, where St. Peter taught, while Clement lived at Alexandria, where St. Mark was probably bishop. Moreover, Clement's office of head-catechist at Alexandria had been previously held by at least three predecessors, who must have handed down traditions of first-rate value. The testimony of Clement with regard to St. Mark is not inconsistent with that of Irenaeus. The

Gospel was probably written while St. Peter was alive, and when he was dead, was given to the Church. Possibly it underwent some revision before publication. Now, as St. Peter evidently had not taught in Rome when St. Paul wrote the Epistle to the Romans in A.D. 56, and as St. Mark was in Rome when he wrote the Epistle to the Colossians in A.D. 60, we may reasonably date this Gospel about A.D. 62. It seems to be later than Colossians, as there is no indication of St. Peter's being in Rome when that Epistle was written.

[Sidenote: Literary Style.]

The internal evidence afforded by the Gospel strongly corroborates the belief that it was based upon the discourses of one who had been with our Lord during His ministry. It is marked by a vivid and dramatic realism. There is a fondness for rapid transitions from one scene to another, as may be illustrated by the fact that the Greek word for "immediately" occurs no less than forty-one times. In i. 27 the actual form of an original dialogue is shown in the abrupt and broken sentences employed. St. Mark uses different tenses of the Greek verb—present, perfect, imperfect, and aorist—with singular freedom, not because he did not know Greek well enough to write with more regularity, but because he is carried away by his interest in the facts which he relates. The student will find good instances of this interchange of tenses in v. 15 ff.; vi. 14 ff.; viii. 35; ix. 34 ff. St. Mark's language shows that he was well acquainted with the Greek version of the Old Testament, which has exercised considerable influence on his style.

There are many picturesque phrases, such as "the heavens rent" (i. 10) and "devour houses" (xii. 40). There are little redundancies in which the author repeats his thoughts with a fresh shade of meaning, as "at even, when the sun did set" (i. 32); "he looked steadfastly, and was restored, and saw all things clearly" (viii. 25); "all that she had, even all her living" (xii. 44). There is a frequent use of popular diminutives, such as words for "little boat," "little daughter," "little dog." This is probably due to provincial Custom, and may be compared with the fondness shown in some parts of Scotland for words such as "boatie," "lassie" or "lassock," etc. There are several Hebraisms. Some of the Greek words are frankly plebeian, such as a foreigner would pick up without realizing that they were inelegant. There are also some Aramaic words and phrases which the writer inserts with a true artistic sense and then interprets—*Boanerges* (iii. 17), *Talitha cumi* (v. 41), *Corban* (vii. 11), *Ephphatha* (vii. 34), *Abba* (xiv. 36), and *Eloi, Eloi, lama sabachthani*[4] (xv. 34). The Greek also contains numerous grammatical irregularities which betray the hand of a foreigner, as in ii. 26; iv. 22; vi. 52; vii. 4, 19; ix. 18, xi.32; xiii. 34. The use of participles is clumsy, especially in the account of the woman with the issue of blood (v. 25 ff.). Finally, there are more Latin words and idioms than in any of the other Gospels. Latin idioms may be seen in v. 23 and xv. 15, and instances of Latin words are *speculator* (vi. 27), *centurion* (xv. 39), *sextarius* (vii. 4), *denarius* (vi. 37), *quadrans* (xii. 42). In xii. 42, xv. 16, Greek words are explained in Latin.

These facts corroborate the tradition that the writer was a Palestinian who stayed in Rome, and knew personally some one who had exceptional knowledge of our Lord's actual words.

The narrative is particularly fresh, and abounds in vivid details such as would have been likely to linger in St. Peter's memory. The green grass whereon the crowds sat, and the appearance of flower-beds which they presented in their gay costume (vi. 39, 40); the stern of the boat, and the pillow whereon our Lord slept (iv. 38); the Gerasene demoniac cutting himself with stones (v. 5); the woman who was a Syro-Phoenician but spoke Greek (vii. 26); Jesus taking children in His arms (ix. 36; x. 16); the street where the colt was tied (xi. 4); the two occasions on which the cock crew (xiv. 68, 72); and St. Peter warming himself in the light of the fire (xiv. 54);—such are some of the instances of the writer's fidelity in recording the impressions of his teacher. This Gospel also abounds in proper names, both of places and persons. Among the latter may be mentioned the name of Bartimaeus, the blind beggar (x. 46); the names of Alexander and Rufus, the sons of Simon of Cyrene (xv. 21); Salome, the mother of Zebedee's children (xv. 40); and Boanerges, their surname (iii. 17). Equally remarkable is the manner in which the emotions of our Lord and others are recorded. We notice the indignation and grief which He felt in the synagogue (iii. 5); His compassion for the unshepherded people (vi. 34); His deep sigh at the sceptical demand for a sign from heaven (viii. 12), His displeasure at the disciples for keeping the children from Him (x. 14); His undisguised love for the rich young man who yet lacked one thing (x. 21); His tragic walk in front of the apostles (x. 32); the intensity of feeling with which He was driven into the wilderness (i. 12), and overturned the tables and seats in the temple (xi. 15). St. Mark always seems to be painting our Lord from the life.

In spite of the fact that St. Mark shows that he knew well how to compress the material which was at his disposal, there is hardly a story which he narrates in common with the other synoptists without some special feature. We may notice the imploring words of the father of the lunatic boy (ix. 2), the spoken blessing on little children (x. 16), the view of the temple (xiii. 3), and Pilate's question of the centurion (xv. 44). None of these things are narrated in the other Gospels. In ix. 2-13 we have the story of the Transfiguration, with the statement that the garments of our Lord "became glistering, exceeding white; *so as no fuller on earth can whiten them.*" We are also told that St. Peter then addressed our Lord as "Rabbi," and that "he wist not what to answer." The same significant phrase, "they wist not what to answer Him," occurs in St. Mark's account of the agony in the garden (xiv. 40). These are only a few instances out of many which show St. Mark's originality, and they are just such personal reminiscences as we might expect St. Peter to retain.

[Sidenote: Character and Contents.]

Just as the style is realistic and the narrative circumstantial, so the contents are practical. "He went about doing good" is the impression which this Gospel gives us of our Lord. The teaching which He announced to the people is made less prominent than in Matt. If we count even the shortest similitudes as parables, we find only nine parables in Mark. Equally remarkable is the absence of quotations made by the writer. He records numerous references made by our Lord to the Old Testament, though fewer than Matt. or Luke, but the only quotations made by St. Mark himself are in i. 2, 3 (Mal. iii. 1; Isa. xl. 3) and xv. 28 (Isa. liii. 12). On the other hand, we find eighteen miracles, only two less than in the much longer Gospel of St. Matthew. The theological tone of Mark may be described as neutral. There is no trace of the innocent preferences which Matt. and Luke show toward this or that aspect of the teaching of Jesus. In Mark we do not find so strong an approval of the more permanent parts of the Jewish Law, or so strong a denunciation of the Pharisees who exalted the external adjuncts of the Law, as we find in Matt. Nor do we find such parables as the Good Samaritan and the Prodigal Son, by which Luke lays emphasis upon the truth that the Jews have no monopoly of holiness, and that the outcast is welcome to the gospel. Mark is less Jewish than Matt., less Gentile and Pauline than Luke. It used to be said that this was the result of "trimming," and intended to bridge over the differences between two different schools of theology. But the charge has broken down. St. Mark, though not anti-Jewish, regards Christ as above the law of the sabbath (ii. 28), and teaches the necessity of new external religious forms (ii. 22). Though he is not Jewish, and though he omits the statement made in Matt. xv. 24, a statement indicating that the Jews had the first right to be taught by the Messiah, he does record, like Matt., the still harder statement of the same fact made to the Syro-Phoenician woman (vii. 27). The truth is that St. Mark is neutral simply in the sense that he faithfully records a story which was moulded before doctrinal conflicts had taken place between Christian believers. The doctrine of St. Mark is archaic.

One of the most distinctive features of this Gospel is the decisive clearness with which it shows how Jesus trained and educated His disciples. The simplicity with which St. Mark describes the faults of the friends of our Lord is as remarkable as the vigour with which the gestures and feelings of our Lord are portrayed. St. Mark relates how that early in the ministry of Jesus, His friends (iii. 21) said that He was mad, and that "His mother and His brethren" (iii. 31) sought to bring Him back. The discipline and education of the disciples are recorded with a plain revelation of their mistakes and their spiritual dulness. When they had settled in Capernaum Christ shows them that He must find a wider sphere of work (i. 38); He meets with a significant silence their obtrusive remonstrance when the woman with the issue of blood caused Him to ask, "Who touched My clothes?" (v. 30, 31); He tells them with affectionate care "to rest a while," when they had been too busy even to eat (vi. 31); He rebukes them gravely when they put a childish interpretation upon His command to beware of the leaven of the Pharisees and of Herod, the formalists and the Erastian (viii. 17); they are unintelligent and uninquiring when He prophesies His death and resurrection (ix. 32), and after this prophecy they actually dispute about their own precedence (ix. 34); when Christ goes boldly forward to Jerusalem, they follow with fear and hesitation (x. 32); He rebukes the niggardly criticism of those who were indignant with the "waste" of the perfume poured upon His head (xiv. 6); and in Gethsemane "they all left Him and fled" (xiv. 50).

Among these disciples, St. Peter is prominent, and though his confession of the Messiahship of Jesus is recorded, a confession which is necessarily central in the Gospel (viii. 29), St. Mark neither records that our Lord designed him as the rock, nor his commission to feed the Lord's lambs and sheep. On the other hand, St. Mark inserts things which were often of a nature to humble St. Peter. He records the crushing reprimand which he received when he criticized the Lord's mission (viii. 33); it was Peter's fanciful plan to erect three tabernacles on the scene of the Transfiguration (ix. 5), it was Peter who informed the Lord that the fig tree had withered after His curse (xi. 21), it was Peter whom Christ awoke in Gethsemane by uttering his name "Simon" (xiv. 37); and Peter's denial appears doubly guilty in this Gospel, inasmuch as he did not repent until the cock crew *twice* (xiv. 68, 72). At the beginning (iii. 16) and at the end (xvi. 7) Peter occupies a special position. But the conduct of Peter is narrated in a fashion which renders the notion of fiction quite impossible. The Gospel cannot have been written by a hero-worshipper wishing to glorify a saint of old, but must surely have been written by "the interpreter of Peter."

In comparing the contents of Mark with those of Matt. and Luke, we are struck by the absence of many of our Lord's discourses. Yet we find an eschatological discourse about the second coming in xiii., though much shorter than those in Matt. xxiv. and xxv. The genuineness of Mark xiii. has been assailed, and it has been described as an apocalyptic "fly-sheet," which was somehow inserted in the Gospel. There is no reason for believing this theory to be true. The chapter was in Mark when it was incorporated into Matthew, and its teaching agrees with that attributed to our Lord in the collections of Logia. We have also the beginning of the charge given to the apostles (vi. 7-11; cf. Matt. x.). There are a few echoes of the Sermon on the Mount, and only a specimen of the final denunciation of the Pharisees, which occupies a whole chapter in Matt. (Mark xii. 38-40, cf. Matt. xxiii.). We find a few statements made by our Lord which are peculiar to this Gospel: *e.g.*—"the sabbath was made for man, and not man for the sabbath" (ii. 27), "foolishness" coming from the heart (vii. 22); "every sacrifice shall be salted with salt" (ix. 49); "Father, all things are possible unto Thee," in the touching filial appeal during the agony (xiv. 36). Here alone have we the tiny parable about the growth of the blade of corn (iv. 26), and that of the porter commanded to watch until the master's return (xiii. 34). There are two miracles peculiar to Mark, the cure of the deaf-mute (vii. 32) and of the blind man at Bethsaida (viii. 22). Among the miracles recorded in Mark, the cures of demoniacs are prominent. This is in peculiar contrast with John, where we find no cure of demoniacs recorded.

In marked contrast to St. Luke, St. Mark appears indifferent to the political conditions of the countries where our Lord worked. Thus Herod Antipas is simply called "the king" (vi. 14), whereas both in Matt. and Luke he is correctly called by the title of "tetrarch," which only implies governorship of a portion of a country. Yet the narrative of St. Mark shows that he was quite aware of facts which can only be explained by the political conditions which he does not describe. He knows that Tyre and Sidon, Caesarea Philippi and Bethsaida, which were not under Herod Antipas, were more safe for our Lord than Capernaum. And he knows that in travelling to Jerusalem He was in greater danger than while He remained in Galilee, and was meeting His doom at the sentence of Gentile officials. Although St. Mark is silent as to the names of many of the places which our Lord visited, he gives us numerous indications of the various scenes of our Lord's labours. We are thus able to fix the geographical surroundings of nearly all the more important events, and construct an intelligible plan of our Lord's ministry. We can see how He made the shores of the lake of Gennesaret the focus of His mission, and went on evangelistic journeys from Capernaum into Galilee. The time of these journeys was largely determined by circumstances, such as the unregulated enthusiasm of the mob, the spite of the scribes at Capernaum, or the anger of Herod's court at Tiberias. Towards the end of the ministry in Galilee our Lord devoted Himself to the deeper instruction of His Apostles and their initiation into the mystery of His death (vii. 24 ff.; viii. 27 ff.). For such teaching the mountain slopes of Lebanon and Hermon afforded scenes of perfect calm and beauty.

ANALYSIS

A.

Winter A.D. 26 till after Pentecost 27.

The preparation for the ministry; i. 1-13.—The mission of John the Baptist and the baptism of Jesus, the temptation.

B.

Pentecost A.D. 27 till before Passover 28.

The ministry of Jesus in Galilee, journeys from Capernaum; i. 14-vi. 13.—The call of the four fishermen, Jesus preaches and heals at Capernaum (i. 14-34).

First missionary journey, in towns of Galilee: leper cleansed, return to Capernaum (i. 38-ii. 1). Work in Capernaum, five grounds of offence against Jesus, Jesus followed by crowds of hearers on the sea-shore (ii. 2-iii. 12). Appointment of the twelve, Christ accused of alliance with Satan, the unpardonable sin, Christ's relation to His mother and brethren. He begins to teach in parables about the kingdom (iii. 13-iv. 34).

Second missionary journey, on the eastern shore of the lake of Gennesaret: the storm calmed, Gerasene demoniac and swine (iv. 35-v. 20). Return to the western shore, the cure of the woman who touched His garment, Jairus' daughter raised (v. 21-43).

Third missionary journey, in the western highlands, including Nazareth, where He is rejected, and adjacent villages, the mission of the twelve (vi. 1-13).

[Perplexity of Herod and death of John the Baptist, vi. 14-29.]

C.

Passover A.D. 28 till before Tabernacles 28.

Climax of missionary work in Galilee, journeys from Capernaum; vi. 30-ix. 50.—Christ in a desert place feeds the 5000, visits Bethsaida, walks on the sea, returns to Gennesaret, heals many (vi. 30-56). Teaching about defilement (vii. 1-23).

Fourth missionary journey, to the north-west into Phoenicia: the Syro-Phoenician woman, departure from Tyre and Sidon, approach to the sea of Galilee through Decapolis, cure of the deaf-mute (vii. 24-37). Christ feeds the 4000 (viii. 1-9) Christ takes ship to Dalmanutha, Pharisees seek a sign, Jesus takes ship to the other side, the leaven of the Pharisees and of Herod, cure of a blind man at Bethsaida (viii. 10-26).

Fifth journey, to towns of Caesarea Philippi, special teaching of the select few: Peter's confession of Christ, Christ's first prediction of His death (viii. 27-ix. 1). Transfiguration, lunatic boy cured, journey through Galilee, second prediction of death, arrival at Capernaum, the value of a child's example, the danger of causing one to stumble (ix. 2-50).

D.

Tabernacles, September A.D. 28 until early 29.

Journey to Jerusalem through Peraea: x.—Christ forbids divorce, blesses children, the rich young man, the difficulties of the rich, Christ's third prediction of His death, the request of Zebedee's sons, Christ's announcement of His mission to serve, blind Bartimaeus cured at Jericho.

E.

Passover A.D. 29.

Last days at Jerusalem, and afterwards; xi. 1-xvi. 20.—Entry into Jerusalem, the withered fig-tree, cleansing of the temple, the duty of forgiveness, Christ challenged (xi.). The parable of the vineyard, three questions to entrap Christ, His question, denunciation of scribes, the widow's mites (xii.).

Predictions of destruction of temple, of woes and of the second coming (xiii.).

The Council discuss how they may arrest Jesus, the woman with the ointment, Judas' bargain, the Passover, Gethsemane, the betrayal, the trial before the Council, Peter's denial (xiv.). Jesus delivered to Pilate, trial, Jesus and Barabbas, the mockery, crucifixion, burial by Joseph of Arimathaea (xv.).

The women at the sepulchre, the angel (xvi. 1-8).

Appendix with summary of appearances of the Lord (xvi. 9-20).

Note on the Concluding Section.—The origin of xvi. 9-20 is one of the most difficult of questions, (a) The section is not found in the two famous Greek MSS., the Vatican and the Sinaitic, nor is it found in the very ancient Sinaitic Syriac MS. It is also lacking in one Latin MS. (k), which represents the Latin version used before St. Jerome made the Vulgate translation, about A.D. 384. The great scholar Eusebius, A.D. 320, omitted it from his "canons," which contain parallel passages from the three Gospels. (b) The language does not resemble the Greek employed in other parts of the Gospels, differing from it in some small particulars which most strongly suggest diversity of authorship. (c) Much of the section might have been constructed out of the other Gospels and Acts; *e.g.* ver. 9 is thought to be derived from John xx. 14, and ver. 14 from John xx. 26-29. (d) Mary Magdalene is introduced as though she had not been mentioned previously; but she has already appeared thrice in Mark (xv. 40, 47; xvi. 1). On the other hand, it is obvious that the Gospel could never have ended with the words "for they were afraid," in ver. 8. All the old Latin MSS. contain the present section except k, and perhaps originally A. The evidence of the Vatican and the Sinaitic MSS. is not so strong as it appears to be at first sight. The end of Mark in the Sinaitic was actually written by the same scribe as the man who wrote the New Testament in the Vatican MS. And the way in which he has arranged the conclusion of the Gospel in both MSS. suggests that the MSS. from which the Sinaitic and the Vatican were copied, both contained this or a similar section. Moreover, there is considerable reason for thinking that he acted under the personal influence of Eusebius. The verses are attested by Irenaeus, and apparently by Justin and Hermas, and were therefore regarded as authentic, or at least as truthful, by educated men at Lyons and Rome, in the 2nd century. A possible solution is offered by an Armenian MS. (A.D. 986), which assigns the section to the "presbyter Ariston." This is probably the presbyter Aristion whom Papias describes as a disciple of the Lord (Eusebius, *H. E.* iii. 39). The conclusion of St. Mark's MS. probably became accidentally detached, and vanished soon after his death, and the Church may well have requested one who knew the Lord to supply the deficiency.

[1] Eusebius, *H. E.* iii. 39.

[2] *Op. cit.* iii. 39.

[3] Eusebius, *H. E.* vi. 14.

[4] Also in Matt. xxvii. 46. Observe also the explanation of Beelzebub (iii. 22), Gehenna (ix. 43), Bartimaeus (x. 46), Golgotha (xv. 22). Also the explanation of Jewish customs in vii. 3, 4; xiv. 12.

CHAPTER V THE GOSPEL ACCORDING TO ST. LUKE

[Sidenote: The Author.]

The evidence for believing that the third Gospel was written by St. Luke, the friend of St. Paul, is very strong. In the 2nd century both this Gospel and Acts were attributed to him. St. Irenaeus, about A.D. 185, writes: "Luke, also, the companion of Paul, recorded in a book the gospel preached by him." [1] A few years earlier the author of the *Muratorian Fragment* wrote the words, "The third book of the Gospel, that according to Luke."

According to Eusebius and Jerome and an unknown writer of the 3rd century, St. Luke was a native of Antioch in Syria. Of this we seem to have confirmation in the full account given in Acts of the Church at Antioch. It is shown by Col. iv. 14 that he was a Gentile, as there is a distinction drawn between him and those "of the circumcision." From the same passage we learn that he was a physician. Traces of his profession have been discovered in the frequency with which he describes the *healing* wrought by Christ and His apostles (iv. 18, 23; ix. 1, 2, 6; x. 9; xxii. 51), and the occasional use of terms which a physician was more likely to employ than other people (iv. 38; v. 12; vi. 19; xxii. 44). It is very possible that it is St. Luke who is described (2 Cor. viii. 18) as "the brother whose praise in the gospel is spread through all the Churches." This tradition can be traced as far back as Origen. The fact that he was a dear friend of St. Paul is shown by the epithet "beloved" in Col. iv. 14; by the fact that he is one of the "fellow-workers" who send greetings from Rome when St. Paul, who was imprisoned there, wrote to Philemon; and by the touching statement in 2 Tim. iv. 11, where St. Paul, as he awaits his death, writes, "Only Luke is with me."

St. Luke's relations with St. Paul are further illustrated from Acts. The literary resemblances between this Gospel and Acts are so numerous and so subtle that the tradition which ascribes both books to one author cannot reasonably be controverted. The passages in Acts which contain the word "we" show that the writer of Acts accompanied St. Paul from Troas to Philippi in A.D. 50, when the apostle made his first missionary journey in Europe (Acts xvi. 10-17). The apostle left him at Philippi. About six years afterwards St. Paul was again at Philippi, and there met St. Luke, who travelled with him to Jerusalem (Acts xx. 5-xxi. 18); he also was with the apostle when he made the voyage to Rome, and was shipwrecked with him at Malta. A writer of the 3rd century (quoted in Wordsworth's *Vulgate*, p. 269) tells us that St. Luke had neither wife nor children, and died in Bithynia at the age of seventy-four. A writer of the 6th century asserts that St. Luke was a painter, and attributes to him a certain picture of the Blessed Virgin. Another such picture is preserved in the great church of S. Maria Maggiore at Rome. The legend finds no support in early Christian writers. At the same time, it bears witness to the fact that this Gospel contains the elements of beauty in especial richness. It is the work of St. Luke that inspired Fra Angelico's pictures of the Annunciation, and the English hymn "Abide with me."

Although St. Irenaeus is the first writer who names St. Luke as the author of the third Gospel, the Gospel is quoted by earlier writers. Special mention must be made of (1) *Justin Martyr*. He records several facts only found in this Gospel, *e.g.* Elisabeth as the mother of John the Baptist, the census under Quirinius, and the cry, "Father, into Thy hands I commend My spirit." (2) *Celsus*, the pagan philosopher, who opposed Christianity. He refers to the genealogy which narrates that Jesus was descended from the first man. (3) The *Letter of the Churches of Lyons and Vienne*, written in A.D. 177. (4) *Marcion.* He endeavoured to found a system of theology which he pretended to be in accordance with the teaching of St. Paul. He rejected the Old Testament as the work of an evil god, and asserted that St. Paul was the only apostle who was free from the taint of Judaism. The only Gospel which he kept was that according to St. Luke, which he retained as agreeing with the teaching of St. Paul. The contents of Marcion's Gospel can be largely discovered in Tertullian. The differences which existed between Marcion's Gospel and our Luke can be easily accounted for. Here, as in St. Paul's Epistles, he simply altered the passages which did not agree with his own interpretation of St. Paul's doctrine. For instance, in Luke xiii. 28, instead of "Abraham, and Isaac, and Jacob," he put "the righteous." The account of our Lord's birth and infancy he omitted, because he did not believe that our Lord's human body was thoroughly human and real. An interesting modern parallel to Marcion's New Testament can be found in England. At the beginning of the 19th century the English Unitarians circulated large numbers of an English version of the New Testament in which were altered all the passages in the English Authorised Version which imply that Jesus is God. The translators of this Unitarian version accepted the Gospels of the New Testament as genuine, although they used unscrupulous methods to support their assertion that the New Testament is Unitarian. In the same way Marcion, although he made unscrupulous alterations in Luke in order to prove that it was really Marcionite, obviously accepted it as a genuine work of the apostolic age.

The Preface of the Gospel begins with a ceremonious dedication to a person of high rank, named Theophilus. He is called by the title "most excellent," which ordinarily implies that the person so designated is a member of the "equestrian order." The evangelist tells Theophilus that many had taken in hand to draw up a narrative of those things which are "most surely believed among us." The preface shows us that many attempts to give an account in order of what our Lord did and said had already been made. The literary activity of the earliest Christians is thus demonstrated to us. The preface suggests to us that substantial accuracy marked these early efforts, and, in a still higher degree, St. Luke's own Gospel. He does not speak of the earlier works as inaccurate, and he does distinctly give his reader to understand that he possesses peculiar qualifications for his task. He asserts that his information is derived from "eye-witnesses and ministers of the Word," and that he has himself "traced the course of all things accurately from the first." This preface certainly shows us that the writer took real pains in writing, and that he had personally known men who accompanied our Lord.

The date can hardly be later than A.D. 80, unless the evangelist wrote in extreme old age. And the date must be earlier than Acts, as the Gospel is referred to in that work (Acts i. 1, 2). Can we fix the date more accurately than this? Many critics think that we can. They say that it must be later than the fall of Jerusalem, A.D. 70. It is said that the Gospel presupposes that Jerusalem was already destroyed. The arguments for this are: (1) In Luke xxi. 20-24 the utter destruction of Jerusalem is foretold with peculiar clearness. We have already seen that a similar argument is employed by many in speaking of Matt., an argument which seems to imply that our Lord did not foretell that destruction because He could not. This argument must be dismissed. (2) In Luke xxi. 20 there is no editorial note like that in Matt. xxiv. 15, to emphasize the necessity of paying peculiar attention to our Lord's warning about the coming destruction, and in Luke xxi. 25 the final judgment is not so clearly connected with the fall of Jerusalem as in Matt. xxiv. 29, where it is foretold as coming "immediately, after the tribulation of those days." Moreover, xxi. 24 suggests that the writer was well aware that an interval must elapse between the two great events. This is the only good argument for placing Luke later than Matt., and it certainly deserves careful attention. At the same time, we must observe the following facts: (a) St. Luke probably did not know St. Matthew's Gospel, otherwise he would not have given such very different, though not contradictory, accounts of the infancy and the resurrection of our Lord; (b) St. Luke may perhaps owe the superior accuracy of his report of the eschatological discourse of Christ to persons whom he knew at Jerusalem in A.D. 56; (c) St. Luke himself possibly thought that the end of the world would follow soon after the destruction of Jerusalem, for in xxi. 32 he seems to connect the final judgment with his own generation. But the statement is not so strong as in Matt. and Mark. For St. Luke says, "This generation shall not pass away till all be accomplished," while Matt. and Mark say, "until all *these* things be accomplished," evidently including the final judgment.

On the whole, it seems reasonable to date the Gospel according to St. Luke soon after A.D. 70, but it contains so many primitive touches that it may be rather earlier. It has been urged that both the Gospel and Acts betray a knowledge of the *Antiquities* of Josephus, and must therefore be later than A.D. 94. This theory remains wholly unproved, and the small evidence which can be brought to support it is far outweighed by the early features which mark St. Luke's books.

[Sidenote: Literary Style.]

The style is marked by great delicacy and power. It is in better Greek than the other Synoptic Gospels, and the evangelist seems to deliberately avoid some of the racy, popular words which are employed by St. Mark. But the beginner should be warned that this Gospel is not very easy to translate, for it contains a good many words with which he is not likely to be familiar. The language of St. Luke contains many proofs that he is writing as a Gentile for Gentiles. Thus he calls the Apostle Simon, who belonged to the fanatically devout party known as the "Cananaeans," by the corresponding Greek name "Zealot" (vi. 15); he seldom uses the Hebrew word "Amen," and he never uses the word "Rabbi" as a form of address. He adds the word "unclean" before the word "devil" (iv. 33), as the Greeks believed that some devils were good and kind, while the Jews believed all devils to be evil. He also substitutes the word "lawyer" for "scribe." But while the preface is written in what is perhaps the best Greek in the New Testament, the evangelist allows his language to be penetrated by his visions of Jewish scenes. Partly from his study of the Old Testament, partly from his knowledge of the books and the lives in which he found a testimony to Jesus, he acquired the art of breathing into his Greek the simple manner and the sweet tone of a Hebrew story. There is nothing in all literature more perfectly told than the story of the walk to Emmaus. Nothing can be better than the delineation of character which is suggested to us in the story of Zacharias, or of Anna, or of Zacchaeus. There is always a freshness to remind us that the Gospel is "good tidings of great joy" (ii. 10), and the Magnificat (i. 46-55), the Benedictus (i. 68-79), the Gloria in Excelsis (ii. 14), and the Nunc Dimittis (ii. 29-32), have become for ever part of the praises of the Christian Church. More often than in any other Gospel we find such expressions as "glorifying God," "praising God," "blessing God." Again, St. Luke, in choosing incidents from the life of home, and more especially in choosing incidents in which women are prominent, gives a new solemnity to a life which men had hitherto despised. We always think of the Blessed Virgin as "highly favoured," of Martha "cumbered about much serving" (x. 40), of the widow with the two mites, of the daughters of Jerusalem weeping on the way of the cross (xxiii. 28), of the double joy of Elisabeth to bear a son in her old age and to be visited by the mother of her Lord (i. 43); and we think all this because St. Luke has told us their story. These passages with their smiles and tears, their simplicity and their depth, are a divine contrast to the grotesque passage in the Jewish liturgy, where the men thank God that they are not women.

The last point in St. Luke's literary style is his use of phrases which resemble phrases in St. Paul's Epistles. He writes as a man who has lived in familiar intercourse with St. Paul. There is a striking similarity between the words attributed to our Lord in *the institution of the Eucharist* (xxii. 19, 20) and those in 1 Cor. xi. 24, 25, a similarity which is probably to be accounted for by the fact that St. Luke must often have heard the apostle use these words in celebrating this Sacrament. Besides this, there are phrases which are parallel with phrases in every Epistle of St. Paul. A few instances are—Luke vi. 36 (2 Cor. i. 3); Luke vi. 39 (Rom. ii. 19); Luke viii. 13 (1 Thess. i. 6); Luke x. 20 (Phil. iv. 3); Luke xii. 35 (Eph. vi. 14); Luke xxi. 24 (Rom. xi. 25); Luke xxii. 53 (Col. i. 13).

[Sidenote: Character and Contents.]

It has been well said that St. Matthew's Gospel is in a peculiar sense *Messianic*, St. Mark's is in a peculiar sense *realistic*, and St. Luke's is in a peculiar sense *Catholic*. And while St. Matthew takes pains to connect Christianity with the religion of the past, and St. Mark allows his interest in the past and the future to be overshadowed by his resolve to speak of Jesus as actually working marvels, St. Luke seems, like St. Paul, to be essentially progressive and to have a wider horizon than his predecessors. He does not manifest the least antipathy towards Judaism. He has none of that intolerance which so often marks the men who advertise their own breadth of view. He represents our Lord as fulfilling the Law, as quoting the Old Testament, and declaring that "it is easier for heaven and earth to pass away than for one tittle of the Law to fail" (xvi. 17). But he writes as a representative Gentile convert. He takes pleasure in recording all that can attract to Christ that Gentile world which was beginning to learn of the new religion. We may note the following points which illustrate this fact: (1) Luke traces the genealogy of our Lord, not like Matt. by the legal line to Abraham, the father of the Jews, but by the natural line to *Adam*, the father of humanity (iii. 38), thus showing Jesus to be the elder Brother and the Redeemer of every human being. (2) While the true Godhead of our Lord is taught throughout, His true *manhood* is brought into prominence with peculiar pathos. We note His condescension in passing through the various stages of a child's life (ii. 4-7, 21, 22, 40, 42, 51, 52), the continuance of His temptations during His ministry (xxii. 28), His constant recourse to prayer in the great crises of His life, His deep *sobbing* over Jerusalem (xix. 41), His sweat like drops of blood during His agony in Gethsemane (xxii. 44), a fact recorded by none of the other evangelists. St. Luke seems to be filled with a sense of the divine compassion of Jesus, and thus he relates the facts which prove the reality of the grace, the undeserved lovingkindness, of God to man. Rightly did the poet Dante call him "the scribe of the gentleness of Christ." (3) Corresponding with this human character of the incarnate Son of God, we find the offer of *universal salvation*. St. Luke alone—for the words are wrongly inserted in Matt.—records the tender words of Jesus, "The Son of man came to seek and to save that which was lost" (xix. 10). St. Paul knew no distinction between Jew and Greek, rich and poor, but taught that to be justified by God is a privilege which can be claimed not by birth but by faith; and what St. Paul enforces by stern arguments which convince our minds, St. Luke instils by the sweet parables and stories which convince our hearts. It is here that we find kindness shown to the *Gentile* (iv. 25-27; xiii. 28, 29), and the *Samaritan* (ix. 51-56; xvii. 11-19); here we are told of the publican who was "justified" rather than the Pharisee (xviii. 9), the story of the penitent thief who had no time to produce the good works which his faith would have prompted (xxiii. 43), of the good Samaritan who, schismatic though he was, showed the spirit of a child of God (x. 30). Last, and best, there is the parable of the Prodigal Son (xv. 11), and the story of the woman who was a sinner (vii. 37). To her Christ says, "Thy faith hath saved thee," and to His host He says, "Her sins, which are many, are forgiven, for she loved much"—words which no one but the Son of God could dare to say of any "woman who was in the city, a sinner." In recording these words, St. Luke proves that Jesus Christ Himself taught the Pauline doctrine that man is saved by faith; and yet not by an empty faith, but by "faith working through love" (Gal. v. 6). In this Gospel Jesus is especially the Refuge of sinners, and the teaching of our Lord may be best described by the happy phrase which records His address in the synagogue of Nazareth: "words of grace."

It is important to notice that in no Gospel do we find such an especial sympathy shown for the poor. The poverty of the holy family (ii. 7, 8, 24); the beatitude on the poor[2] (vi. 20), with the corresponding woes pronounced upon the rich (vi. 24 ff.); the parable of Dives and Lazarus (xvi. 19), the invitation of the poor to the supper of the King (xiv. 21), show this sympathy. In consequence of this, St. Luke's Gospel has been said to show an *Ebionite* tendency. But the word is misleading. It is possible that some early Christians may have called themselves by the name *Ebionim*, a Hebrew word which designated the poor and oppressed servants of God. And it is known that in the 2nd century and afterwards there was a heretical semi-Christian Jewish sect of that name. But St. Luke's Gospel is utterly opposed to the main tenets of these heretics, which were a repudiation of Christ's real Divinity and an insistence upon the necessity of circumcision for all Christians.

Perhaps it is the gentleness of the evangelist, and his preference for all that is tender and gracious, which causes his account of the twelve apostles to differ considerably from that in Mark. Their slowness, their weakness of faith, their rivalries, are set in a subdued light. He does not tell us that Christ once called St. Peter "Satan," or that Peter cursed and swore when he denied Christ. He omits the rebuke administered to the disciples in the conversation concerning the leaven (Mark viii. 17), the ambitious request of the two sons of Zebedee, and the indignation of the disciples at Mary's costly gift of ointment (Matt xxvi. 8). When St. Mark speaks of the failure of the disciples to keep awake while their Master was in Gethsemane, he says that they were asleep, "for their eyes were heavy" (xiv. 40). When St. Luke speaks of it, he says that they were "sleeping for *sorrow*" (xxii. 45). Doubtless both accounts are true, and we can reverently wonder both at the rugged honesty with which St. Peter must have told St. Mark about the faults of himself and his friends, and at the consideration shown by St. Luke towards the twelve in spite of the fact that he was more closely connected with St. Paul than with them.

About one-third of this Gospel is peculiar to itself, consisting mainly of the large section, ix. 51-xviii. 14. St. Luke here seems to have used an Aramaic document; the beginning of the section is full of Aramaic idioms. In places where St. Luke records the same facts as the other Synoptists, he sometimes adds slight but significant touches. The withered hand restored on the sabbath is the *right* hand (vi. 6); the centurion's servant is one *dear* to him (vii. 2); and the daughter of Jairus an *only* daughter (viii. 42; cf. the son of the widow at Nain, an *only* son, vii. 12). Among the remarkable omissions in this Gospel we may notice two sayings which are found in Matt. and Mark, and which seem to us to have been peculiarly appropriate for St. Luke's general purpose. The first is the saying of Christ that He had come "not to be ministered unto, but to minister, and to give His life a ransom for many" (Matt. xx. 28; Mark x. 45). The second is the statement that the Gospel "shall be preached in the whole world" (Matt. xxvi. 13; Mark xiv. 9). With the omission of these sayings we may compare the omission of any record of the visit of the Gentile wise men to the cradle of the infant Saviour of the world—an incident which would probably have appealed most strongly to the heart of St. Luke, if he had known it. Its absence from this Gospel is one of the many proofs that St. Luke was not familiar with the Gospel according to St. Matthew.

We have already noticed that much of the freshness of this Gospel is due to its being in a peculiar sense the Gospel of praise and thanksgiving. It is also peculiarly the Gospel of *prayer*. All the three Synoptists record that Christ prayed in Gethsemane. But on seven occasions St. Luke is alone in recording prayers which Jesus offered at the crises of His life: at His baptism (iii. 21); before His first conflict with the Pharisees and scribes (v. 16); before choosing the Twelve (vi. 12); before the first prediction of His Passion (ix. 18); at the Transfiguration (ix. 29); before teaching the Lord's Prayer (xi. 1); and on the Cross (xxiii. 34, 46). St. Luke mentions His insistence on the duty of prayer in two parables which no other evangelist has recorded (xi. 5-13; xviii. 1-8). He alone relates the declaration of Jesus that He had made supplication for Peter, and His charge to the Twelve, "Pray that ye enter not into temptation" (xxii. 32, 40).

As the Gospel according to St. Luke is more rich in parables than any other Gospel, we may conclude by giving a few words of explanation concerning our Lord's parables. The word "parable" means a "comparison," or, more strictly, "a placing of one thing beside another with a view to comparing them." In the Gospels the word is generally applied to a particular form of teaching. That is to say, it means a story about earthly things told in such a manner as to teach a spiritual truth. The Jews were familiar with parables. There are some in the Old Testament, the Book of Isaiah containing two (v. 1-6; xxviii. 24-28). The rabbinical writings of the Jews are full of them. But the Jewish parable was only an illustration of a truth which had already been made known. The parables of our Lord are often means of conveying truths which were not known. They must be distinguished from (a) fables, (b) allegories, (c) myths. A fable teaches worldly wisdom and prudence, not spiritual wisdom, and it is put into somewhat childish forms in which foxes and birds converse together. An allegory puts the story and its interpretation side by side, and each part of the story usually has some special significance. A myth takes the form of history, but it relates things which happened before the dawn of history, as they appear to the child-mind of primitive men.

The parables of our Lord were intended to teach the secrets of the kingdom of God (see p. 44). They unfold these secrets and at the same time veil them in the illustrations which are employed. These illustrations attract the attention and inquiry of those who are spiritually receptive. On the other hand, those who are unworthy or hardened do not recognize the truth. Nevertheless, the parables were such miracles of simplicity and power, were so easy to remember, and so closely connected with everyday objects, that even the dullest man would awake to the truth if he retained a spark of life. It is difficult to divide the parables into separate groups. But they may perhaps be divided into two groups. The first group is drawn from man's relations with the world of nature and from his simpler experiences, and the second is drawn from man's relations with his fellow-men, relations which involve more complicated experiences. The parables of the second group were sometimes spoken in answer to questions addressed to our Lord in private; such is the parable of the good Samaritan, and that of the rich fool. If we desire to study the parables in special relation to the kingdom of God, we can divide them into three groups. The first consists of those collected in Matt. xiii., delivered in and near Capernaum, and referring to the kingdom of God as a whole. The second consists of those collected in Luke x.-xviii., delivered on Christ's journeys from Galilee to Jerusalem, and referring to the character of the individual members of the kingdom. The third consists of parables spoken during our Lord's last days at Jerusalem, and referring to the judgment of members of the kingdom.

It is difficult to decide whether some of the shorter parables ought to be regarded as parables or not, but the number is usually estimated at about thirty, of which eighteen are peculiar to Luke. In John there are no parables, strictly so called, and St. John never uses the word "parable." But he uses the word *paroimia*, or "proverb," and records several proverbial sayings of our Lord which are rather like parables (John iv. 34; x. i-3; xii. 24; xv. 1-6; xvi. 21).

ANALYSIS

The infancy of our Lord: i. 1-ii. 52.—Similarity and contrast between the predictions of the birth of John the Baptist and Jesus, and also between their birth. The circumcision, the visit of Jesus to the temple in boyhood.

A.

Winter A.D. 26 till after Pentecost 27.

The preparation for the ministry: iii. 1-iv. 13.—The ministry of John the Baptist and the baptism of Jesus, the genealogy from Adam, the threefold temptation.

B.

Pentecost A.D. 27 till before Passover 28.

Missionary work of Jesus in Galilee: iv. 14-ix. 6.—Jesus preaches, is rejected at Nazareth, goes to Capernaum, various miracles (iv.). Call of Simon, leper cleansed, five grounds of offence against Jesus (v.-vi. 11). Appointment of the twelve, the sermon (vi.). The centurion's servant, the widow's son, Christ's description of John and of the age, the penitent (vii.). Parables, Christ's relation to His mother and brethren, various miracles (viii.). The mission of the twelve (ix. 1-6).

[Perplexity of Herod, ix. 7-9.]

C.

Passover A.D. 28 till before Tabernacles 28.

Climax of missionary work in Galilee: ix. 10-50.—Christ feeds the multitude, Peter's confession, Christ's first prediction of His death, transfiguration, lunatic boy cured, second prediction of death, two rebukes to apostles.

D.

Tabernacles, September A.D. 28 until early 29.

Later ministry, chiefly in Peraea: ix. 51-xix. 28.—Jesus rejected by Samaritans, discouragements (ix.). Mission of the seventy, lament over cities of Galilee, the good Samaritan, Mary and Martha (x.). Prayer and the Lord's Prayer, Jesus accused of alliance with Beelzebub, His saying about His mother, denunciation of a generation which will not believe without signs, and of the Pharisees and lawyers (xi.). The leaven of the Pharisees, confidence in God, warnings against covetousness, anxiety and lack of watchfulness, Christ's coming "baptism," signs of the times (xii.). The meaning of calamities, parable of the fig tree, cure on the sabbath, the mustard seed and the leaven, Gentiles to replace Jews, the Pharisees try to persuade Jesus to leave the dominions of Herod, Christ's first lament over Jerusalem (xiii.).

Lawfulness of healing on the sabbath, humility, inviting the poor, the King's supper, counting the cost (xiv.). Parables to illustrate Christ's care for the lost (xv.). The use and abuse of money (xvi.). Occasions of stumbling, the increase of faith, the truth that we cannot purchase God's favour by doing more than He commands, the ten lepers, the coming of the Son of man (xvii.). Answer to prayer, the Pharisee and publican, little children, the rich young man, Christ's third prediction of His death, the blind beggar at Jericho (xviii.). Zacchaeus, the parable of the pounds (xix. 1-28).

E.

Passover A.D. 29.

Last days at Jerusalem, and afterwards: xix. 29-xxiv. 53.—Entry into Jerusalem, Christ's second lament over Jerusalem, cleansing of the temple (xix. 29-xx.). Christ challenged, parable of the vineyard, two questions to entrap Christ, His question (xx.). The widow's mites, predictions of the destruction of the temple, siege of Jerusalem, the second coming (xxi.). Judas' bargain, the Passover, agony on the mount of Olives, the betrayal, Peter's denial, Jesus tried before the elders (xxii.). Jesus before Pilate, Herod, Pilate again, Simon of Cyrene, the daughters of Jerusalem, the crucifixion, burial by Joseph of Arimathaea (xxiii.).

The women at the sepulchre, and Peter, the walk to Emmaus, Jesus appears to the disciples and eats, His commission, the Ascension (xxiv.).

The Date of our Lord's Birth.—It is fairly well known that the dates of our Lord's Birth and of His Death are both, in all probability, misrepresented in popular chronology. The best ancient chronology fixes the date of the Crucifixion in A.D. 29. The Birth was probably about six years before the commencement of our present era. Various reasons make this date probable, including the fact that there was at that time a conjunction of Jupiter, Saturn, and Mars, which must have presented a most brilliant appearance in the sky, and would certainly have attracted the star-loving sages of the East. The great astronomer Kepler was of opinion that this conjunction was followed by the brief appearance of a new star, which is the star mentioned in Matt. ii. 2. This is of importance in considering the statements of St. Luke. Several objections have been made to his account of the census held under Quirinius. (1) It is said that Quirinius was not governor of Syria when Jesus was born; his administration was from A.D. 6 to A.D. 9, and Quinctilius Varus was governor in A.D. 1. But St. Luke cannot be proved to say that Quirinius was governor; he describes his office by a participle which may mean "acting as leader," and there is proof that Quirinius was engaged in a military command in the time of Herod, and also proof that some high official twice governed Syria in the time of Augustus. St. Luke's expression might fit either of these two facts. (2) It is said that Herod was reigning as king in Palestine, and that his subjects would not be included in a Roman census. But in the year 8-7 B.C. Augustus wrote to Herod, saying that he would henceforth treat him as a subject. His dominions must henceforth have been treated like the rest of the dominions of Augustus. (3) It is said that no census took place at that time, and that if there had been a census, it would have been carried out by households, according to Roman custom, and not by families. But there seems to have been a census in Egypt and Syria in B.C. 8, and after Augustus determined to put Herod under his authority, the census would naturally be extended to Judaea. Herod would probably be allowed to carry out the census on his own lines, so long as it was really carried out. And he would plainly prefer to do it in the Jewish fashion, so as to irritate the Jews as little as might be.

The question is still involved in some obscurity, but St. Luke's accuracy has not been in the least disproved by the controversy. He is the only evangelist who connects his narrative with the history of Syria and of the Roman empire, and we have every reason to believe that he did his work with care as well as sympathy.

[1] *Adv. Har.* iii. 1.

[2] Matt. v. 3 has "poor in spirit." The same Aramaic word might be used for both "poor" and "poor in spirit."

CHAPTER VI THE GOSPEL ACCORDING TO ST. JOHN

[Sidenote: The Author.]

We learn from the Gospels that St. John was the son of Zebedee, a Galilean fisherman, and was a follower of the Baptist before he joined our Lord. The Synoptists show that he was one of the most prominent and intimate of our Lord's followers. With St. Peter and St. James he was permitted to witness the raising of Jairus' daughter, and to be present at the Transfiguration, and with them was nearest to Christ at the agony in Gethsemane. With St. Peter he was sent to prepare the last Passover. Like his brother St. James, he shared in the fervour of his mother, Salome, who begged for them a special place of dignity in the kingdom of Christ. They both wished to call down fire on a Samaritan village, and St. John asked Jesus what was to be done with the man whom they found casting out devils in His name. Their fiery temperament caused our Lord to give them the surname of Boanerges ("sons of thunder"). In the fourth Gospel the name of John the son of Zebedee is never mentioned, but there are several references to an apostle whose name is not recorded, but can be intended for no other than St. John. At the crucifixion this apostle was bidden by our Lord to regard Mary as henceforth his mother, and the writer claims to have been an eye-witness of the crucifixion. In the last chapter very similar words are used to assert that the writer is he whom Jesus loved.

In Acts St. John appears with St. Peter as healing the lame man at the Beautiful Gate of the temple, and with St. Peter he goes to Samaria to bestow the Holy Ghost on those whom Philip had baptized. He was revered as one of the pillars of the Church when St. Paul visited Jerusalem in A.D. 49 (Gal. ii. 9). It is remarkable that the Synoptic Gospels, the fourth Gospel, Acts, and Galatians, all show St. John in close connection with St. Peter. St. John's name occurs in the Revelation, which has been attributed to him since the beginning of the 2nd century.

Numerous fragments of tradition concerning St. John are preserved by early Christian writers. Tertullian, about A.D. 200, says that St. John came to Rome, and was miraculously preserved from death when an attempt was made to kill him in a cauldron of boiling oil. Tertullian and Eusebius both say that he was banished to an island, and Eusebius tells us that the island was Patmos, and that the banishment took place in the time of Domitian. On the accession of Nerva, St. John removed from Patmos to Ephesus, where he survived until the time of Trajan, who became emperor in A.D. 98. Polycrates, Bishop of Ephesus, writing about A.D. 190, speaks of St. John's tomb in that city, and says that he wore the *petalon*, the high priest's mitre used in the Jewish Church. We are told by other writers how he reclaimed a robber, how he played with a tame partridge, how when too old to preach he was carried into church and would repeat again and again, "Little children, love one another." On one occasion a spark of his youthful fire was seen. It was when the old man indignantly refused to stay under the roof of the same public baths as Cerinthus, the heretic who denied that Mary was a virgin when she bore our Lord, and asserted that the Divinity of Jesus was only a power which came upon Him and went from Him.

The residence of St. John at Ephesus is attested by the Revelation. Even if that book were a forgery, no forger at the close of the 1st century would have ventured to place the hero of his book in a neighbourhood where he had not lived. Many threads of evidence lead us back to the statement made by Polycrates about the apostle's tomb. It was not until long after that date that the Christians began to carry the relics of saints from place to place, and churches rivalled one another in producing shrines for the severed members of one body. There is therefore no reason whatever to doubt that the tomb at Ephesus marked the resting-place of the apostle. It was known two hundred years later in the time of Jerome, and visited in 431 by the members of the great Church Council which met at Ephesus. The Emperor Justinian built a sumptuous church on the site, and near a modern Turkish mosque may still be seen the remnants of the church of St. John.

Until the end of the 18th century the authorship of this Gospel was not seriously challenged. The only party which ever denied that it was written by the Apostle St. John was an ignorant and insignificant body of people mentioned by Irenaeus and Epiphanius. They were known as the *Alogi*, or "unbelievers in the Word." Their views in no wise undermine the tradition of the Catholic Church. For the Alogi asserted that this Gospel was written by Cerinthus, who lived at Ephesus where St. John lived, and was himself a contemporary of St. John. We have sufficient knowledge of the teaching of Cerinthus to be perfectly certain that he could not have written a Gospel which so completely contradicts his own theories. Therefore the opinion of the Alogi is absolutely worthless where it negatives the tradition of the Church, and on the other hand it agrees with that tradition in asserting that the book was written in the apostolic age.

During the last hundred years the men who deny that Jesus Christ was truly "God of God, Light of Light," have strained every nerve to prove that the fourth Gospel was not written by St. John. It is, of course, almost impossible that they should admit that the writer was an apostle and an honest man and continue to deny that the Christ whom he depicts claimed to be the Lord and Maker of all things. During the controversy which has been waged during the last three generations with regard to St. John's Gospel, it has been evident throughout that the Gospel has been rejected for this very reason. The book has driven a wedge into the whole band of New Testament students. The critics who deny that Jesus was God, but are willing to grant that He was the most holy and the most divine of men, have been forced to side with those who are openly Atheists or Agnostics. The clue to their theories was unguardedly exposed by Weizsäcker, who said, with regard to St. John's Gospel, "It is impossible to imagine any power of faith and philosophy so great as thus to obliterate the recollection of the real life, and to substitute for it this marvellous picture of a Divine Being." [1] This remark shows us that the critic approached the Gospel with a prejudice against the doctrine of our Lord's Divinity, and rejected the Gospel mainly because it would not agree with his own prejudice. But the determination to fight to the uttermost against the converging lines of Christian evidence has now driven such critics into a corner. Many have already abandoned the position that the book is a semi-Gnostic forgery written in the middle of the 2nd century, and they are now endeavouring to maintain that it was written about A.D. 100 by a certain John the Presbyter, whom they assert to have been afterwards confounded with the Apostle John.

Of John the Presbyter very little indeed is known. Papias, about A.D. 130, says that he was, like Aristion, "a disciple" of the Lord, and that he had himself made oral inquiries as to his teaching. He seems to have been an elder contemporary of Papias. Dionysius of Alexandria, about A.D. 250, mentions that there were two monuments in Ephesus bearing the name of John, and we may reasonably suppose that one of these was in memory of the presbyter mentioned by Papias. But a little reflection will soon convince us that nothing has been gained by the conjecture that this John wrote the Gospel. If John the Presbyter was personally acquainted with our Lord, as some writers understand Papias to mean, then the sceptics are forced to admit that one who personally knew Jesus, describes Jesus as a more than human Being—as, in fact, the Divine Creator. This is the precise fact which keeps these writers from admitting that an apostle wrote the Gospel. If, on the other hand, they suppose, as some do, that John the Presbyter was very much younger than the apostles, the sceptics are confronted with the following difficulties:—

(a) There is the important external evidence which shows how widely the Gospel was regarded in the early Church as the work of St. John.

(b) There is the minute knowledge displayed of the topography, customs, and opinions of Jerusalem and the Holy Land as they existed in the time of Christ.

(c) There is the impossibility of supposing that Irenaeus, who was probably not born a year later than A.D. 130, would not have known that the Gospel was written by John the Presbyter.

(d) There is the fact that the evidence for St. John having lived in Ephesus is better than the evidence for a renowned presbyter of the same name having lived in Ephesus. This has been wisely pointed out by Jülicher, even though he himself denies that the apostle wrote St. John's Gospel. And the justice of this argument proves that it is sheer paradox to maintain, as some now maintain, that the *only* John who lived in Ephesus was the Presbyter.

It is constantly urged by the opponents of the authenticity of this Gospel that, as it was published at Ephesus at a late period, it cannot be the work of the apostle, because he never went to Ephesus, and "died early as a martyr." [2] This is a most unscrupulous use of an inexact quotation made by some later Greek writers from a lost book of Papias. It can be traced to Philip of Side (5th century), and it is to the effect that "John the Divine and James his brother were killed by the Jews." Papias does not say that they died together, and his statement is compatible with the belief that St. John survived his brother very many years. We know from Gal. ii. 9 that he was alive some time after his brother's death, which was about A.D. 44. And George Hamartolus, one of the Greek writers who quote the above passage in Papias, expressly says that the Emperor Nerva (A.D. 96) recalled John from Patmos, and "dismissed him to live in Ephesus."

[Sidenote: The External Evidence.]

The external evidence for the authenticity of this Gospel is in some respects stronger than that which is to be found in the case of the other Gospels. Thus the Christian may recognize with gratitude that his Divine Master has especially added the witness of the Church to the work of His beloved disciple. All through the 2nd century we have the links of a chain of evidence, and after A.D. 200 the canon of the Gospels is known to have been so fixed that no defender of the faith is called upon to show what that canon was. The earliest traces of the phraseology of St. John are to be discovered in the *Didaché*, which was probably written in Eastern Palestine or Syria about A.D. 100. The prayers which are provided in this book for use at the Eucharist are plainly of a Johannine type, and are probably derived from oral teaching given by the apostle himself before he lived at Ephesus. In any case, the *Didaché* seems sufficient to disprove the sceptical assertion that theological language of a Johannine character was unknown in the Christian Church about A.D. 100. The letters attributed to St. Ignatius, the martyr bishop of Antioch, are now universally admitted to be genuine by competent scholars. They may most reasonably be dated about A.D. 110, and they are deeply imbued with thought of a Johannine type. It has been lately suggested that this tendency of thought does not prove an actual acquaintance with the Gospel of St. John. But when we find Christ called "the Word," and the devil called "the prince of this world," and read such a phrase as "the bread of God which is the flesh of Christ," it is almost impossible to deny that the letters of Ignatius contain actual reminiscences of St. John's language. Nor is there the least reason why Ignatius should not have been acquainted with this Gospel. His younger contemporary St. Polycarp, whose letter to the Philippians was also written about A.D. 110, quotes from the First Epistle of St. John. And Papias, who probably wrote about A.D. 130, and collected his materials many years earlier, also quoted that Epistle, as we learn from Eusebius. Now, the connection between the Gospel and the Epistle is, as has been cleverly remarked, like the connection between a star and its satellite. They are obviously the work of the same author. If Polycarp, who had himself seen St. John, knew that the Epistle was genuine, he must have known that the Gospel was genuine.

The evidence which can definitely be dated between A.D. 120 and A.D. 170 is of extreme interest. It proves conclusively that a belief in the authenticity of this Gospel was so firmly engrained in the Christian mind that men holding the most opposite opinions appealed to its authority. It is true that the "irrational" Alogi rejected it, and that Marcion repudiated it, not because it was not by an apostle, but because St. Paul was the only apostle whom he admired. But it was used by the Catholics, the Gnostics, and the Montanists. St. Justin Martyr was acquainted with it, and before he wrote, Basilides, the great Gnostic of Alexandria, borrowed from it some materials for his doctrine. The equally celebrated Gnostic Valentinus used it, and his followers also revered it. About A.D. 170 Heracleon, an eminent Valentinian, wrote a commentary upon this Gospel, of which commentary some fragments still remain. The Montanists arose in Phrygia about A.D. 157. Montanus, their founder, endeavoured to revive the power of prophecy, and his followers maintained that "the Paraclete said more things in Montanus than Christ uttered in the Gospel." It can easily be proved that their teaching was an attempt to realize some of the promises of our Lord contained in St. John's Gospel. And the fact that the Montanists were strongly opposed to the Gnostics makes it all the more remarkable that both sects regarded this Gospel as so important. Somewhat before A.D. 170 St. John's Gospel was inserted by the great Syrian apologist, Tatian, in his *Diatessaron*, or harmony of the Gospels, and the apocryphal Acts of John composed near the same date contain unmistakable allusions to this Gospel.

The evidence of Irenaeus is the culminating proof of the genuineness of the Gospel according to St. John. He became Bishop of Lyons in A.D. 177, and remembered Polycarp, who suffered martyrdom at Smyrna in A.D. 156, at the age of eighty-six. Irenaeus, in writing to his friend Florinus, says, "I can describe the very place in which the blessed Polycarp used to sit when he discoursed, and his goings-out and his comings-in, and his manner of life, and his personal appearance, and the discourses which he held before the people, and how he would describe his intercourse with John and the rest who had seen the Lord, and how he would relate their words. And whatsoever things he had heard from them about the Lord and about His miracles, Polycarp, as having received them from eye-witnesses of the life of the Word, would relate, altogether in accordance with the Scriptures." [3]

Now, it is perfectly certain that Irenaeus, like his contemporaries Heracleon and Tatian, accepted the fourth Gospel as the work of the Apostle John. And can we believe that he would have thus accepted it, if it had not been acknowledged by his teacher Polycarp, who knew St. John, and was nearly thirty years old at the time of St. John's death?

[Sidenote: The Internal Evidence.]

The Gospel itself contains manifest tokens that it was written by a Jew of Palestine, by one who held no Gnostic heresy, and by a contemporary of our Lord.

I. *The author was a Jew and not a Gentile.*

He makes frequent quotations from the Old Testament, and some of these quotations imply an acquaintance with the Hebrew. This is especially the case in the verse from the 41st Psalm (xiii. 18), and in that (xix. 37) from Zech. xii. 10, "They shall look on Him whom they pierced." The Septuagint of Zech. xii. 10, translating from a different form of the Hebrew, has, instead of the words "whom they pierced," "because they mocked." It is, therefore, plain that John xiii. 18 is not derived from the Septuagint. The Gospel is also Hebraic in style. The sentences are broken up in a manner which is at variance with Greek idiom. Whereas in St. Luke's two writings the style becomes more Greek or more Hebraic in proportion to his writing independently or employing the writings of Jewish Christians, the style of this Gospel is the same throughout. We may particularly notice the Hebraic use of the word "and" to signify both "and" and "but" (*e.g.* in v. 39, 40, where "and ye will not come" means "but ye will not come"). We may also notice the correct use of certain Hebrew proper names: *e.g.* Judas is called "the son of Iscariot," showing that the writer did not regard the word Iscariot as the fixed name of Judas only, but knew that it might be applied to any man of Kerioth. In fact, the Greek of St. John is exactly like the English of a Scottish Highlander who has only spoken Gaelic in his earlier days, and, when he has acquired English, shows his origin by the continued use of a few Gaelic idioms and his knowledge of Highland proper names.

He shows a minute acquaintance with Jewish social and ceremonial customs. We may notice iii. 25; iv. 9, 27; vii. 2, 23, 37; x. 22; xi. 44; xix. 7, 31; and especially the waterpots (ii. 6), the purification previous to the Passover (xi. 55), the fear of our Lord's accusers to defile themselves by entering the praetorium (xviii. 28), and the Jewish method of embalming (xix. 40). Jewish opinions are faithfully reflected, *e.g.* as to the importance attached to the religious schools (vii. 15); the disparagement of the Jews of the "dispersion" (vii. 35); the scorn felt by many Jews for the provincials of Galilee (i. 46; vii. 41, 52), and the idea of the soul's pre-existence (ix. 2).

II. *The author was a Jew of Palestine.*

He shows a minute acquaintance with the geography of the Holy Land. At the present day elaborate guide-books and histories make it possible for a very clever writer to disguise the fact that he has not visited the land in which he lays the scene of his story. But even at the present day such procedure is dangerous, and likely to be detected. In ancient times it was almost impossible. Yet no one has ever detected an error in the geography of this Gospel. The writer mentions Cana of Galilee (ii. 1, 11), a place not noticed by any earlier writer, and Bethany beyond Jordan (i. 28); he knows the exact distance from Jerusalem to the better-known Bethany (xi. 18); the "deep" well of Jacob at Sychar (iv. 11); the city of Ephraim near the wilderness (xi. 54); Aenon near to Salim, where John baptized (iii. 23). This word Aenon is an Aramaic word signifying "springs," and even Renan ridicules the notion of such a name having been invented by Greek-speaking sectaries at Ephesus. The place was too obscure to be known to ordinary travellers, and, on the other hand, such a name cannot have been invented by a Gentile.

The topography of Jerusalem is described with equal nicety. We may notice viii. 20; ix. 7; x. 23; xviii. 1, 15; xix. 17, 41; and particularly the pool near the sheep-gate, having five porches (v. 2), and the place which is called the Pavement, "but in the Hebrew Gabbatha" (xix. 13). Even a person who had heard of Solomon's porch and of Golgotha might well have been ignorant of the sheep-gate and the Pavement, unless he had been in Jerusalem.

Lastly, the writer shows an acquaintance not only with the Jewish feasts, but also with facts connected with them which imply special knowledge on his part. He could not have gathered from the Old Testament the fact that the later Jews were in the habit of keeping a feast in honour of the dedication of the temple after its profanation by Antiochus Epiphanes (x. 22), nor would he have learned how to introduce an allusion to the rite of pouring forth water from the pool at Siloam at the Feast of Tabernacles (vii. 37).

The only important argument which can be urged against the author having been a Jew is that founded on the use of the phrase "the Jews," which is said to imply that the writer was not a Jew. Now, in some passages (as vii. 1), "the Jews" may mean the inhabitants of Judaea, as distinct from those of Galilee, and such passages are therefore indecisive. But in other passages the phrase "the Jews" does not admit this interpretation, and is used with a decided suggestion of dislike. But when we remember the bitter hostility which the Jews soon manifested towards the Christians, and remember that in Asia Minor this hostility was active, the phrase presents no real difficulty. St. Paul was proud to reckon himself a Jew, but long before the Jews had shown their full antagonism to Christianity, St. Paul spoke of "the Jews" (1 Thess. ii. 14-16) with the same condemnation as the writer of the fourth Gospel.

The only important arguments in favour of the author having absorbed Gnostic views are drawn: (1) *From the alleged Dualism of the Gospel.* In theology the word Dualism signifies the doctrine that the world is not only the battle-ground of two opposing forces, one good and the other evil, but also that the material world is itself essentially evil. Such was the doctrine of the great Gnostic sects of the 2nd century. But this Gospel, in spite of the strong contrast which it draws between God and the world, light and darkness, is not Dualist. It teaches that there is one God, that the world was made by the Word who is God, that this Word was made flesh and came to save the world. In thus teaching that the material world was made by the good God, and that God took a material human body, this Gospel opposes the fundamental tenet of Gnostic Dualism. (2) *From the alleged condemnation of the Jewish prophets by Christ in x. 8.* Other passages make it perfectly plain that this is not a condemnation of the Jewish prophets, but of any religious pretenders who claimed divine authority. In this Gospel an appeal is made to Moses (v. 46), to Abraham (viii. 56), to Isaiah (xii. 41), and, what is most remarkable of all, our Lord says, "Salvation is of the Jews," *i.e.* the knowledge and the origin of religious truth came from the Jews. The Jewish Scriptures are ratified (v. 39; x. 35). It is impossible to find a shred of the anti-Jewish theories which the Gnostics taught. And though it is true that some Gnostics were fond of using such words as "life" and "light" in their religious phraseology, it is much more probable that they were influenced by the fourth Gospel than that this Gospel was tinged with Gnosticism.

We conclude, therefore, that the author was a Jew of Palestine, and that he was not a Gentile or in any sense a Gnostic.

III. *The author was a contemporary and an eye-witness of the events described.*

His knowledge of Jerusalem and of the temple, which we have already noticed, strongly suggests that he knew the city before its destruction in A.D. 70. So far as can be tested, his treatment of the Messianic ideas of the people is exactly accurate, and of a kind which it would have been difficult for a later writer to exhibit. This Gospel represents the people as pervaded by a nationalist notion of the Messiah as of a king who would deliver them from foreign powers (vi. 15, xi. 48; xix. 12), a notion which was dispelled in A.D. 70, and apparently did not revive until the rising of Bar Kocheba in A.D. 135, a date which is now almost universally recognized as too late for this Gospel to have been written. We also find the two contradictory ideas as to the place of the Messiah's origin then current (vii. 27, 42), and the writer distinguishes "the prophet" (i. 21, 25; vi. 14; vii. 40), who was expected to precede Christ, from Christ Himself. At a very early date the Christians identified "the prophet" with

Christ, and it is in the highest degree improbable that any but a contemporary of our Lord would have been aware of this change of belief.

It is claimed that the author is an eye-witness in i. 14; xix. 35; and xxi. 24. We may add 1 John i. 1, for the author of the Epistle was obviously the author of the Gospel. Numerous details, especially the frequent notes of time, suggest the hand of an eye-witness. And the delicate descriptions of the inner life of the disciples and of Christ Himself point to the same conclusion. The description of the Last Supper and the words spoken at it suggest with overwhelming force that the writer knew the peculiar manner of seating employed at this ceremony. Another Jew would have known where the celebrant sat, but he would scarcely have been able to make the actions of our Lord and Judas, St. John and St. Peter, fit their places at the table with such perfection.[4]

The Gospel claims that the disciple who "wrote these things" is the disciple "whom Jesus loved," and who reclined "in Jesus' bosom" at the Supper. It was not Peter, for Peter did not recline "in Jesus' bosom." The presumption therefore is that it was either James or John, these two being with Peter the closest friends of Jesus. It could hardly have been James, who was martyred in A.D. 44, as the whole weight of tradition and external evidence is against this. It must, then, have been John, or a forger who wished to pass for that apostle. And to suppose that an unknown forger, born two generations, or even one generation, later than the apostles, could invent such sublime doctrine, and insert it in so realistic a story, and completely deceive the whole Christian world, including the district where St. John lived and died, is to show a credulity which is without parallel in the history of civilization.[5]

Now that we have reviewed the internal evidence for the authenticity, we are able to return with renewed vigour to deal with the popular rationalistic hypothesis that the author was a Christian who had learned some genuine stories about Jesus current in the Church at Ephesus, and then wove them into a narrative of his own composing. We have observed that the marks of an eye-witness and contemporary of Jesus are scattered over the whole surface of the Gospel. If the Gospel is not by St. John, only one other explanation is possible. It must be composed of three distinct elements: (a) some genuine traditions, (b) numerous fictions, (c) a conscious manipulation of the narrative contained in the Synoptists. But the internal evidence is absolutely opposed to any such theory. We can trace no manipulation of the Synoptic narrative. The writer seems to be aware of St. Mark's Gospel, and possibly the other two, but he evidently did not write with them actually before him. He plainly had a wholly independent plan and an independent source of information. And if we turn to the passages which tell us facts not recorded by the Synoptists, it is quite impossible to separate the supposed fictions from the supposed genuine traditions. Both style and matter proceed from one and the same individuality. One passage alone can be separated from the rest without interrupting the flow of the story, and that passage is absent in the best manuscripts. It is the story of the woman taken in adultery (vii. 53-viii. 11). It seems to have been originally placed after Luke xxi. 36, and was inserted into St. John's Gospel after it was completed. We cannot apply the same process to any other passage in the Gospel. It is an organic whole, as much as any play of Shakespeare or poem of Tennyson. And over the whole book we find the same morsels of history and geography. They are of a kind which tradition never hands down unimpaired, and which no Ephesian disciple of an apostle would be likely to commit to memory. In spite of all attempts to divide the Gospel into parts derived straight from an apostle and parts invented by later minds, the Gospel remains like the seamless coat which once clothed the form of the Son of man.

[Sidenote: Date.]

It is important to observe that even the most hostile criticism has tended to recede in its attempt to find a probable date for this Gospel. Baur fixed it about A.D. 160-170, Pfleiderer at 140, Hilgenfeld 130-140; Jülicher and Harnack will not date it later than 110, and the latter grants that it may be as early as 80. The year 80 is as early a date as the most orthodox Christian need desire, and we can reasonably believe that it was written by the apostle at Ephesus between A.D. 80 and A.D. 90. We learn from Irenaeus that St. John survived until A.D. 98.

[Sidenote: Literary Style.]

Several points in the literary style of the apostle have been noticed in dealing with the internal evidence which they afford to the authenticity of his Gospel. But it is necessary to add something more, for there is no writer to whom we can more fitly apply the profound saying that "the style is the man." The language of St. John is the result of a long and impassioned contemplation. Whether he writes down his own words, or records the words and deeds of our Lord, his language shows the result of careful reflection.

The teaching of Jesus exhibits a development different from that in the Synoptists. We find in chs. ii., iii., and iv. that our Lord definitely taught that He was the Son of God and Messiah quite early in His ministry, while in the earlier part of Mark our Lord's teaching about His Messiahship is far less definite. And the method of teaching is also different. In the Synoptists we find picturesque parables and pointed proverbs, while in John we find long discourses and arguments. In the Synoptists the teaching is generally practical, in John it is much more openly theological. This difference between the Synoptists and St. John can be partly accounted for by the fact that St. John's Gospel contains much more of the instruction given by our Lord to His intimate friends, and that this instruction was naturally more profound than that which was given to the multitude. But there is another reason for the difference. If we attend to such passages as xiv. 15-21, 25-26; xv. 26-27, we see that our Lord teaches that there are two manifestations of His Person, one during the time between His birth and His death, and the other after the outpouring of the Holy Spirit. The Spirit is not a substitute for an absent Christ; His coming brings with it an inward presence of Christ within the Christian soul (xiv. 18). By the aid of the Spirit, St. John condenses and interprets the language of our Lord in a manner which can be understood by the simplest of simple souls who live the inner life. In St. John we find a writer who is writing when Jesus spoke no longer in parables and proverbs, but "plainly" (xvi. 25, 29). He records the teaching of Jesus, as it had shaped itself *in* his own mind, but not so much *by* his own mind as by perpetual communion with the ascended Christ.

[Sidenote: Character and Contents.]

We have noted on p. 31 the fact that St. John's Gospel shows that he was acquainted with facts in the Synoptic Gospels which he does not himself narrate. Yet the broad difference between the character of the Synoptic writers and that of St. John is that the Synoptists are historical, he is mystical. We do not mean that St. John does not trouble about historical accuracy. His history is often more minute than that of the Synoptists. But his purpose is to bring his readers into deeper life through union with the God who is in Christ and is Christ. The true mystic ever desires to maintain the knowledge of this inward union in life with God. It is a knowledge which is made possible by obedience, made perfect by love, and causes not new ecstasies, but a new character. St. John adjusts all his material to this one purpose. "These are written that ye may believe that Jesus is the Christ, the Son of God; and that believing ye may have life in His name" (xx. 31).

The Introduction or Prologue (i. 1-18) teaches that Jesus Christ is that personal manifestation of God to whom the Jews had given the name of the Word. The Palestinian Jews were accustomed to describe God acting upon the world by the name *Memra*, or "Word" of the Lord. The Alexandrian Jews also were in the habit of giving the title *Logos*, which means both "Word" and "Reason," to an idea of God which perfectly expressed all that God is. The Greek Stoics had used the name in a similar sense, and thus St. John, having realized that Jesus is truly God made manifest, called Him by a name which every educated Jew and Greek would understand. Unlike Philo, the great Alexandrian Jew who tried to combine Greek philosophy with Jewish religion, St. John teaches that this divine Word is a Person, and took human flesh and revealed Himself as the Messiah. The whole Gospel shows how this revelation met with increasing faith on the part of some, and increasing unbelief and hatred on the part of others. The crises of this unbelief are represented chiefly in connection with our Lord's visits to Jerusalem, when He made His claims before the religious leaders of Judaism. His revelation is attended by various forms of *witness*. There is that of the apostle himself (i. 14); that of the other apostles who also witnessed His "glory," as displayed by His miracles (ii. 11). There is that of John the Baptist (i. 34); and when we remember that there had existed at Ephesus an incomplete Christianity which had only known the baptism given by John the Baptist (Acts xix. 3), we see how fit it was that the apostle should record the Baptist's testimony to Christ's superiority. There is the witness of His works, and that which the Father Himself bore (v. 34-36). We should notice that the miracles are called "signs," and are carefully selected so as to give evidence to the reader concerning particular aspects of our Lord's glory.[6] Even the Passion is described as containing an element of glory (xii. 28, 32), it contains a secret divine triumph (cf. Col. ii. 15), and is a stage towards the glory of the Ascension. The "darkness" contends with the divine "light," but cannot "suppress" it. After the "world" has done its worst, the final victory of faith is seen in the confession of St. Thomas, "My Lord and my God" (xx. 28).

We find other points of doctrine corresponding with the mystical teaching that "eternal life" does not begin after the last judgment, but may be enjoyed here and now by knowing "God and Jesus Christ whom He hath sent" (xvii. 3). Thus the judgment is shown to be executed in one sense by the mere division which takes place among men when they come in contact with Christ, according as they are good or bad (v. 30; viii. 16; ix. 39). The principle of this moral testing is made plain in iii. 19. Those who stand the test, and believe in Christ, undergo a resurrection

41

here (xi. 26). On the other hand, there is also a future judgment (v. 22, 29) and a future consummation (v. 28, 29; vi. 39 f., xiv. 3).

Similar beautiful paradoxes are found in the teaching that the "work" which God requires of us is to believe in His Son (vi. 28, 29); and that to fulfil God's will is the mark not of servants but of friends (xv. 14). And those who hope that they are numbered among the friends of Jesus will find in this Gospel all the deepest experiences of the soul—the new birth, the finding of the living water and the true light, and that abiding in Christ which is made complete by the eating of His flesh and the drinking of His blood.

To realize the meaning of Jesus it is necessary to follow the guidance of the Holy Spirit. The Synoptists tell us comparatively little of His work, though they show us the Spirit descending on Christ at His baptism, driving Him into the wilderness to be tempted, speaking in His disciples, pervading His work (Luke iv. 18), and possessed of a personality into which the Christian is baptized (Matt. xxviii. 19), and against which blasphemy is unpardonable (Luke xii. 10). In John we find a much fuller doctrine of the Holy Spirit. The fact that He is not a mere impersonal influence of God is very clearly shown. And it is impossible to accept the modern rationalistic hypothesis that the Holy Spirit is only a phrase for describing the idea which the apostles had about the invisible presence of Christ. He is called "another Advocate" (xiv. 16). Christ was an Advocate or Helper; the Spirit will be another. Again, it is the work of the Spirit to refresh the memory and strengthen the apprehension of the disciples concerning Christ (xiv. 26); and our Lord definitely says, "If I go, I will send Him unto you" (xvi. 7). With regard to the unbelieving world, the Spirit will prove the sinfulness of opposition to Christ, will convince the world of His righteousness as testified by the Father's approval manifested in the Ascension, and will procure the verdict of history that by the crucifixion the evil spirit who inspires worldliness was condemned (xvi. 8-11). The Spirit's work is the same in kind as the work of Christ, but the two Persons are distinct. That Christ continues His advent and His work in the world through the Spirit implies neither that the Spirit is an impersonal influence nor that He is personally identical with Christ.

This Gospel gives us invaluable help in determining the chronology of our Lord's ministry. His ministry is connected with six Jewish feasts (ii. 13; v. 1; vi. 4; vii. 2; x. 22; xii. 1). All are named except that in v. 1, which is probably Pentecost, A.D. 27. The forty-six years in ii. 20 are correct. Herod began to rebuild the temple in 20-19 B.C. Therefore the Passover in ii. 13 cannot be before A.D. 27.

ANALYSIS

Introduction: i. 1—i. 18.—The Word ever with God and Himself God, manifested in creation, in conscience, in the incarnation.

A.

Winter A.D. 26 till after Passover 27.

The preparation and beginning of the ministry: i. 19-iv. 54.—The testimony of John the Baptist to Jesus and his baptism of Jesus, his disciples come to Jesus, the gathering of other disciples, the promise of seeing heaven opened (i.). Jesus and Mary at the marriage at Cana, the disciples believe. Jesus at Capernaum. At the Passover Jesus goes to Jerusalem and cleanses the temple (ii). At Jerusalem Jesus teaches Nicodemus of the new birth, He labours in Judaea while John is at Aenon (iii.). The woman of Samaria converted; Jesus returns and is welcomed in Galilee, is again at Cana, cures the Capernaum nobleman's son (iv.).

B.

Pentecost A.D. 27 till before Passover 28.

The increased self-revelation of Jesus at Jerusalem: v.—Jesus cures the infirm man at the pool of Bethesda, is accused of sabbath-breaking. He co-ordinates His work and His honour with the work and honour of the Father, claims to give life now and execute judgment, claims the testimony of John, of His own miracles, of the Scriptures.

C.

Passover A.D. 28 till before Tabernacles 28.

Full self-revelation of Jesus in Galilee: vi.—Christ sustains physical life by feeding the 5000, the people wish to make Him King. He again shows power over nature by walking on the sea. He reveals Himself as the Bread sustaining all spiritual life, commands the eating of His flesh and drinking of His blood. The effect of this teaching is increased enmity, the desertion by nominal disciples, and intensified faith as shown by Peter's confession.

D.

Tabernacles, September A.D. 28 till early 29.

Further self-revelation at Jerusalem: conflict: journey to Peraea; vii. 1-xi. 57.—Jesus at the feast, is accused of having a devil, defends His former action on the sabbath, attempt to seize Him, His invitation to all who thirst, the people divided, the officers refuse to arrest Him (vii.). [Interpolated story of the woman taken in adultery, vii. 53-viii. 11.]

Jesus reveals Himself as the Light of the world, the Jews no longer Abraham's children, the Jews reject His claim to pre-existence, and attempt to stone Him (viii.). Jesus gives sight to the blind man at Siloam, discussion about healing on the sabbath (ix.). Jesus the good Shepherd, at the feast of the Dedication in December the Jews try to stone Him and He goes east of Jordan (x.).

Jesus as Conqueror of death goes to Bethany, raises Lazarus and proclaims Himself as the Resurrection and the Life. On the advice of Caiaphas, the Council propose to put Jesus to death. After raising Lazarus Jesus retires to Ephraim, a city on the edge of the wilderness to the north-east of Jerusalem (xi.).

E.

Passover A.D. 29.

Last public ministry at Jerusalem: xii.—Mary anoints Jesus for burial, the entry into Jerusalem, the Greeks who desire to see Jesus, a voice from heaven promises to glorify Him. Rejecting or receiving Christ.

Full self-revelation of Jesus to His apostles: xiii.-xvii.—At the Passover He washes the disciples' feet. Judas pointed out and departs. The question of Peter (xiii. 37), of Thomas (xiv. 5), of Philip (xiv. 8), of Judas (xiv. 22). The work of the Advocate who is to come (xiv. 26). Abiding in Christ, the new commandment to love one another, the hatred of the world, future testimony of the Spirit of truth (xv.). The Spirit will convict the world, guide the disciples. Sorrow only for a little while, final assurances, warm expression of faith on the part of the apostles, Christ's warning (xvi.).

Christ's intercession (xvii.).

The death of Jesus, the apparent triumph of unbelief: xviii.-xix.—Betrayal in the garden, trial before Annas and Caiaphas, Peter's denial, trial before Pilate, Jesus or Barabbas (xviii.).

The scourging, Pilate's futile endeavour to release Jesus, his political fears, the crucifixion, "behold thy mother," the spear-thrust, the writer's personal testimony, the burial by Joseph of Arimathaea (xix.).

The resurrection, the victory over unbelief: xx.—Mary Magdalene, Peter and the writer at the sepulchre, the writer records his own conviction. Jesus manifests Himself to the Magdalene, to the ten disciples, most of whom had deserted Him, and to Thomas who doubted. Thomas is convinced of the Divinity of Jesus, the writer states that this Gospel was written "that ye might believe."

Epilogue: xxi.—The manifestation of Jesus by the sea of Galilee, the solemn charge to Peter. The editors of the Gospel assert that the author was the beloved disciple.

(John xxi. 24 was probably written by the Ephesian presbyters who knew St. John. The rest of the chapter is evidently by the apostle himself, although, it may have been added at a time later than the rest of the Gospel, which seems to come to an end with the impressive words in xx. 31. The most contradictory hypotheses have been broached by writers who have denied the authenticity of ch. xxi. Some have held that it was added in order to exalt St. John, the apostle of Asia Minor, over St. Peter, the patron of Rome. Others have held that it was added to exalt St. Peter. Those who deny the authenticity of the whole Gospel are compelled to regard ch. xxi. 24 as deliberate false witness.)

St. John's Oral Teaching.—It seems that before St. John wrote his Gospel, he had adapted it to oral teaching. This is shown by the arrangement of facts in combinations of 3, possibly suggested by the 3 manifestations of the Word recorded in the Introduction. There are 3 Passovers recorded, 3 feasts besides the Passovers, 3 journeys to Judaea, 3 discourses on the last day of Tabernacles before the address to believing Jews (viii. 31), 3 sayings from the Cross. If we regard ch. xxi. as added later by St. John, we find in the rest of the Gospel 3 miracles in Judaea, 3 in Galilee, and 3 appearances of the risen Lord.

[1] *Apostolic Age of the Church*, vol. ii. p. 211. (English translation.)

[2] Dr. James Moffat, *Introduction to the Literature of the New Testament*, p. 601.

[3] Eusebius, *H. E.* v. 20. It is worth noting that Dr. Moffat, *op. cit.* p. 609, admits that "if Irenaeus is correct, his testimony to John the Apostle is of first-rate importance." So he adds, "he must be held to have mistaken what Polykarp said, and to have confused John the Presbyter with John the Apostle."

[4] See Edersheim, *Life and Times of Jesus the Messiah*, vol. ii. p. 494.

[5] The difficulties which arise from the difference between the history of our Lord's ministry as given by St. John, and by the Synoptists, have been discussed on p. 27, ff.

[6] He changes the good into better (ii. 9); saves the dying (iv. 50); gives power (v. 8); gives food (vi. 11); gives sight (ix. 7); is Lord over death (xi. 44); blesses the work done in faith (xxi. 11). It should be noticed that St. John never mentions that our Lord cured any one possessed with a devil, which according to the Synoptists was a common kind of miracle. But St. John does not therefore contradict the other evangelists. He recognizes that there are visible works of the devil (viii. 41; cf. 1 John iii. 8), and mentions "the prince of this world" as causing the trials of our Lord.

CHAPTER VII THE ACTS OF THE APOSTLES

[Sidenote: The Author.]

The Christian Church has never attributed the Book of Acts to any other writer than St. Luke. The external proofs of the primitive date of the book are important, and point to the apostolic age as the date of its composition. St. Clement of Rome, about A.D. 95, in referring to Ps. lxxxviii. 20, quotes it in words which are almost certainly based on Acts xiii. 22. There are two apparent quotations from Acts in the letters of St. Ignatius and one in the letter of St. Polycarp. It is also quoted in the works of Justin Martyr, Tatian, and Athenagoras, and in the letter of the Churches of Vienne and Lyons written in A.D. 177. It was evidently read throughout the 2nd century, and it is definitely assigned to St. Luke by Irenaeus, the *Muratorian Fragment*, Tertullian, and Clement of Alexandria.

In opposition to this tradition, a persistent effort has been made to prove that the book belongs to the early part of the and century. There are certain passages in which the writer uses the *first person plural*, implying that he was personally present on the occasions described. The sections of the book in which that peculiarity is found are ordinarily called the "we sections," and it has been asserted that though the "we sections" are primitive they have been worked into the narrative of a later writer.[1] Furthermore it is asserted that the book was deliberately intended to be a fictitious account of the primitive Church, and that its special purpose was to balance the story of St. Peter with that of St. Paul in such a manner as to completely disguise the fundamental antagonism of the two apostles.

The force of this argument has been weakened by the general admission of non-Christian writers that the differences of opinion between the two apostles were grossly exaggerated by the critics of fifty years ago. It is therefore granted that there was less necessity for the forgery than there was said to be by the critics in question. It is also very obvious that we cannot fairly charge a historian with dishonesty because he wishes to balance one great character with another. No one would assert that a modern writer was a partisan or a liar because he devoted in the same book twenty appreciative pages to the Evangelical Revival and twenty appreciative pages to the Oxford Movement. In spite of this fact, the trustworthy character of the book is still vigorously assailed. It is said that no statement in the book deserves ready belief except the "we sections," that those sections were written by an unknown companion of St. Paul, and impudently "appropriated" by a Christian who wrote between A.D. 105 and A.D. 130.

This argument about the "we sections" can be completely overthrown by a consideration of the *linguistic evidence* of Acts. If language implies anything, the peculiarities of Acts imply that the author of the "we sections," who was a companion of St. Paul, was the author of the whole book. And they also show that the author of the whole book was the person who wrote the third Gospel. There are many words and phrases found only in the "we sections" and in the rest of Acts. There is, too, a large number of words and phrases in the "we sections" which are rarely used in those books of the New Testament which are *not* attributed to St. Luke, and occur frequently in the rest of Acts and in St. Luke's Gospel. If we compare Acts with St. Luke's Gospel, we find that Acts contains 108 out of 140 which are characteristic of this Gospel, whereas it contains only about a half of those which are characteristic of Matt. and Mark. There are 58 Greek words which are found in both Acts and Luke and nowhere else in the New Testament.[2] Among the terms which serve as connecting links between St. Luke's Gospel and Acts, including the "we sections," occur various medical phrases. It is becoming more and more widely recognized that these phrases imply that the writer was a physician, such as we know St. Luke to have been (Col. iv. 14). It is all the more remarkable that many of the words peculiar to Acts are found in St. Luke's contemporary, the physician Dioscorides.

It is true that the sections taken from Mark show numerous "Lucan" characteristics as they appear in our third Gospel, but these characteristics are due to the third evangelist, and not to St. Mark. So, it can be urged, the "Lucan" characteristics in the "we sections" are due not to the author, but to an expert editor of a later time. In reply, we can answer that the cases are not strictly parallel. For if the "we sections" are not by the writer of Acts, he must have almost entirely rewritten them, and, at the same time, have been guilty of a gross fraud, which he stupidly dropped in passages where it could have been effectively used.

To this linguistic evidence of authenticity we can add *archaeological evidence*. The discoveries of the last thirty years have greatly confirmed the accuracy of the writer in points where a writer of the 2nd century would have betrayed his ignorance. In fact, we are able to compare his accuracy with the inaccuracy of the writing known as the *Acts of Paul and Thecla*, a 2nd century blend of sensationalism and piety based on a document of the 1st century. Now, in almost every point where we are able to test the knowledge possessed by the author of Acts with regard to the topography of Asia Minor and the details of Roman government, it can be pronounced correct. This has been admirably shown by Prof. Ramsay's works on *The Church in the Roman Empire and St. Paul*. St. Luke knows that Cyprus was governed by a pro-consul, which had ceased to be the case early in the 2nd century; that the magistrates at Philippi were called *strategoi*, and were attended by lictors, while those at Thessalonica were called *politarchai* (xvii. 6), a title which has been verified by inscriptions. He is aware that the governor of Malta was only called the head-man (xxviii. 7). He knows that Derbe and Lystra, but not Iconium, were cities of Lycaonia, and that "great Artemis" was the cry used at Ephesus in invoking the patronal goddess of the city (xix. 28). We must not assert that these and similar details absolutely prove that the writer was a companion of St. Paul; but we can say that he was peculiarly well acquainted with the life of that period. The account of St. Paul's voyage and shipwreck is equally accurate.

A very favourite argument against the genuineness of Acts is that Acts xv., in its account of St. Paul's third visit to Jerusalem, A.D. 49, is inconsistent with Gal. ii. It is asserted that the author deliberately falsified the story in order to represent the older apostles as promoting the union of Gentile and Jewish Christians, some modern critics assuming that the apostles would never have done anything so Catholic. But there is no real discrepancy between the two accounts, if we are ready to believe that St. Luke gives the public and exterior view of the proceedings, while St. Paul, as is natural, describes the personal aspect of those proceedings. According to Acts xv. 2, St. Paul and St. Barnabas were *deputed* to go to Jerusalem by the Church at Antioch; according to Gal. ii. 2, St. Paul went there "by revelation." The internal motive is surely compatible with the external. Again, both Acts xv. and Gal. ii. show that the momentous Council at Jerusalem included private and public meetings. The two accounts fit one another all the better in consequence of the fact that Acts lays stress upon the public settlement (xv. 7 f.) and Galatians upon a private conference (ii. 2). Acts shows that there was much dispute, and Galatians shows that the dispute included opposition to St. Paul's methods. Acts shows that St. Paul greatly desired to be on good terms with the older apostles, Galatians shows that they gave him the right hand of fellowship. The historical situation, the occasion of dispute (viz. the attempt to impose circumcision on the Gentiles), the chief persons concerned and the feelings which they entertained, are the same in both books.[3]

As to the fact that St. Paul in Galatians makes no mention of a second visit to Jerusalem about A.D. 46, he ignores it because it was devoted to the specific business mentioned in Acts xi. 30; xii. 25. Nothing arose out of it affecting his relations with the first apostles or his own apostleship. A description of this visit was therefore quite beside the argument of Galatians. We cannot therefore say that its omission in Galatians proves that it was an invention of the author of Acts.

The fact that Acts does not depend upon St. Paul's writings and nevertheless shows many undesigned points of contact with them, leads us to a very important conclusion. This conclusion is that the writer of Acts was a companion of St. Paul. It is incredible that a later writer, who took an eager interest in St. Paul's adventures, should have made no use of St. Paul's letters. Those letters made a deep impression upon St. Paul's contemporaries (cf. 2 Cor. x. 10), and they were carefully treasured by all succeeding generations. We can only explain the relation between Acts and the Pauline Epistles by the theory that the author of Acts was sufficiently intimate with the apostle to be able to write his book without feeling the necessity of enriching it by references to those Epistles. The theory, then, fits with the theory which is suggested to us by the "we sections." The only remaining question is whether this companion was, or was not, St. Luke. He was evidently with St. Paul at Rome, and this makes it impossible to attribute the authorship of Acts to Titus, as there is no hint in the New Testament of Titus being there. Nor was the author Silas, for Silas was not with St. Paul on the third missionary journey, while the author of Acts was. Acts xx. 5, 6 seems to prove that the book was not written by Timothy. No one seems so likely to have been the author as St. Luke. For the writer of Acts xxvii. 1-xxviii. 16 evidently accompanied St. Paul to Rome, and we learn from Col. iv. 14 and Philem. 24 that St. Luke was with the apostle during his first imprisonment in that city. We may therefore say that every line of evidence points to the truth of the ancient tradition that St. Luke wrote Acts.

The sources of information employed by St. Luke can sometimes be determined with a high degree of probability. Where he did not draw upon his own recollections he could often rely upon those of St. Paul. The apostle was, as we should expect, in the habit of narrating his own experiences (cf. 2 Cor. i. 8-10; xii. 9; Gal. i. 11-ii. 14; Phil. iii. 3-7; Rom. xv. 16-32). Acts xxi. 19; xiv. 27; xv. 3, 12, 26, show how St. Paul related his travels. Acts i.-v. probably incorporates an early Jewish Christian document, and contains features which unmistakably point to the truthfulness of the record. A good deal of information was probably obtained from John Mark: it was to the house of Mark's mother that St. Peter made his way after his escape from prison recorded in ch. xii. As St. Mark was with St. Luke and St. Paul at Rome, and acted as St. Peter's interpreter, St. Luke had the opportunity of learning from him many facts concerning St. Peter. St. Barnabas also perhaps furnished some details concerning the history of the early Church at Jerusalem. Some of the converts who fled from Judaea to Antioch (xi. 19) were probably men who witnessed the wonders of the Day of Pentecost. And if St. Luke was a Christian of Antioch, as tradition says, he may have made inquiries of these converts.

From Philip the evangelist, St. Luke may have learnt the history of events with which Philip was concerned, as he stayed with him at Caesarea (xxi. 8-12), and he also knew Mnason, who was one of the "original" disciples of Pentecost (xxi. 16). Finally, we notice that St. Luke had intercourse with St. James, the Bishop of Jerusalem, himself (xxi. 18).

[Sidenote: Date.]

We have seen above (p. 68) that St. Luke's Gospel was probably written soon after A.D. 70. As Acts i. 1 shows that Acts was written later than the Gospel, and as there is just enough difference in style between the two books to encourage the idea that Acts was not written immediately after the Gospel, we may reasonably place Acts between A.D. 75 and 80.

One obvious objection to placing the date of Acts so late is the fact that the writer does not record the death of St. Paul. This is certainly startling, for the martyrdom of the great apostle would have formed an impressive conclusion to the book. But there are several reasons which may be appropriately suggested to account for the omission. Possibly the author intended to write a third "treatise," in which the story of the martyrdom of his two great heroes, St. Peter and St. Paul, would be recounted; possibly Acts, which ends very abruptly, was never completed by the author. It is also possible that, after showing that the Roman civil power had generally been tolerant towards Christianity, he did not wish to endanger the circulation of his book by giving an account of Nero's brutal persecution of the Christians. If the book had contained any such history, the possession of it would have been regarded as no small offence by the civil authorities. Several years later, when the Church was probably much stronger, St. John, in writing the Revelation, disguised his description of Nero in symbolical language. In any case, St. Luke may have wished both to show Theophilus that Christianity was compatible with loyalty to the government, and that the government had for a long time been tolerant towards Christianity.

[Sidenote: Character and Contents.]

The general plan of the book may easily be seen by a glance at the Analysis printed below. We may describe it by saying that the ruling ideas are the progress and the continuity of the Church. That is to say, St. Luke shows how the Church, the divinely organized society which promotes the kingdom of God, lives and develops through various stages and crises. It spreads from one upper room in Jerusalem to Rome, the world's mightiest city. From the election of Matthias, the new apostle, until the decision reached by the Council at Jerusalem twenty years afterwards, and recorded in ch. xv., we behold a slow but sure progress. The secret of this progress is dependence upon the risen Christ. We cannot conceive how the apostles could ever have come out of the perplexity and dismay caused by the death of their Lord, and laboured with such enthusiasm, unless they were certain that the Lord was indeed risen. Without the resurrection, the Church would have collapsed at once. Knowing that it could not be possibly disproved, the apostles appeal to it as their reason for advancing out of Judaism. Two points with regard to the doctrine implied in chs. i.-xv. deserve special attention.

(1) *The doctrine of Christ's Person.* The doctrine is of the simplest kind, but the facts asserted by the apostles imply that He is divine. He is the Messiah, anointed by God, and the Holy One, and He is in a special sense the Holy Servant or Child of God (iii. 14; iv. 27). He is seated at the right hand of God (v. 31), He is Prince and Saviour. He fulfils divine functions. It is He who has poured out the Holy Spirit (ii. 33). He is the object of man's faith, and His name or revealed personality is declared to have just restored a lame man to soundness (iii. 16); signs and wonders are expected to be done through Him (iv. 30). There is "salvation" in none other (iv. 12), and He is to be "the Judge of quick and dead" (x. 42). St. Stephen in dying prays to Him. He is perpetually called Lord, and the fact that the same name is applied to Jehovah in the Septuagint makes it impossible to suppose that Christ is not regarded as possessed of divine attributes.

(2) *The doctrine of the salvation of the world.* Rationalist critics have asserted that the first apostles had no idea that the gospel was meant for the world, and that they limited its light to the children of Abraham. The unfairness of this assertion is shown by the consistent manner in which the same doctrine of the salvation of all men is interwoven in different parts of Acts, including the early chapters, which are generally acknowledged to be derived from an early Jewish Christian source. The doctrine is that salvation is offered to the Jews first (iii. 26), but "all that are afar off" may share in it (ii. 39; iii. 25). This is exactly the doctrine expressed by St. Paul in Rom. i. 16. And the conversion of Gentiles of different classes, as recorded in Acts, testifies that the apostles acted up to the doctrine. They did not doubt that the Gentiles had a right to the gospel. The point which did agitate them was, how much of the Jewish ceremonial ought the Gentiles to be required to observe. When the Gentile converts became numerous the question became acute, being sharpened by the demand of certain Jewish Christians that all converts should be circumcised.

St. Peter and St. James set their faces against this demand, and it was determined on their advice that the Gentiles should only be required to abstain from "meats offered to idols, and from blood, and from things strangled, and from fornication" (xv. 29). The rule was primarily meant for Antioch, Syria, and Cilicia. It prohibits complicity in idolatry, and in the immorality with which Syrian idolatry had been historically associated. And it prohibits the eating of blood and things strangled, a practice which might cause friction in the presence of Jewish communities. Nothing is said about circumcision or the sabbath. It is impossible to reconcile Acts xv. with the theory that the original apostles were merely Jewish Unitarians who detested St. Paul. And the Rationalists who have propagated this theory gain no help either from Galatians or from Acts xxi. For St. Paul, in writing to the Galatians, asserts the two central facts which we find in Acts xv., viz. (i.) that his policy of an open gospel was opposed by a party which appealed to the original apostles, (ii.) that the original apostles gave him the hand of fellowship and repudiated the Judaizers. In Acts xxi. 24 we find St. Paul himself performing a Jewish ceremonial act at the request of St. James. The request was made in order to counteract the falsehood that he had been trying to make the Hebrew converts desert the old Jewish customs. It cannot be interpreted as a proof of the supposed blind Judaism of St. James. For St. Paul *voluntarily* performed a similar act at Cenchreae, and we have no ground for believing that he always claimed for himself that entire freedom from Jewish usages which he always claimed for his Gentile converts. His own words contradict such a notion emphatically (1 Cor. ix. 20).

The truth is that it is only by doing violence to all the evidence which we possess, that anything can be done to support either the theory of Baur and his school that the apostles of the Church were divided with regard to the *Law*, or the more recent theory of Harnack and others that they were divided with regard to the *Person of Christ*. All the apostles believed that the gospel was for all men on equal terms, and that Christ was the divine Lord of all.

In addition to these points, it is necessary to say a few words about *the ministry of the Church* which is described in Acts. It is asserted by such writers as Martineau, Sabatier, and Schmiedel, that the state of the Church and the ministry in Acts betrays the fact that the author did not write in the apostolic age. It is said that "hierarchical ideas" or "hierarchical pretensions" can be detected in such passages as i. 17, 20; viii. 14-17; xv. 28; xx. 28, and that such ideas could not have been entertained by the apostles. It is not possible to give a full discussion of such a theory in this book.[4] We must be content with noting that, in order to give it any appearance of validity, it is necessary to reject every part of the New Testament which does not happen to agree with it. Schmiedel, who places Acts between A.D. 110 and 130, says that "Acts xx. 18-35 has many ideas in common with those of the Pastoral Epistles," but that "the author has not yet reached the stage in the development of Church government which characterizes the First Epistle to Timothy." [5] He says this simply because that Epistle, which he regards as a late forgery, shows a form of Church government practically identical with Episcopacy, while he thinks that Acts xx. shows a form of government intermediate between the genuine apostolic form and Episcopacy. To this we may make two answers; (a) that the Church government in Acts and 1 Timothy is practically the same, the work of the apostle being in r Timothy partly delegated to an apostolic vicar; (b) as there is excellent evidence for regarding 1 Timothy as a genuine writing of St. Paul, it gives us an additional cause for believing that the description of Church government in Acts is not fictitious.

ANALYSIS

The outline of the book is laid down in the words of our Lord quoted in i. 8, "Ye shall receive power after that the Holy Ghost is come upon you: and ye shall be My witnesses both in Jerusalem, and in all Judaea, and Samaria, and unto the uttermost parts of the earth."

A.

From A.D. 29 to ? 34,

The Church at Jerusalem: i.-viii. 1.—Introduction; the commission to the apostles, the Ascension, choice of Matthias in place of Judas (i.). Outpouring of the Holy Spirit at Pentecost, Peter's speech, the unity of the Church (ii.). Cure of a lame man, Peter's speech on the occasion (iii.). Peter and John imprisoned and before the Council, their dismissal and return to the Church, community of goods in the Church (iv.). Ananias and Sapphira, miracles of healing, especially by Peter, second imprisonment of Peter and John, Peter's speech, Gamaliel's advice to refrain from persecution (v.). Appointment of the seven deacons, Stephen's ministry and arrest (vi.). Stephen's defence, in which he shows that the Jews have always opposed the chief servants of God and that *true worship is independent of the Jewish temple*, Stephen's martyrdom (vii.-viii. 1).

B.

From A.D. ? 34 to 46.

Christianity spreads through Judaea and Samaria and to the Gentiles, St. Paul's conversion: viii.-xii.—Church scattered by persecution, Philip in Samaria, Simon Magus, Peter and John at Samaria, Philip baptizes an Ethiopian proselyte to Judaism (viii.). Conversion of Paul, his baptism, he is introduced to the apostles, Peter at Joppa and Lydda, raising of Tabitha by Peter (ix.). Peter and Cornelius, Peter's trance, he eats with and has baptized *Gentiles* who had previously believed in God but were *uncircumcised* (x.). He explains his conduct and the Church approves (xi. 1-18).

Christianity spreads to Phoenicia, Cyprus, and Antioch, where it is preached to *pagan Greeks* (xi. 19-30). Herod's persecution, murder of James, Peter's third imprisonment and escape, death of Herod in A.D. 44, Paul returns from his second visit to Jerusalem (xii.).

C.

From A.D. 47 to 49.

St. Paul's First Missionary Journey: xiii. 1-xv. 35.—Barnabas and Paul receive the laying on of hands at Antioch, journey through Cyprus, Elymas the sorcerer blinded, visit to Antioch in Pisidia, Paul's speech in the synagogue, he turns to the Gentiles (xiii.). Paul preaches at Iconium, cures lame man at Lystra, is stoned, returns to Antioch (xiv.). *Persecution of the Christians by Jews.*

The Jerusalem Church Council decides that *Gentiles need not be circumcised* (xv. 1-35).

D.

From A.D. 49 to 52.

St. Paul's Second Missionary Journey: xv. 36-xviii. 22.—Paul with Silas visits the Churches founded during the first journey, Timothy circumcised (xv. 36-xvi. 5). Paul crosses to Europe, imprisoned at Philippi, conversion of the jailor (xvi.). At Thessalonica and Beroea, at Athens, Paul's speech at the Areopagus (xvii.). At Corinth, brought before Gallic the Roman proconsul, travels by Ephesus and Caesarea to Jerusalem and Antioch (xviii. 1-22). *Persecution by Jews, or by Gentiles whose pockets are affected* (xvi. 19).

E.

From A.D. 52 to 56.

St. Paul's Third Missionary Journey: xviii. 23-xxi. 16.—Paul revisits Galatia and Phrygia; Apollos, a converted Jew, defends Christianity at Corinth (xviii. 23-28). Paul stays at Ephesus, great riot (xix.). *Roman officials tolerant to Christianity, craftsmen whose pockets are affected show violence.* Journey to Macedonia and Greece, Paul at Troas, Eutychus' fall and cure, journey to Miletus where Paul meets the presbyters of Ephesus (xx.). Voyage to Tyre and Caesarea (xxi. 1-16).

F.

From A.D. 56 to 61.

St. Paul arrested at Jerusalem, imprisoned at Caesarea, voyage to Rome: xxi. 17-xxviii. 31.—Paul visits James and the presbyters, the Jews try to kill him, he is rescued and taken to the castle (xxi. 17-40). His speech to the Jews, is removed by the chief captain (xxii.). His speech before the Jewish Council, is taken to Caesarea (xxiii.). Appears before the procurator Felix (xxiv.). Appears before the procurator Festus, appeals to the emperor, speaks before Agrippa (xxv., xxvi.). *Roman officials still tolerant, but obliged to interfere.* The voyage and shipwreck (xxvii.). Paul at Melita (xxviii. 1-10). He journeys to Rome and expounds the gospel at Rome, where the Jews had not previously heard anything against him. He preaches the kingdom of God for two years (xxviii. 11-31).

Similar Characteristics of St. Luke's Gospel and Acts.—Among such are the continued interest in Samaritans (Acts i. 8; viii. 5-25) John the Baptist (Acts i. 22; x. 37; xiii. 24; xviii. 25; xix. 3), women (Acts i. 14; ix. 36; xii. 12; xvii. 4), the poor (Acts ii. 45; iii. 3; iv. 32; ix. 39, etc.). In both books Christ is specially called "Lord," and is the great Prophet (Luke vii. 16, 39; xxiv. 19-27; cf. Acts iii. 22; vii. 37), also the suffering "Servant" (Luke xxiv. 36, 45; cf. Acts iii. 13, 18; iv. 27; viii. 32). Notice, too, in both books the long reports of prayers and speeches.

[1] The "we sections" contain 97 verses. They are xvi. 10-17, xx. 5-15; xxi. 1-18, xxvii. 1-xxviii. 16.

[2] See Rev. Sir John C. Hawkins, Bart., M.A., *Horae Synopticae*.

[3] See Lightfoot, *Commentary on Galatians*.

[4] The reader is referred to Dr. Gore, *The Church and the Ministry*, p. 234 f. (fourth edition).

[5] *Encyclopaedia Biblica*, vol. i. p. 49.

CHAPTER VIII THE EPISTLES OF ST. PAUL

Although the Christian cannot regard the Epistles contained in the New Testament as having quite the same importance as the Gospels which record the life and sayings of his Divine Master, he must regard them as having a profound significance. They deal with the creed and the conduct of the Church with an inspired insight which gives them an undying value, and they are marked by a personal affection which gives them an undying charm. They lend, too, a most powerful support to the historical evidence of the truth of Christianity. We have already noticed that the earliest Gospel was probably not written before A.D. 62, while St. John's Gospel is probably as late as A.D. 85. But several of the twenty-one Epistles in the New Testament are certainly earlier than A.D. 62, and out of the whole number only the three by St. John can be confidently placed at a later date than St. John's Gospel. Now, these twenty-one Epistles assume the truth of the story contained in the Gospels. They do more than this. For they prove that during the lifetime of men who had personally known Jesus Christ, there were large numbers of earnest men and women who were at home with the same ideas as those which Christians have cherished until modern times. Some of these ideas explain what we find in the Gospels. For instance, the doctrine of the Atonement is more plainly expounded in the Epistles than in the Gospels. This doctrine, together with those which concern the Person of Jesus Christ, the Holy Trinity, the sacraments, the Church, and the ministry, could be shown to have existed about A.D. 60, even if the Gospels had perished or were proved to be forgeries. The indirect evidence which the Epistles give to the life and teaching of our Lord is therefore of immense importance. If the infidel says that these doctrines are mere theories, we can ask him how these theories arose, and challenge him to produce a cause which so adequately accounts for them as the incarnation of the Son of God.

The origin of "spiritual letters" or "epistles" was perhaps due to the wisdom and originality of St. Paul. At any rate, there is nothing improbable in this conjecture, nor need it draw us into any sympathy with the recent attempts to use it as a means for discrediting those Epistles in the New Testament which bear the names of other authors. It is possible that the earliest Epistle is that of St. James, and we have no means of telling whether St. Paul did or did not anticipate him in writing Epistles. In any case, if St. Paul is not the pioneer, he is the captain of epistle-writers. St. Cyprian, St. Jerome, St. Bernard, and in modern times Archbishop Fenelon and Dr. Pusey, have illustrated the power of making a letter the vehicle of momentous truths. But on the greatest of them there has fallen only a portion of the mantle of St. Paul.

We possess thirteen Epistles written by St. Paul. There is no real reason for doubting the genuineness of any of them, and a remarkable change has lately taken place in the manner in which the opponents of orthodox Christianity have treated them. When the ingenious attempt was made, sixty years ago, to prove that St. Paul invented a type of Christianity which was not taught by Christ, it was held that only Galatians, Romans, and 1 and 2 Corinthians were genuine. The other Epistles attributed to St. Paul were said to be forgeries written after St. Paul's death, and intended to act as certificates for the Catholic faith of the 2nd century. Since then criticism has grown wiser. The genuineness of Philippians and 1 Thessalonians was first conceded. Then it became necessary to admit the genuineness of Colossians and Philemon; and 2 Thessalonians and Ephesians are now being placed in the same list even by some extreme critics. In fact, the use made of St. Paul's Epistles in the 2nd century, and the impossibility of finding any one who had the genius to personate the great apostle, are two things which have disabled fancy-criticism. The Epistles to Timothy and Titus are still confidently rejected by some authors, but this confidence is being undermined. Some special attention is given to the question of their genuineness in this book.

The writings of St. Paul fall into four groups, each group being shaped by something which is unmistakably novel and by something which it has in common with the other groups.

I. A.D. 51. 1 and 2 Thessalonians.

II. A.D. 55-56. 1 and 2 Corinthians, Galatians, Romans.

III. A.D. 59-61. Colossians, Philemon, Ephesians, Philippians.

IV. A.D. 61-64. 1 Timothy, Titus, 2 Timothy.

St. Paul was in the habit of dictating his letters. In Rom. xvi. 22 occurs the name of Tertius, who was then acting as his secretary. But St. Paul wrote the little letter to Philemon himself, and in Gal. vi. 11-18 we find a postscript which the apostle wrote in his own large handwriting. Similar instances are found in 1 Cor. xvi. 21-24 and Col. iv. 18, while in 2 Thess. iii. 17 he shows us that he sometimes made these additions in order to protect his converts from being deceived by forged letters written in his name.

In order to enter into the spirit of St. Paul's letters it is necessary to understand his history, a brief outline of which will now be given.

Saul, who changed his name to Paul, was born at Tarsus in Cilicia, a city which prided itself upon its good education. The language of the city was Greek; Saul's father was a Jew and a Roman citizen. He was trained at Jerusalem by Gamaliel, a renowned Pharisee. The future apostle was therefore born a member of the most religious race in the world, spoke the language of the most cultivated race in the world, and lived under the most masterly and fully organized government. All these three influences left their mark on a soul which was always impressible towards everything great and noble. But his nature was not only impressible; it was endowed as well by God with a strong pure heat which could fuse truths together into an orderly and well-proportioned form, and purge away the falsehoods which clung to truths. It is plain that he was not a Pharisee of the baser sort, even when he believed that the Messiah was a pretender. Righteousness was his ideal, and because he hated sin, a struggle raged between his conscience and his lower instincts (Rom. vii. 7-25). He fiercely persecuted the Christians, whom he regarded as traitors to their race and their religion. On his way from Jerusalem to Damascus with a warrant from the high priest to arrest the Christians, he was converted (about A.D. 35) by a direct interposition of the risen Lord. Every effort has been made by modern rationalists to explain this revelation as either an imaginary vision or an inward light in his conscience. The fact remains that St. Paul never speaks of it as a merely inward reality, that he does not number his conversion among the ecstatic states to which he was subject (2 Cor. xii. 1), and that he reckons the appearance of Christ to himself as an outward appearance like the appearances to the older apostles (1 Cor. xv. 5-8). We cannot get behind the statements made by St. Paul and those made in Acts by his friend, St. Luke. They show that he was met and conquered by Christ. The appearance of Christ changed his whole career, transformed his character, convinced him that Jesus was the Messiah, and that salvation can only be obtained by faith in Him—that is, by a devoted adherence to His Person and His teaching. After preaching Christ in Damascus, he retired into the keen air and inspiring solitude of the Arabian desert. During this period the outline of his creed seems to have grown clear and definite. It afterwards expanded and developed, as truly as youth passes into manhood, but there is no evidence for any material alteration having taken place after his return from Arabia. Many Christians doubted the sincerity of his conversion, but St. Barnabas, a conciliatory and kind evangelist, introduced him to St. Peter and St. James at Jerusalem, A.D. 38. His life being threatened by the Greek-speaking Jews, he departed for Tarsus. In due time he was brought by St. Barnabas to aid the new mission to the Gentiles at Antioch, a large and splendid city, admirably adapted for the first propagation of the gospel among the heathen. In A.D. 46 he paid with Barnabas a second visit to Jerusalem, taking thither a contribution from Antioch to relieve the famine which raged there. In A.D. 47 he went from Antioch in company with Barnabas on his first missionary tour, visiting Cyprus and part of Asia Minor. On his return, A.D. 49, he attended the Council at Jerusalem (Acts xv.; Gal. ii.), at which he insisted that converts from paganism should not be required to submit to circumcision and the other ceremonial rules of the Jewish Church. Only once again has any Council of the Church had to discuss such a burning and weighty question, and that once was at the Council of Nicaea in 325, when it was determined to describe the fact that Jesus is God in language which would admit of no possible mistake or jugglery. At Jerusalem, in A.D. 49, the Church had to determine whether it was sufficient for a man to be a Christian, or necessary for him to become a Jew and a Christian simultaneously. Some Judaizing Christians maintained the latter. Faithful to the teaching of our Lord, who laid on no Gentile the necessity of adopting Judaism, the Church decided that Gentile converts need not be circumcised.

In A.D. 49, soon after the Council at Jerusalem, St. Paul began a second missionary journey, and crossed over into Europe, where he founded several Churches, including those of Philippi and Thessalonica. At Athens he seems to have made but little impression, but at Corinth, the busy and profligate centre of Greek commerce, he was more successful. He stayed there for eighteen months, and during this stay he wrote the Epistles to the Thessalonians. They are marked by the attention given to *eschatology*, or doctrine of "the last things"—the second coming of Christ, the resurrection of mankind, and the judgment.

This second journey closed with a visit to Jerusalem, and was followed by an incident which shows that the apostle's long warfare with Judaism was not over. The Judaizers had been defeated at the Council of Jerusalem, and they were aware that the Gentiles were pouring into the Church. So they attempted a new and artful plan for securing their own predominance. They no longer denied that uncircumcised Christians were Christians, but they tried to gain a higher status for the circumcised. They asserted that special prerogatives belonged to the Messiah's own people, and to the apostles whom He had chosen while He was on earth. When St. Paul went from Jerusalem to Antioch in A.D. 52, St. Peter, fearing to offend these Judaizers, was guilty of pretending to believe that he agreed with them.[1] He refused to eat with Gentile (uncircumcised) Christians. He thereby tried to compel the Gentiles to "Judaize" (Gal. ii. 14), treating them as if they were an inferior caste. St. Barnabas was carried away by St. Peter's example. St. Paul then openly rebuked the leader of the apostles. It is on this incident that F. C. Baur and the Tübingen school founded their fictitious history of a doctrinal struggle between St. Paul and the original apostles. The fundamental falsehood of this history lies in the fact that there was no real difference of opinion between St. Peter and St. Paul. The latter rebuked the former for "dissembling," *i.e.* for acting on a special occasion in a manner contrary to his convictions and openly professed principles.

The Judaizing party not only tried to inoculate the Church with Judaism, but strained every nerve to undermine the authority of St. Paul. They said that he had no authority to preach Christ unless it was derived through the Twelve, and they showed "letters of commendation" (Gal. ii. 12; 2 Cor. iii. 1), to the effect that they represented the first apostles and came to supply the defects of St. Paul's teaching. With these opponents he was in conflict during his third missionary journey, which began about August, A.D. 52. On this journey he revisited Galatia and Phrygia, made a long stay at Ephesus, and went to Macedonia and Greece. During this third missionary journey he wrote 1 and 2 Corinthians, Galatians, and Romans. It is hard to determine the exact order in which they were written, as Galatians may have been written before 1 Corinthians. These Epistles are the noblest work of St. Paul. The persistent efforts of his opponents compel him to defend both his principles and his character. Amid the perplexity of the time, his clear and clarifying mind formulated Christian doctrine so perfectly that he compels his readers to see what he sees. This group of Epistles is mainly devoted to *soteriology*, or the method by which God saves man. It contains abundant teaching about God's purpose of saving us, the use of the Jewish law, the struggle between our flesh and our spirit, the work of Jesus Christ in dying and rising for us, the work of the Holy Spirit, and the morals and worship of the Church. St. Paul's arguments are mainly addressed to believing Christians, whom he wishes to preserve from Jewish or heathen error. They are marked by the strongest light and shade. Nowhere does sin appear more awful, and the love of God to undeserving man appear more generous. At one moment the apostle writes as a logician, at another as a mystic. Now he is stern, and now he is pathetic. In compass, in variety, in depth, these four Epistles are great works of art, and all the greater because the writer esteems his intellectual powers as nothing in comparison with the story of the Cross.

In May, A.D. 56, St. Paul was arrested at Jerusalem, after which he was detained by the Roman procurator Felix for two years at Caesarea, and then sent to Rome because he appealed to have his case tried by the emperor. He arrived at Rome early in A.D. 59, and was imprisoned for two years in his own hired house before his trial. During this imprisonment he wrote the Epistles to the Colossians, Ephesians, and Philippians, and the exquisite private letter to Philemon. In Philippians there is a strong reprimand of the infatuation of trusting in Jewish privileges, but it is plain from Colossians and Ephesians that Gentile Christianity was already firmly established, and that in Asia Minor the Judaizing heresies were becoming fainter and more fanciful. St. Paul criticizes a Judaic Gnosticism, a morbid mixture of Jewish ritual with that Oriental spiritualism which fascinated many devotees in the Roman empire at this period. The Philippians do not seem to have been infected with the same religious malaria as the Christians who dwelt in the valley of the Lycus. But St. Paul in writing to them, as to the Colossians and Ephesians, takes great pains to show who Christ is and what our relation towards Him ought to be. This group is therefore distinguished by its *Christology*.

St. Paul was released from his first imprisonment at Rome, though we know no details of his release. He again resumed his missionary life, and wrote the First Epistle to Timothy and that to Titus. According to a tradition of very great antiquity, he visited Spain. But the changed attitude of the Roman government towards the Christians soon cut short his work. Earlier in his career the Roman officials had regarded the new religion with easy though somewhat supercilious toleration. In 2 Thessalonians we find St. Paul apparently describing the Roman authorities as the restraining power which hindered the malice of antichristian Judaism from working revenge upon the Church. At Ephesus he had been personally protected from the mob by the men who were responsible for the public worship of the Roman emperor. But under Nero an active persecution of the Christians was set on foot, and St. Paul was again imprisoned at Rome. During this last imprisonment he wrote his Second Epistle to Timothy. This letter, like the First Epistle to Timothy and that to Titus, deals specially with the organization and ministry of the Church, and was intended to consolidate the Church before the apostle's death. The martyrdom of the apostle probably took place in A.D. 64. His tomb, marked by an inscription of the 4th century, still remains at Rome in the church of "St. Paul outside the walls," which stands near the scene of his martyrdom. Unless the relics were destroyed by the Saracens who sacked Rome in 846, they probably remain in this tomb. The festival of June 29, which in mediaeval times was kept in honour of St. Peter and St. Paul, and which in our present English Prayer-book is wrongly dedicated to St. Peter only, is probably not the day on which either of the apostles suffered. It is the day on which their relics were removed for safety to the catacombs in the time of the persecution of the Christians by the Emperor Decius, A.D. 258.

[1] The above account places the dispute at Antioch before the third missionary journey. Some writers of deserved repute place it in the winter of A.D. 48, before the Council of Jerusalem.

CHAPTER IX 1 AND 2 THESSALONIANS

THE FIRST EPISTLE OF PAUL THE APOSTLE TO THE THESSALONIANS

[Sidenote: The Author.]

Among all schools of thought there has been an increasing conviction that this Epistle is genuine. It was included in Marcion's *Apostolicon*, or list of Pauline writings, it is contained in the *Muratorian Fragment*, it is quoted by the great Fathers of the close of the 2nd century, and is found in the Old Latin and Peshitta Syriac versions of the New Testament. The earnest and affectionate tone of the Epistle is thoroughly Pauline, and the argument that it is not genuine because it does not contain the same pronounced anti-Jewish teaching as we find in Romans is precarious, though it has seemed to some sceptics to be convenient. The argument might be turned in the opposite direction. For it would be just as reasonable to say that the absence of anti-Jewish doctrine proves that the Epistle was written before the great conflict with the semi-Christian Jews began, as to say that it proves that it was written by a forger after the conflict was over. One paragraph in the Epistle points decisively to an early date. In iv. 13-18 we find that some Thessalonians were under the delusion that it would be an exceptional thing for a Christian to die before the second coming of our Lord, and that those who did so die would miss some of the felicity appointed for the rest. Such a delusion must have been dispelled at a very early date. Moreover, the comfort which St. Paul administers to those who are agitated by this notion gives us the idea that he expected Christ to return in his own lifetime. In this respect he writes to the Thessalonians something very different from what he writes in his later Epistles (Phil. i. 21-24; 2 Tim. iv. 6), or even in 2 Cor. v. 1. We need not be surprised that God left the great apostle in ignorance of an event which it is not given even to the angels to understand (Matt. xxiv. 36). But a forger, living after the apostle's death, would not be at all likely to represent his hero as falling into such a mistake.

[Sidenote: To whom written.]

Thessalonica, the modern Saloniki, was the capital of part of Macedonia, situated in the middle of the bend of the Thermaic Gulf, and not far from Mount Olympus, the snow-clad home of the gods of Greece. It was a busy mercantile town, and in ready communication with Italy, as the great road called *Via Egnatia* passed through its walls. It contained then, as now, a considerable number of Jews among its inhabitants. In Christian times it became a great ecclesiastical centre, and was influential in the conversion of the Slavs and Bulgarians. It is still famous for its splendid Byzantine churches, though the finest have long since been converted into mosques by the Turks.

The Church was planted there by St. Paul on his second missionary journey, in A.D. 50 (Acts xvii.). He preached first to the Jews, and after his third visit to the synagogue he was rejected by the Jews, and he turned to the Gentiles. Some of these Thracian Gentiles were converts to Judaism, but they were people whose character could be trusted. In the mean time his Philippian converts twice sent aid to him (Phil. iv. 16). Previous to this the apostle had been earning his own bread, no doubt by tent-making. St. Paul was forced to leave Thessalonica in consequence of a riot stirred up by the Jews. He visited it again before his last journey to Jerusalem in A.D. 56.

1 Thess. i. 9 shows that the majority of the Christians had been Gentile idolaters, though there were a few of Jewish blood. It was among the sturdy people of Macedonia that St. Paul won his steadiest recruits for Christ. Here, as in the letter to Philippi, we find that he uses words of more than ordinary affection. These converts are to St. Paul his "joy and crown" (1 Thess. ii. 19; Phil. iv. 1). He compares his relation with them to that of a nurse with her own children (1 Thess. ii. 7). When he wrote to the Corinthians he displayed his Macedonians as brilliant examples of Christian liberality and Christian loyalty (2 Cor. viii. 1-5). In this passage he alludes to their poverty, and these Epistles show that they had to work for their bread. They were exposed to bitter and continuous persecution from Jews, who were capable of inciting the roughs of the town to set on St. Paul (Acts xvii. 5).

[Sidenote: Where and when written.]

The Epistle was written from Corinth on the occasion of St. Paul's first visit there. When St. Paul had to leave Beroea in A.D. 50, Silas and Timothy remained (Acts xvii. 14, 15; xviii. 5). He sent for them to meet him at Athens, and when they had come, he despatched Timothy to Thessalonica (1 Thess. iii. 2). In October A.D. 50, St. Paul arrived at Corinth from Athens: Timothy and Silas rejoined him at Corinth, and the letter was written soon afterwards, probably early in A.D. 51.

[Sidenote: Character and Contents.]

The immediate cause of the Epistle was the arrival of Timothy with news from Thessalonica. The apostle's reasons for writing were: (a) to calm and encourage the converts whom he had so abruptly left; (b) to urge them to perform their ordinary duties. They had fallen into a state bordering on religious hysteria. Quite determined to be true to Christ, they had been demoralized by the strain of facing constant hostility. They had begun to take excessive interest in unfulfilled prophecy and eschatological speculation. The result was that individuals had become careless as to the performance of simple duties.

The apostle comforts the Thessalonians by reminding them of the happiness and reality of their own spiritual experience. He wishes them to see plainly the working of God both in his own preaching of the gospel and their acceptance of it. On the one hand, he gladly recognizes the *faith, charity, hope,* and constancy under persecution: the story of their conversion, as it had been known everywhere, has won many friends for the Faith (i.). On the other hand, St. Paul is aware that his own conduct has not been unworthy of an apostle. Probably to vindicate himself against Jewish calumnies, he declares that his ministry at Thessalonica was bold, pure, honest, and gentle. Moreover, he did not quarter himself upon his converts; he worked with his hands, and was just and fatherly (ii. 1-12).

After a thanksgiving for the manner in which they received the word of God, he speaks of his eager wish to see his friends again. He had sent Timothy that he might comfort them, and Timothy has returned with glad tidings. He prays for their establishment in holiness (ii. 13-iii. 13).

He goes on to exhort them to avoid impurity and work quietly, and then he speaks of the eschatological difficulties. The Thessalonians wondered whether the Christians already dead would miss a share in the joy of Christ's second coming. St. Paul replies that those who are alive at Christ's appearing will have no advantage over the dead (iv. 15). On the contrary, the dead will rise first, and then the living Christians will be caught up together with them to meet the Lord. The day will come with surprise, and will terrify the unprepared (iv. 1-v. 3).

He then calls them to watchfulness and sobriety. There follows an exhortation to obey the clergy, and the early date of the Epistle is again suggested by the fact that the titles which are used in his later epistles are not given to the clergy of Thessalonica. The existence of an order of prophets seems implied (v. 20). The Epistle has a special blessing for these troubled Christians who look so wistfully for "the coming of our Lord Jesus Christ."

ANALYSIS

Salutation, thanksgiving, and congratulation. The good fruit borne by Christianity at Thessalonica is known of through all Macedonia and Achaia (i.).

The character of the apostle's ministry there, a fresh thanksgiving, the apostle desires to see his friends, but is hindered by Satan working through adverse circumstances (ii.).

Timothy's expedition, a prayer (iii.).

Encouragement to obedience, exhortation against impurity and to work; the blessed dead and Christ's second coming. The sudden coming of the Lord (iv. 1-v. 3).

Practical conclusion based on the above doctrine (v. 4-28).

THE SECOND EPISTLE OF PAUL THE APOSTLE TO THE THESSALONIANS

[Sidenote: The Author.]

The external evidence for the genuineness of the Second Epistle is even stronger than that of the First. It is mentioned by Polycarp,[1] and apparently by Justin Martyr.[2] It is also supported by the same versions of the New Testament and by the same Fathers as the First Epistle. In modern times it has been rejected even by some who accept 1 Thessalonians. Some of the objections which have been raised are almost too trivial to deserve attention. But the prophetic and apocalyptic passage in ii. 1-12 has been regarded by many critics as a serious stumbling-block. It has been urged (a) that 1 Thessalonians implies that St. Paul believed Christ would return immediately, whereas 2 Thessalonians implies that certain important occurrences must first intervene. But there is no real contradiction. For 1 Thessalonians represents the return of Christ as certainly sudden and *possibly soon*; it does not represent it as certainly immediate. A thief may come suddenly in the night, and yet the man who gives warning that the thief will come, does not necessarily mean that the thief is coming without delay. It has been urged (b) that the doctrine of Antichrist in 2 Thessalonians is un-Pauline, and depends on the Book of Revelation. But there is not the least improbability in supposing that St. Paul was in touch with these ideas about the end of the world. We know that such ideas were common among the Jews at this period. Nor is there any proof that the teaching of 2 Thessalonians on this subject is derived from the Revelation of St. John. Moreover, on the least Christian view with regard to Christ and the Gospels, it is irrational to deny that our Lord made various predictions about His second coming. We find a list of such predictions in Matt. xxiv. and in the parallel passages of the other Gospels. It is therefore natural to find St. Paul speaking about the end of the world in language which resembles that used by our Lord, or that found in Daniel, Ezekiel, and the later Jewish Apocalypses.

[Sidenote: Where and when written.]

St. Paul sent this Epistle from Corinth, probably towards the end of the year 51.

Several modern writers have dated 2 Thessalonians earlier than 1 Thessalonians. The grounds for this view are the references in this Epistle to the teaching lately given by St. Paul while at Thessalonica. But although these references would be natural in any Epistle written first after his departure from that place, they do not necessarily imply that 2 Thessalonians was the first. Moreover, ii. 2 probably contains a reference to the First Epistle, and this letter was apparently written to clear up a difficulty which the First Epistle did not solve. Persecution had continued at Thessalonica, and higher excitement and wider confusion prevailed. The Thessalonians were more sure than ever that Christ's advent was coming immediately, on the strength, perhaps, of some words in St. Paul's earlier letter to them, supported by a forged letter which pretended to be his and by feigned revelations. The result was entire neglect of daily duties. "There is no reason," men said, "why I should work for my living or try to be provident, because the Lord is sure to come to-day or to-morrow."

As the circumstances are so similar to those in the First Epistle, and as Silvanus (otherwise Silas) and Timothy are still with the apostle, we may be sure that 2 Thessalonians was written during St. Paul's first stay at Corinth.

[Sidenote: Character and Contents.]

The Epistle consists of instruction and exhortation. The most characteristic passage is ii. 1-12. The apostle declares that he never taught that the day of the Lord is about to dawn immediately (ii. 2). It must be preceded by several events. There will be an apostasy, the revelation of "the man of sin, the son of perdition," who will assume equality with God and sit in the temple of God. Over against this "man of sin" we find placed "one that restraineth now." Many strange interpretations of these two phrases have been devised, and the fancy of commentators has ranged over various historical monsters from Mohammed to Napoleon Bonaparte. One favourite idea is that the description of the man of sin "setting himself forth as God" refers to the worship offered to the Roman emperors, and to the attempt made by Caligula in A.D. 39 to place his statue in the temple at Jerusalem. But it seems far better to regard the man of sin as hostile Judaism, personified in an Antichrist who pretends to be the representative of God foretold in Mal. iii. 1. The other force which St. Paul personifies is the curbing power of a strong government as then seen in the administrative system of the Roman empire. The power of Rome protected him against Jewish fanaticism at this period (Acts xix. 35-41; xxii. 22-29), but in this truly irreligious fanaticism he discerned a latent mysterious evil (ii. 7) which would afterwards reveal itself in hideous excesses. While "the man of sin," or "wicked one," thus wreaks his will, Christ will come and consume him with the breath of His mouth.

St. Paul understood the real genius of the antichristian Jews. Early in the 2nd century they began a series of rebellions against the power of Rome, committing horrible atrocities. These rebellions culminated between A.D. 132 and 135. The Jews then rallied round a pretended Messiah, Simon Bar Kocheba, whom they named "Prince of Israel"; they killed the Christians who refused to blaspheme Jesus, and they captured Jerusalem from the Romans. After a fierce struggle the Romans took Jerusalem again, and crowds of Jews were either massacred, or sold as slaves by the oak of Abraham at Hebron and in the markets of Egypt.

ANALYSIS

Salutation, thanksgiving for faith, charity, steadfastness, the certainty of Christ's coming to "render vengeance" and "to be glorified in His saints" (i.).

Apocalyptic passage, renewed thanksgiving, exhortation to hold the traditions already received, invocation of Christ and our Father to comfort and stablish the converts (ii.).

St. Paul requests their prayers for himself, anticipates their Christian progress, excommunication of disorderly brethren commanded. The apostle had worked for his living, they must do likewise. He commends them to the Lord, and appends a salutation in his own hand as a seal of authenticity (iii.).

[1] *Ad Phil.* ii.

[2] *Trypho*, 110.

CHAPTER X THE FIRST EPISTLE OF PAUL THE APOSTLE TO THE CORINTHIANS

[Sidenote: The Author.]

The genuineness of 1 and 2 Corinthians, Galatians, and Romans is admitted by almost every modern critic, Christian or not Christian. It was always acknowledged by F. C. Baur, who rejected all the Epistles bearing the name of St. Paul except these four. This Epistle is referred to in several writings of the 2nd century, and is unmistakably mentioned in the letter written to the Corinthians by St. Clement of Rome about A.D. 95. He says, "Take up the Epistle of the blessed Paul the apostle. What did he first write to you in the beginning of the Gospel? Of a truth he sent a letter to you by the Spirit concerning himself, and also Cephas and Apollos, because you had even then formed parties" (cf. 1 Cor. i. 12). The style of the Epistle is spontaneous, vivid, and coherent. The authenticity is only disputed by a tiny group of infidel writers who, in reaction against Baur, have endeavoured to make good their unbelief by asserting the genuineness of the Scriptures which Baur rejected, and rejecting what Baur defended.

[Sidenote: To whom written.]

"Unto the Church of God which is at Corinth" (i. 2). In former times Corinth had been the most important city in Greece after Athens itself. It was one of the earliest homes of Greek art, and its position made it so favourable for commerce that it attracted a colony of Phoenician traders at a very remote period. When its art declined, it remained celebrated for its wealth and its extreme licentiousness. The patron deity of the Corinthians was Aphrodite, who was no other than the foul Phoenician Astarte. Her temple on the rock of the Acrocorinthus dominated the city below, and from it there came a stream of impure, influences "to turn men into swine."

In B.C. 146 the city was captured by the Roman general Mummius. It was left desolate until B.C. 46, when Julius Caesar refounded it as a Roman colony. The Romans called the whole of Greece the province of Achaia, and constituted Corinth the capital of it. While Athens was still the seat of the greatest university in the world, where lived most vigorously the glorious memories of bygone Greece, the government of the province was directed from Corinth. When St. Paul visited it, it was under a proconsul, Junius Gallio, the brother of the philosopher Seneca. The possession of two good harbours, and its position on the quickest route from Rome to the East, caused a rapid revival of Corinthian wealth and Corinthian manners. There was also a good deal of literary and philosophic culture. In the time of St. Paul the descendants of the original Roman colonists probably formed a small aristocracy among the mass of Greek dwellers at Corinth, and some settlements of various nationalities, including one of Jews, were living there. A few miles away, at the shrine of Poseidon, were held the athletic Isthmian games, and still by the sea-shore there grow the pine trees, such as furnished the quickly withering wreaths which were given to the victors in the race.

The Church of Corinth was founded by St. Paul on his second missionary journey, during his first visit to Europe. His stay at Corinth lasted for eighteen months. There is an account of it in Acts xviii. He laboured at tent-making, and found a home with a devout Jewish couple, Aquila and Priscilla. At first he preached in the synagogue, where he converted the ruler of the synagogue, Crispus. Being rejected by the Jews, he turned to the Gentiles, and held his meetings in the house of Justus, a converted proselyte. The Jews prosecuted St. Paul before Gallio, who, however, dismissed the case with contemptuous indifference. The converts to Christianity were numerous. They were mostly Gentiles (1 Cor. xii. 2), but there were a few influential Jewish Christians and some Gentiles who had been proselytes of Judaism. It is clear that the Church contained a few men of good birth and education (1 Cor. i. 26), but the majority were from the poorer classes. The Corinthians as Christians were by no means entirely free from the characteristics which had marked them as citizens. They were ready to form cliques and quarrel in the name of Christ, and they still showed the same quarrelsome mood in the time of St. Clement. They found it hard to hate the sensuality which in their earlier days they had regarded as divine. They were puffed up with eloquence and philosophic speculation, and forgot that there is no "sweetness and light" comparable to the Gospel.

This Epistle was written from Ephesus in the spring of A.D. 55. The note at the end of the Epistle to the effect that it was written "from Philippi," though ancient, is incorrect, and is due to a misunderstanding of xvi. 5.

When St. Paul left Corinth in April, A.D. 52, to go to Jerusalem, Apollos came to take his place, and preached with much success (Acts xviii. 27). St. Paul returned to Ephesus at the end of the summer of 52, and Apollos left Corinth and joined St. Paul. Soon some Judaizing teachers appeared at Corinth, and the apostle was obliged to go thither, though "in sorrow" (2 Cor. ii. 1; cf. 2 Cor. xii. 14; xiii. 1). After this disciplinary visit he returned to Ephesus, and sent the Corinthians a sharp letter, now lost, about the relations which they should have with open and notorious evil-livers (1 Cor. v. 9).

St. Paul's next news from Corinth caused him to write this letter. Some members of Chloe's household told him of the development of factions there; and a letter was sent, perhaps by the hands of Stephanas, Fortunatus, and Achaicus (xvi. 15-18), asking for advice about matters of grave importance, including litigation between Christians and an unseemly freedom in public worship. Realizing the serious state of affairs, St. Paul determined to visit Corinth a third time, and sent Timothy as his representative to prepare for his coming (1 Cor. iv. 17, xvi. 10). After Timothy's departure he wrote this Epistle.

The above account assumes that St. Paul's *second visit* to Corinth was paid before 1 Corinthians was written, but it is thought by some writers of repute that it was paid after 1 Corinthians was written and before 2 Corinthians.

[Sidenote Character and Contents.]

This Epistle, like each of the three other Epistles belonging to the same group, has a perfectly distinct character of its own. It expounds the doctrine of a crucified Christ as applied to social difficulties. What Romans does as a theological treatise, and Galatians as a controversial admonition, and 2 Corinthians as a record of personal experience and vocation, this 1 Corinthians does as an instruction for influencing a corrupt urban life with the leaven of the gospel. It is very practical in tone, and the doctrine which it contains is not stated separately, but is throughout woven into the cords of the apostle's argument. There is nothing in the New Testament equal to this Epistle in its power of bringing us close to the difficulties of the Church in an ancient city. We seem to see the men and women who composed it—their eagerness for religious novelties, their debased surroundings, their anarchic divisions, their frail sense of moral responsibility. And a modern reader will probably lay the letter down with a conviction that our great modern cities have much to learn from the words written by St. Paul to Corinth, "the light of Greece."

The Epistle is very orderly in arrangement. It deals first with the report which St. Paul had received about the Corinthian Church (i.-vi.); then it answers various questions which the Corinthians had submitted to him (vii.-xi. 1). Then follow directions based on the report and the questions.

The letter opens with a significant salutation and thanksgiving (i. 1-9). St. Paul then proceeds to rebuke the Corinthian *tendency to party spirit*. There were apparently four parties in the Church. The first asserted that they were followers of *Paul*; the second preferred the rhetorical preaching of *Apollos* to Paul's simplicity; the third— probably Judaizers—ranged themselves under the name of *Cephas* as the leader of the original apostles; the fourth repudiated human leaders, and arrogantly named their clique that of *Christ*, thereby insinuating that the other parties were less Christian than themselves. It is evident that all these four names were really used as party watchwords. St. Paul says that he has *transferred by a fiction* (iv. 6) the action of the wranglers to himself and Apollos. He means by this, not that the Corinthians did not employ these names in their strife, but that he and Apollos were in no sense responsible for the strife. Some perplexity has been caused by the name of the Christ-party. It is thought by some that they were rigid Jewish Christians from Jerusalem (2 Cor. iii. 1; xi. 22). But it is more probable that they were only a body of Christians who protested against the parties named after human leaders, and saying, "We are the people," made a new party of their own.

St. Paul shows that this sectarian spirit is entirely alien to the whole principle and history of the Christian faith. That faith, though it is a wisdom which comes from God, does not lend itself to pride of intellect. It is deliberately content to be counted foolish by the world; its sign is the cross, its converts are the poor and insignificant Corinthians, its eloquence the unpolished speaking of the apostle himself. And as to their personal preferences for receiving spiritual benefits from one Christian teacher rather than another, this shows a complete misconception as to the source of the benefit and the position of the teacher. This is explained in iii. 1-iv. 5. All spiritual increase comes from God. Christ is the Foundation. Human teachers are not figure-heads of different schools, but the instruments and the stewards through whom God dispenses His gifts. It is not the duty of Christian teachers to put forward original ideas on religion.

Then the apostle, after referring to their ostentatious self-righteousness, pathetically shows the unfitness of pitting against one another teachers who share in an equality of forlorn destitution and contempt (iv. 6-13). He concludes this section with an affectionate but authoritative speech: he says that he has sent Timothy to Corinth, and hopes shortly to come himself (iv. 14-21).

The apostle proceeds with sharp decision to deal with *a case of incest*. The Corinthians had treated this gross offence almost with levity, but St. Paul declares that the offender shall be excommunicated and shall be punished by disease (v. 1-8). After explaining some advice of his earlier letter (v. 9-13), he goes on to rebuke a third abuse—*litigation* between Christians in pagan law-courts. The love of law-suits was mischievous in itself, as involving a breach of Christian brotherhood. It was also scandalous in its effects, as exposing the bickerings of the disciples of Christ to the ridicule of unbelievers. A stern rebuke of vice follows (vi. 1-11). Then comes an indignant and lofty argument against fornication, which is a defilement of the temple of the Holy Ghost (vi. 12-20).

St. Paul now turns to the various questions that the Corinthians have asked him. He first gives some advice about *matrimony*, carefully distinguishing between statements which he makes on his own authority, and rules laid down by Christ, and also between counsels of perfection and the obligations of ordinary Christians. It is excellent to lead a single life, but in view of prevailing sensuality, he recommends marriage as generally more prudent. He advises that when people do marry, there should be a fulfilment of conjugal duties except for occasional devotion "unto prayer." One permanently important assertion in the apostle's teaching is that both marriage and celibacy imply a "gift from God." St. Paul would have had no sympathy with either any mediaeval depreciation of married life, or the modern English notion that a man has not "settled down" until he has married (vii. 1-40).

The next question is whether converts may eat *meat that has been offered to idols*. With strong common-sense, the apostle points out that there is here no alternative between essential right and wrong. You may eat it, because an idol is nothing, but you must take care not to hurt the consciences of other Christians (viii.). You may eat anything that you buy in the market-place, but you must not attend an idolatrous feast in a temple, and if you are at a private house you must not eat food offered to idols if your attention has been directly called to its character (x. 23-32). St. Paul illustrates his meaning by reference to his own self-denial—the policy he had at Corinth of exacting no payment for his ministry, his tactful caution, his severe self-control (ix.). The need of such self-control is proved by the fact that the ancient Jews, in spite of their high privileges, fell into carelessness and sin (x. 1-13). The Corinthians must not be like the Jews. The nature of the Eucharist warns them to be scrupulously careful about temple feasts. There cannot be a drinking of the chalice of Christ and of the cup of devils (x. 14-22).

Chapter xi. deals with public worship. *St. Paul gives directions for women to cover the head in church, and then comes a reference to the Holy Eucharist which is of extreme interest and importance. It was the custom for Christians to meet together before the Eucharist for a common meal called the Agapé, which was intended to commemorate the Lord's Last Supper. St. Paul complains that this meal has been made an occasion of sin among the Corinthians: the richer people had overeaten themselves, while the poor were left hungry and ashamed. The apostle sets off the unfitness of this conduct by a brief exposition of the Eucharist; the preliminary meal, so much misused by these ungracious and ungenerous Christians, was intended to be a preparation for the ineffable Feast, at which the Fare was the very Body and Blood of Jesus Christ, and at which His death was solemnly represented (xi. 2-34).*

St. Paul deals next with *spiritual gifts*, saying that they come from God, and so give no ground for boasting, and that the exercise of them is only pleasing to God if it be joined with charity. After a sublime chapter on charity, he lays down some regulations for those who possessed these abnormal gifts, which, it is evident, were already the cause of disorders in the Church. The Corinthians, with their craving for the miraculous, tended to set a high value on speaking with tongues, but St. Paul upholds the superiority of the more intelligible and useful gift of prophecy (xii.-xiv.).

The Epistle concludes with a splendid argument for the reality of the *Resurrection*. It is directed against some false philosophy. St. Paul claims for the fact of the resurrection of Christ the witness of Scripture, of many honest and intelligent Christians, and of himself. Then he goes on to show to the Corinthian objectors what a denial of the resurrection of the dead involves. It means that Christ did not rise, that I am preaching deceit, that you are believing a lie, that the dead in Christ have no existence except as memories, that we who have foregone the pleasures of this life have done so in pursuit of a delusive phantom. But it cannot be so. Christ is really risen. And St. Paul passes on to demonstrate the happy consequences which follow from this. The Resurrection is the earnest of all that Christ will do for man; and in the light of it Christian baptism for the sake of the dead[1] and Christian heroism have their meaning (xv. 1-34).

In order to remove difficulties from the mind of an objector, St. Paul discusses the kind of body which we shall have at the Resurrection. He shows by analogies from nature (a) that God is able to effect the transformation of a seed-grain into a new product, and can therefore transform us while retaining a connection between our present and future body; (b) that God is able to create a variety of embodiments, and can therefore give us a higher embodiment than we now possess. There will be a spiritual body adapted to the spiritual world, as truly as our natural body is adapted to life in this world. Thus the gospel is truly a gospel for the body as well as for the spirit. Our whole personality will be saved, and nothing will be discarded (xv. 35-58).

St. Paul concludes with an order for the collection of alms on behalf of the faithful in Jerusalem, and says that he hopes to come soon to Corinth. After some personal matters, he characteristically appends with his own hand a curse on those who do not love the Lord, and a prayer and loving message for the faithful.

ANALYSIS

Salutation, thanksgiving (i. 1-9).

(1) Evils in the Church: i. 10-vi. 20.—Sectarianism. This is rebuked on the ground that all the apostles, etc., are working for one end, and all their power is God's. Christ is supreme over all (i. 10-iv. 21).

Incest. The Church is to deliver the sinner to Satan (the severest form of excommunication). St. Paul mentions a previous warning not to associate with immoral Christians (v.).

Going to law with a Christian in the pagan courts is rebuked. Warning against profligacy (vi.).

(2) Answers to a letter from the Corinthians: vii. 1-xi. 1.—Marriage and celibacy. It is well to avoid marriage. But the married must not separate. Under present circumstances, the apostle would prefer others to be unencumbered as he is (vii.).

Food offered to idols. Christian liberty (viii.). St. Paul's example in not claiming one's own rights (ix.). Danger of thinking that we stand. We are "one bread," and must seek each other's good (x.-xi. 1).

(3) Other evils in the Church: xi. 2-34.—Women to be covered. Conduct at the Eucharist and the Agapé. An account of the institution of the Eucharist.

(4) Answer to a question concerning spiritual gifts: xii.-xiv.—Unity in diversity (xii.). Charity the greatest gift (xiii.). Prophesying and tongues compared (xiv.).

(5) Vindication of the Resurrection: xv.—The evidence for Christ's resurrection.[2] The nature of our resurrection.

(6) Some directions and personal details: xvi.

[1] 1 Cor. xv. 29. This verse is very obscure. It has been interpreted as meaning that when a convert died before it was possible for him to be baptized, it was a custom of the Corinthians to allow a friend to undergo baptism in his stead. But perhaps it simply means being baptized for the sake of some dear one who was a sincere Christian, and begged that his or her surviving relatives would be baptized and meet him or her hereafter.

[2] It is important to notice that St. Paul, in writing of the death and resurrection of our Lord, gives powerful evidence in support of St. John's assertion that our Lord died on Nisan 14 (see above, p. 29). In 1 Cor. v. 7, 8 he says, "Our Passover also hath been sacrificed, even Christ: wherefore let us keep the feast"; and in 1 Cor. xv. 20 he calls Christ "the first-fruits of them that are asleep." Now, if Christ died on Nisan 14, when the Passover lamb was sacrificed for a feast, and if He rose on Nisan 16, when the Passover firstfruits were offered in the temple, this double comparison is exquisitely appropriate. But if the statement in John is false, St. Paul's comparison is forced and unnatural.

CHAPTER XI THE SECOND EPISTLE OF PAUL THE APOSTLE TO THE CORINTHIANS

[Sidenote: The Author.]

The genuineness of this Epistle is almost universally admitted, although it is not quoted quite as early as the First Epistle. The two Epistles are interwoven with each other by several threads of thought, such as St. Paul's intention to visit Macedonia, his decision with regard to the incestuous man, and his direction to collect alms for the Christians of Jerusalem. Moreover, this Epistle agrees with the Book of Acts, and at the same time is plainly independent of it. Acts does not mention *Titus*, whose name is prominent in 2 Corinthians, and at the same time Acts xx. 5, 6 corroborates the account of the visit to *Troas* in 2 Cor. ii. 12, 13. The whole style of the Epistle is so natural and impassioned, so wonderful in its light and gloom, that there is only one author to whom we can possibly attribute it.

There is, however, a difficulty with regard to the last four chapters. It is thought by some critics that they are a separate Epistle written by St. Paul to the Corinthians, and afterwards joined to chs. i.-ix. These writers are usually of the opinion that the last four chapters were written before i.-ix., and that their theory will account for the fact that they are more severe and depressed in tone. Now, it is true that i.-ix. seem more hopeful than x.-xiii., and also that i.-ix. contain two references to a previous letter (ii. 4; vii. 8, 9). We find, too, in 2 Cor. i. 23; ii. 1, 4, that the apostle shows a shrinking from the thought of another visit to Corinth, while in 1 Corinthians no such feeling is manifested. If, however, 2 Cor. x.-xiii. had been written in the interval, the feeling is not unreasonable. But the facts of the case seem to be most easily explained by the belief that there was a letter written between 1 and 2 Corinthians, but that this letter has been lost. In spite of the difference in tone between the two parts of 2 Corinthians, there is sufficient continuity of theme to make us hesitate to detach them.

[Sidenote: To whom written.]

"Unto the Church of God which is at Corinth, with all the saints which are in the whole of Achaia." The latter part of the address shows us that St. Paul felt it necessary to vindicate himself to all the Christians in Greece (Hellas). His opponents had evidently been extremely active.

[Sidenote: Where and when written.]

The Epistle was written in A.D. 55, a few months after 1 Corinthians, from some town in Macedonia, probably Philippi. It was sent by the hands of Titus and perhaps St. Luke (2 Cor. viii. 18-23).

The First Epistle was received submissively by the Corinthians, the strife of parties subsided, and the case of incest was dealt with as the apostle required. In consequence of this happy result, it seems that St. Paul decided to visit the Corinthians on his way to Macedonia, sailing straight to Corinth from Ephesus (2 Cor. i. 15), as well as to pay them the visit which he had promised before (1 Cor. xvi. 5).

Timothy, who had arrived at Corinth in accordance with St. Paul's previous wish (1 Cor. iv. 17; xvi. 10), soon returned to Ephesus with news of a second and more serious crisis. We do not know what caused it, or what was precisely its character, but it is certain that St. Paul's motives and authority were harshly and openly challenged. Perhaps Timothy himself was insulted, and therefore, indirectly, the apostle who gave him his commission and authority. St. Paul wrote at once a very sharp letter, which is the *second lost letter* to the Corinthians, and he resolved to return to his earlier plan of visiting them only as he came south from Macedonia. He made this resolution to spare them for the present the pain of meeting him. This lost letter was probably sent by Titus (2 Cor. xii. 18), who also carried instructions with regard to the collection for the poor at Jerusalem. Apparently St. Paul thought that it would be wiser not to entrust Timothy with the delicate task of again calming the Corinthian wranglers. As soon as Titus left, St. Paul was full of nervous apprehension as to the effect which this letter would produce. He set out from Ephesus (2 Cor. i. 8-10) in great anxiety, his departure being perhaps precipitated by the riot so graphically described in Acts. He tells us himself that when he came to Troas he had still no relief for his spirit—no news from Corinth. Though he found an opening for the gospel at Troas, he hurried on into Macedonia, and at last Titus came with joyful news of the penitence and submission of the Corinthians. St. Paul then wrote this Epistle. Towards the end of December, A.D. 55, he reached Corinth, where he stayed for three months.

The Book of Acts fits perfectly with the Epistles. From Acts xx. 1-3 we see that St. Paul did visit Macedonia and Greece at the close of his stay at Ephesus, and from Acts xix. 22 we see that he sent Timothy before him.

The Epistle has the nature of a letter sent by a spiritual father to his children rather than of a doctrinal treatise with an argument carefully built up. Its value for us lies chiefly in the vivid reality with which it reflects the personality of the writer, his love for his converts, his intense conviction that his apostolic commission and power are entirely genuine—a conviction which is set off by his wish always to associate himself with the weakness and fragility of ordinary human nature. Throughout the Epistle there are scattered allusions to Christian doctrine which are of the very highest importance. Before giving an outline of the Epistle, we may notice one or two doctrinal passages of special importance.

First, with regard to the Resurrection. The teaching of 1 Corinthians is further explained. St. Paul shows how entirely he has thrown off the feeling of terror which environed the ordinary Jewish idea of death. The sense of union with God by which a few Jews in some rare flashes of inspiration knew that they would live after death, is here triumphant. St. Paul regards death as a portal to that happy existence which can only be described as being "at home with the Lord" (2 Cor. v. 1-8; cf. Phil. i. 23). Union with Christ *now* absolutely guarantees union with Him hereafter. The resurrection-body which in 1 Corinthians he described as "a spiritual body," he poetically calls the "house from heaven" which God will provide for the redeemed spirit. Then he thinks of this new body as a *robe*. And as he hopes that Christ will come again before we have put off our present body in death, he says that he desires to be clothed with the new body over his present body, "if so be that being clothed we shall not be found naked." The last phrase is obscure, but it probably is a fresh rebuke of those Corinthians who denied the resurrection of the body. If so, it means "assuming, as is indeed the case, that we shall really be found clothed with a body at Christ's coming, and not naked (*i.e.* bodiless spirits)."

Secondly, with regard to the work of Christ. In 2 Cor. iv. 4 He is called the "image of God." Now, St. Paul teaches that we men may reflect the likeness of Christ to God:

"The truth in God's breast
Lies trace for trace upon ours impressed:
Though He is so bright and we so dim,
We are made in His image to witness Him."

But St. Paul also teaches that the relation between the Son and the Father is unique. He means that Christ reveals the Father completely in virtue of this eternal relation between them. We are made to become like God, but the Son is not made; He does not belong to the class of created things (1 Cor. viii. 6). And St. Paul never speaks of Christ *becoming* the Son of God. He regards Christ as having always been the Son, exercising divine functions, and therefore as "God blessed for ever" (Rom. ix. 5). In 2 Cor. iii. 17, 18 he asserts that the Lord is the divine Spirit who animates the new dispensation. The old Jewish dispensation is described as "letter," because it was a system of outward commandments; the Gospel dispensation is described as "spirit," because it is a system of spiritual principles which are summed up in Christ. We by reflecting His glory are transformed into the same image by successive stages of glory. This glory comes from the Lord Jesus, who is the Spirit of Christianity (2 Cor. iii. 18). It is important to notice that St. Paul does not confuse the Second Person of the Trinity with the Third Person, and that for many years the Christians used occasionally to describe the divine nature of the Son by the word "Spirit." They gradually gave up this manner of speaking, as it was ambiguous.

In 2 Cor. v. 18-21 there is an important statement on the Atonement. The close connection between the Atonement and the Incarnation is shown in the assertion that "God was in Christ, reconciling the world unto Himself," and the love of both the Father and the Son is shown in the words that "He made Him to be sin on our behalf." The first statement saves us from the idea that God selected a holy man to reveal His will, and then gave up this best of men to unimaginable suffering. No! it was God Himself who came in the Person of the Sufferer. The second statement implies that Christ, though sinless, was treated as a sinner. He thus by dying accomplished the end which our punishment would accomplish, namely, the expression of God's hatred of sin and love of righteousness.

The Epistle opens with an introduction and thanksgiving, in which there seems to be a note of sadness, marking the effect which the crisis in Corinth has left on the mind of St. Paul. He proceeds to give a personal explanation. The visit to the Corinthians on the way to Macedonia was abandoned only because of the pain which it would have given them; the sharp letter was not written in wrath, but in sorrowful love (i. 23-ii. 1-4). St. Paul goes on to ask pardon for the man who caused the recent disturbance (ii. 5-11).

Then, whilst he is describing his journey to Macedonia (ii. 12-17), he breaks off suddenly into a digression, in which he describes the dignity of the apostolic ministry, its superiority over the Mosaic ministry, the nature of its commission, and the seal of it in a life which is always martyrdom (iii. 1-vi. 13). St. Paul concludes this section with a short appeal to the Corinthians to avoid contamination from heathenism (vi. 14-vii. 1).

He then returns to the situation of ii. 13. He tells us with how much joy he received the news that Titus brought him—joy for the Corinthians, for Titus, and for himself. The next two chapters (viii., ix.) contain instructions and exhortations respecting the fund mentioned in 1 Cor. xvi. 1. The last four chapters follow quite naturally. The apostle speaks with plain severity to rebuke those who created the recent disturbance, and to warn any there may be whose submission perhaps has not been quite entire. The prevailing tone is that of pathetic and sorrowful expostulation. St. Paul repeats the unkind things that have been said of him—how unimposing his presence, that he depends on alms, that he is only eloquent with his pen. But he defends his apostleship with absolute though very humble confidence, counting up the things that he can say for himself—his share in Jewish privileges, his sufferings for Christ, the revelations that God has sent him, the signs of his success, the continual weakness that Christ gives and blesses. Truly, the apostle is even greater than his grief.

The Epistle concludes with a benediction, in which St. Paul co-ordinates the Three Persons of the Holy Trinity. From primitive times these words have been used as the introduction to the most solemn part of the Greek liturgy, from which they were taken into the services of the Church of England.

ANALYSIS

(1) St. Paul's thankfulness and exhortation: i. 1-ii. 17.—Salutation, thanksgiving, the promised visit postponed, the previous letter, the penitent offender. St. Paul's journey to Macedonia, triumph in Christ.

(2) The Apostle's ministry: iii. 1-vii. 1.—His converts are his letters of commendation, the superiority of this ministry of the gospel above that of the Mosaic dispensation (iii.).

Christ the subject of his preaching, present light affliction resulting in eternal glory (iv.).

Inspiring hopes of the resurrection, constraining love of Christ, the ministry of reconciliation based on the atonement (v.).

He persuades and suffers (vi. 1-13).

Warning against being yoked with unbelievers (vi. 14-vii. 1).

(3) The Corinthian Church and Titus: vii. 2-ix. 15.—The visit of Titus to Corinth, the godly sorrow that followed (vii. 2-16).

The collection for the poor at Jerusalem, Macedonian generosity, praise of Titus (viii.).

Exhortation to a generosity like that of the Macedonians (ix.).

(4) A sorrowful expostulation: x.-xiii.—A warning to those who despise his authority (x.).

His rights and his sufferings for Christ (xi.).

Revelations given, but also a thorn in the flesh, the signs of an apostle, how he and Titus had dealt with the Corinthians (xii.).

He repeats that he will come to Corinth a third time, exhortation, benediction (xiii.).

CHAPTER XII THE EPISTLE OF PAUL THE APOSTLE TO THE GALATIANS

[Sidenote: The Author.]

This Epistle, being one of the four Epistles which are almost universally unquestioned, requires little or no defence. The Pauline authorship "has never been called in question by a critic of first-rate importance, and until recently has never been called in question at all." The writings of those Fathers of the Church who lived nearest to the apostolic age contain several possible allusions to it, and it is expressly named by Irenaeus, Clement of Alexandria, and Tertullian. The internal evidence shows that it must belong to the time of the apostles, for the errors which are criticized in it are different from the Ebionite ideas which existed at the beginning of the 2nd century, and from the Gnosticism which existed even before the apostles were all dead. They are evidently earlier than these heresies. Still more convincing is the vehement and pathetic energy which marks this Epistle. There is a ring of reality in its broken sentences and earnest appeals. It displays none of the careful patchwork which we should expect from a forger; it consists only of the quick hot words of a man who is very deeply moved.

[Sidenote: To whom written.]

"Unto the Churches of Galatia." What is the meaning of the name "Galatia"? Students are still divided on the question. If the word "Galatia" is used in a popular sense to describe the country inhabited by the Galatai, then it means North Galatia, a district in the extreme north of Asia Minor. It was mainly inhabited by Celts, who came thither from Europe in the 3rd century B.C., and spoke a Celtic language as late as the 2nd and even 4th century after Christ. This language is mentioned by Pausanias, and St. Jerome says that it was a dialect only slightly varying from that used in Gaul by the Treveri. But if the word "Galatia" is used in a political sense, signifying a particular province of the Roman empire, then it means a large area much further south, including Pisidia, Lycaonia, and part of Phrygia. In this province were Pisidian Antioch, Derbe, Iconium, and Lystra, where St. Paul founded Churches in A.D. 47, on his first missionary journey. The latter explanation is almost certainly correct.

No good argument can be brought forward in favour of North Galatia which cannot be balanced by a better argument in favour of South Galatia. For instance, though St. Luke in Acts uses the popular and not the political names for districts, this cannot be urged in favour of St. Paul's adopting the same usage. On the contrary, he uses Asia, Macedonia, and Achaia in their political sense, and so we may suppose that he would do the same in the case of Galatia. Again, though there were in North Galatia Jews who would tempt the converts to Jewish observances, there were Jews in plenty in South Galatia also. And while many writers have said that the Celtic blood of these recalcitrant Christians is proved by the enthusiasm, fickleness, superstition, love of strife, and vanity which St. Paul rebukes, we may reasonably urge that these defects are not confined to the Celts. The Phrygians doted on a sombre and mysterious religion. In heathen times they loved the worship of Cybele, with its exciting ceremonial and cruel mutilations. And when they adopted Christianity, though their morality was generally austere, their credulity was intense. In the 2nd century many of them embraced the new revelations of Montanus, and in the 4th they largely affected the hard Puritanism of Novatian. In religious matters the Celts are very little inclined to fickleness, and their superstitions are more closely connected with dreaminess than with vehemence.

The following facts also deserve attention; (1) It would be strange if Acts gave us no account of Churches in which St. Paul took so much interest. If Galatia be North Galatia, there is no such account in Acts. If it be South Galatia there is, and the polite and natural manner of addressing the inhabitants of the cities of Antioch, Derbe, etc., would be "Galatians." Their bond of union was association in one Roman province. (2) It is improbable that St. Paul would take the very difficult journey necessary for visiting the Celtic Galatians. His usual plan was to travel on Roman high-roads to the big centres of population. North Galatia was both isolated and half-civilized. Also, he says that he visited the Galatians on account of an illness (iv. 13). It is incredible that he would have chosen the long unhealthy journey to North Galatia when he was ill. But it is extremely probable that he left the damp lowlands of Pamphylia for the bracing air of Pisidian Antioch. The malady was probably the malarial neuralgia and fever which are contracted in those lowlands. (3) The Epistle contains technical legal terms for adoption, covenant, and tutor, which seem to be used not in the Roman but in the Greek sense.[1] They would hardly be intelligible except in cities like those of South Galatia where the institutions were mainly Greek.

Assuming that the "Galatians" are those of South Galatia, we note that in Gal. iv. 13 St. Paul speaks of preaching to them "the first time." This first time must be the occasion mentioned in Acts xiii., xiv. The second time is that in Acts xvi. 1-6. The Christians were mainly converts from heathenism (iv. 8; v. 2; vi. 12), but some were no doubt Jews or proselytes. After the second visit of St. Paul, his converts were tampered with. Some Judaizers had put a perverse construction upon his action in promulgating the decrees of the Council of Jerusalem of A.D. 49, and in circumcising Timothy. They urged that St. Paul had thereby acknowledged his inferiority to the other apostles, and practically advocated a return to Jewish ceremonial. Instigated by other Judaizers from Jerusalem, the Galatians had changed their Christianity into a semi-Judaism, and this all the more readily because of their previous familiarity with the Jewish religion.

[Sidenote: Where and when written.]

The place and date are both uncertain. The words, "I marvel that ye are so *quickly* removing from Him that called you" (i. 6), suggest that it was written not long after the conversion of the Galatians. But we cannot place it, as some writers have done, before 1 and 2 Thessalonians. Its style is allied with that of 1 and 2 Corinthians and Romans. It must be earlier than Romans, as it is like a rough model of that Epistle. If written soon before Romans, it was probably composed at Corinth early in A.D. 56. It may, however, have been written as early as A.D. 52, before St. Paul's third missionary journey.

[Sidenote: Character and Contents.]

The Epistle is intended to recall the Galatians to St. Paul's true gospel. In order to do this, he vindicates his own apostolic authority to preach it, and expounds its great principle—justification by faith, and not by observance of the Jewish law.

After a salutation, without the congratulations which the apostle ordinarily offers, St. Paul expresses his astonishment at their perversion, and vehemently asserts that if any one dares to preach a gospel other than that which the Galatians first received, let him be anathema (i. 1-10). The history of St. Paul's reception of the gospel is then set out. It came to him by revelation of Jesus Christ: this is at once the demonstration of its unique authority, and the decisive fact which settles the relation of St. Paul to the other apostles. He did not receive from them the gospel he preached, and, to emphasize this, St. Paul counts up the various opportunities he had of intercourse with them, and says what use he made of each (i. 11-ii. 10). The best illustration of the independence of his position is the attitude which he adopted towards St. Peter, the prince of the apostles, when at Antioch he deceitfully took the same sort of line with respect to Jewish ceremonial that the Galatians are taking now (ii. 11-13).[2] St. Paul describes the speech he made in opposition to St. Peter, but while he is dictating it, he is carried away by an orator's enthusiasm: he forgets that he is telling the story only of an old debate, and at some points we cannot confidently distinguish the rebuke to St. Peter from the exhortation to the Galatians (ii. 14-21).

Then, still as if he were making a speech, the apostle proceeds to argue as he does later in the Epistle to the Romans. He recalls to the "bewitched" Galatians the happy memories of the days when they first heard of Christ—the out-pouring of the Spirit, the first sharp persecution endured so well. Did not all this happen when they were under the gospel of Faith (iii. 2-5)? The true sons of Abraham are those who accept the gospel (iii. 6-9). On the other hand, the people who still desire to be under the Law can only avoid being under a curse by keeping the whole Law—and this is impossible (iii. 10). God's will is plain: He has said, "The righteous shall live by faith" (iii. 11, 12). Moreover, whatever claim the Law had on us is now discharged by the satisfaction made by Christ (iii. 13, 14). Now St. Paul goes on to show that the promise made by God to Abraham binds Him still. Just as no subsequent transaction can nullify a Greek "covenant," *i.e.* will, so the Law cannot nullify the earlier promise of God (iii. 15-18).[3] Then he compares the promise made to Abraham with the Law. The latter was a contract, a mutual agreement between two parties involving mutual obligations; if the Jews did not keep the Law, God was not bound to bless them. But in the case of the promise, there is no suggestion of contract. Then, lest his readers should suppose that there was an inconsistency in the fact that God was the Author of both the Law and the promise, St. Paul adds an explanation (iii. 19-22). The Law would have been contrary to the promise if it had been intended to produce the same result as the promise by another method. But, on the contrary, the Law was added as a parenthesis in order to make known transgressions, and with the result that it increased them (iii. 19). Scripture shut up all mankind in the fold of sin, that they might look forward to the reign of faith as the only means of escape. To emphasize further the contrast between the Law and the promise, St. Paul asserts that the Law did not come direct from God to man. It came, as Jewish traditions said, from God and the angels to Moses, the mediator, and from him to the Hebrews. The Law had a mediator, therefore it involved two parties—God and the Hebrew people. But there was no such mediator in the case of the promise. God spoke directly to Abraham. And God in the Person of Christ spoke directly to mankind. Thus the promises are greater and more gracious than the Law. It is important to observe that the argument implies the Divinity of Christ.

Before Faith came, the Law played the part of a Greek "tutor," *i.e.* a trusted servant who attended a child. He took the child to the house where he was taught, and kept him from harm and mischief. And we, if we wish to be still under the Law, shall be as foolish as a grown-up son who wishes to be under a steward and a guardian. We must leave the mere rudiments of religion now that we have reached a stage at which we have been taught that God is indeed our Father (iii. 23-iv. 11).

St. Paul supports this conclusion from his arguments by a touching appeal, in which he gratefully recalls the kindness he received from the Galatians when he came to them in all the weakness and distress of fever (iv. 12-20). Then he interprets for them the story of Hagar, probably in answer to a reference in a letter which they had sent him (iv. 21-v. 1). The Jew is in bondage like Hagar's child, the Christian is free like Sarah's child.

After this we have another appeal, a medley of exhortation, warning, denunciation, and pathetic entreaty: the apostle, himself so appreciative of great ideas, tries to make the unaspiring Galatians understand that they are called to the perfect freedom which is the service of God (v. 2-26). The Epistle closes with some plain words which the apostle wrote with his own hand in large characters so as to emphasize them for his readers. The motive of the Judaizers is boldly labelled. Then, as if there had been a question of his own humility, he associates himself with the crucified Christ, for whose sake he bears in his flesh the eloquent marks of the Roman rods and the stones of the Jews. It was the cruel custom in Asia Minor, a custom not yet extinct, for masters to wound their slaves with marks which made it impossible for them to escape recognition. And so St. Paul glories in the pitiful scars on his body, because they prove Whose he is and Whom he serves.

ANALYSIS

Salutation, rebuke (i. 1-10).

(1) St. Paul defends his apostleship: i. 11-ii. 21.—He was called by God in spite of his fanatical Judaism, God's Son was revealed in him, he conferred with no man, but retired to Arabia, then three years after his conversion he stayed fifteen days with Cephas, and afterwards preached in Syria and Cilicia (i.).

Fourteen years after his conversion[4] he again went to Jerusalem "by revelation." False brethren attempted to get Titus circumcised, but in vain. James, Cephas, and John were most friendly to Paul and Barnabas, agreeing that they should go to the Gentiles while remembering the poor in Jerusalem. Cephas rebuked at Antioch by St. Paul (ii.).

(2) St. Paul defends justification by faith: iii. 1-v. 1.—Galatian fickleness, even Abraham was justified by faith, and in the Old Testament the righteous live by faith, the Jewish Law merely a parenthesis between God's promise and its fulfilment, the Law a tutor to bring us to Christ (iii.).

Judaism is the state of a son who is a minor, Christianity is the state of a son who has attained his majority. Why return to the beggarly rudiments of knowledge? The Jew is like the child of Hagar, the Christian is like the child of Sarah (iv.-v. 1).

(3) Practical exhortation: v. 2-vi. 18.—Circumcision useless, freedom and love are the allies of the true Law, the works of the flesh and the fruits of the Spirit (v.). Bearing one another's burdens, supporting our teachers. A conclusion in St. Paul's handwriting (vi.).

[1] The law implied in Gal. iv. 2 is in accordance with Syrian law. If a father died, he left his son under the authority of a steward until he was fourteen, and left his property in the hands of a guardian until he was twenty-five. It is probable that in South Galatia as in Syria this law was made under the reign of the Seleucids.

[2] For the explanation of this quarrel, see p. 121.

[3] The argument about "seeds" and "seed," in iii. 16, looks like a mere verbal quibble in English. But it becomes quite intelligible when we remember that in rabbinical Hebrew the word "seed_s_" was used in the sense of descendant_s_.

[4] See Gal. ii. 1, "at an interval of fourteen years." This third visit to Jerusalem (the second mentioned here) was in A.D. 49. The verse probably means fourteen years after his *conversion*, and eleven years after his first visit. If we reckon the fourteen years from his *first visit* to Jerusalem, the first visit would be in A.D. 33. This will not agree with Acts ix. 25, 26; 2 Cor. xi. 32, which show us that the first visit was made while Aretas ruled at Damascus. Aretas became master of Damascus in A.D. 37.

CHAPTER XIII THE EPISTLE OF PAUL THE APOSTLE TO THE ROMANS

[Sidenote: The Author.]

The genuineness of this Epistle, like that of Galatians and 1 and 2 Corinthians, is practically undisputed. No one ever seems to have questioned it between the time that Marcion drew up his *Apostolicon*, about A.D. 140, and A.D. 1792. Before the time of Marcion it is quoted by St. Clement of Rome, St. Ignatius, and St. Polycarp. And there seem to be some reminiscences of it in 1 Peter. It is first definitely mentioned by name in the writings of St. Irenaeus, who quotes it several times. This early and frequent use postulates for the Epistle a very authoritative source. There is no one that we know of among the first Christians who could have written it except St. Paul. What he tells the Romans about his personal wishes and intentions is exactly consonant with what he says elsewhere. The notices that he gives them of his movements perfectly accord with the notices in Acts. The primary conceptions of the Epistle are more or less common to all St. Paul's works. They are concerned with the guilt and the power of sin, the eternal purpose which God has for man, the meaning of Christ's death and the effect of His resurrection, the nature of our acquittal by God and our new spiritual life.

The only serious question with regard to the criticism of the outward letter of the Epistle, is connected with the last two chapters (xv., xvi.). Baur rejected both as spurious compilations, intended to reconcile "Paulinism" with the more Jewish school of early Christian thought. But Baur's habit of pronouncing spurious every book or part of a book which did not agree with his peculiar estimate of St. Paul, is now discredited. In spite of this, many critics think that xv. and xvi. do not belong to this Epistle. They are generally admitted to be by St. Paul, but it is thought that they are simply pages which have become detached from some other writings of the apostle. Chapter xvi. in particular is supposed to be a fragment of an Epistle to Ephesus. It abounds in personal greetings to intimate friends; and yet it is difficult to believe that St. Paul had many friends in Rome before he visited it. And among these friends are Prisca and Aquila (xvi. 3), who certainly stayed at Ephesus, where St. Paul had laboured for two years and must have had many friends. The tone of xvi. 17-20 is thought to imply sectarian divisions which the rest of the Epistle ignores. And the final doxology appears in different places in different MSS., a fact which suggests that the early Church doubted where the Epistle ended. No real importance need be attached to another argument used by some critics, viz. that Marcion omitted xv. and xvi. He would have rejected them, whether genuine or not, on account of the sanction given to the Old Testament in xv. 4.

On the other hand, the integrity of the Epistle is maintained by some of the best recent critics, including Sanday, Zahn, and Godet. The best MSS. place the final doxology in its present position. The fact that the majority of cursive MSS. and some valuable versions, such as the later Syriac and the Armenian, place it at the end of xiv. seems to be accounted for by the fact that the last two chapters were often omitted in the lessons read in church, being considered unimportant for the purposes of general edification. The fact that the Epistle seems to come to an end at xv. 33, and also at xvi. 20, before the final doxology in xvi. 27, suggests the best solution. It is that the apostle, after concluding the argument of the Epistle, made various additions of a personal nature with reference to himself and his friends as they occurred to his mind. He then summed up the whole argument in xvi. 25-27, where the obedience of *faith* is stated to be the purpose of God's final revelation. The number of friends mentioned in xvi. is not incredibly large when we remember the easy and frequent intercourse which existed between Rome and the east.

[Sidenote: To whom written.]

"To all that are in Rome, beloved by God, called to be saints." It has been well said that the universality of the gospel made St. Paul desire to preach it in the universal city. He longed to "see Rome;" he was conscious that Christ had called him to "bear witness at Rome." He himself had the freedom of the city of Rome, and he was inspired with the hope, which was fulfilled three hundred years afterwards, that the religion of Christ would be the religion of the Roman empire. The territory then ruled by Rome more nearly embraced the whole of the civilized world than any empire that has since been seen. It included London and Toledo, Constantinople and Jerusalem. Roman soldiers kept their watch on the blue Danube, and were planting outposts on the far-off grey Euphrates. The city of Rome itself contained about a million and a half of inhabitants. It was well governed and sumptuously adorned. A real belief in the homely vulgar gods of their forefathers had declined among educated people, and the humane principles of Stoic philosophy were instilling a new regard for the less fortunate classes of mankind. Strange foreign devotions were satisfying some of the yearnings which found no nourishment in the hard old Roman paganism. Men who took no interest in Jupiter were attracted by Mithras, the Eastern god of the light. Women who could obtain no entrance into the exclusive sisterhood of the Vestal Virgins, could find occupation in the worship of the Egyptian Isis. Some vague belief in a Divine One was rising in minds who thought that Jupiter Mithras and Isis were only symbols of a power behind the mists of human wisdom. Jews of all classes were numerous, though the majority were as poor as those of East London. They made some converts, and Poppaea, the mistress of Nero in A.D. 58, dallied with Judaism as with a new sensation. Men and women of every race were included among the slaves of Rome, and the arts and elegance of Greek and Syrian slaves often proved a staircase by which new religions found a way into the chambers of the great and wealthy. In spite of some signs of moral vigour, society was cankered with pride of class and with self-indulgence. It possessed no regenerating force capable of checking the repulsive vice which was encouraged by the obscenity of actors and the frivolity of sceptics.

We are told that "sojourners from Rome," both Jews and proselytes, were in the crowd which listened to St. Peter's address on the Day of Pentecost (Acts ii. 10). It is possible that these men brought news of the gospel to the large body in Rome of Jews, and of Gentiles influenced by Jewish ideas. In any case, communication between the chief cities of the empire was at this time so frequent that we may be sure that the principles and attractions of Christianity were soon heard of at Rome. Gradually a small band formed there of people who were interested and pleased by what they had learnt of Christ; it is probable that St. Paul sent Aquila and Prisca from Ephesus to give them definite instruction. It does not seem that they had been visited by an apostle (xv. 20). The Epistle is addressed to a community consisting of Jews and Gentiles, but the Gentiles are by far the more numerous.

The apostle's claim in ch. i. to address this Church as within the jurisdiction of "the apostle of the Gentiles," his direct appeal to the Gentiles in xi. 13, and the statement of his priestly office exercised over the Gentiles in xv. 16, show that the Church of Rome was Gentile in character. The proper names in the Epistle afford us little indication of the proportion of Jews and Gentiles. The majority of the names are Greek, and four names are Latin; but the Jews of that time, like the Jews of the present day, often passed under Gentile names. We know how the English Jews now disguise Moses as "Moss" Judah as "Leo," and Levi as "Lewis."

The majority of the converts were probably in a humble social position. When St. Paul wrote to the Philippians, there were Christians in the imperial household itself, and it is possible that the Narcissus mentioned in Romans may be the freedman of the Emperor Claudius, put to death in A.D. 54. Ordinary slaves and freedmen seem to have been the principal element among those who were first "called to be saints" at Rome, but before long there were people of good birth and cultured intelligence who turned gladly from the lifeless old Roman religion and the fantastic new-fashioned Eastern cults to this original faith in the incarnate God.

[Sidenote: Where and when written.]

St. Paul wrote this letter towards the end of his stay at Corinth, at the close of A.D. 55 or the beginning of A.D. 56 (see xvi. 1; xv. 23-26, and Acts xix. 21).

[Sidenote: Character and Contents.]

St. Paul writes as the apostle of the Gentiles to the Christians of the greatest of all Gentile cities. He does so with a solemn sense of special responsibility. Profoundly impressed with the grandeur of the Roman name, the position of this promiscuous little body of converts is to him enormously significant. They are the representatives of the faith of Jesus in the capital of the world; they are the first members of a Church to which God seems to give the most magnificent of all opportunities. And the thought is scarcely absent from his mind that this may be the last Epistle he will ever send. He is going to Jerusalem, and has a sad foreboding of what may await him there (xv. 31).

The manner and style which give the Epistle a unique place among the works of St. Paul are caused by these considerations. He wishes to tell the Roman Christians his very best ideas in the very best way: this may be his last chance of doing so. He puts aside, then, all clamour of personal debate, and sets himself to produce an ordered theological treatise. Never elsewhere does the apostle write with so careful method, so powerful concentration, so effective marshalling of arguments, so stirring yet measured eloquence.

The Epistle opens with a brief introduction. Paul, the apostle of Christ, wishes to preach the gospel to those in Rome whom Christ has called. Then he begins at once to describe the set of circumstances which the gospel is intended to meet. The Gentiles have not been true to such knowledge as they had of God, and by an inevitable process they have passed on to unnatural and vicious excess (i. 18-32). And when St. Paul turns to the Jews, he finds they are in no better case. With fuller knowledge they have sinned scarcely less. Strict justice will be meted out by God to all, the Jew coming first and then the Gentile. The Gentile will not escape, for the Gentiles, whom we conceive of as having no law, have a law in that moral sense which makes them instinctively put in practice the precepts of the Law, and their inward thoughts accuse or defend them (ii. 1-16). The Jew may boast of his

Law and his knowledge of revelation, but he is no better in practice than a Gentile. And as for his circumcision, it is worthless unless he is also spiritually circumcised in the heart (ii. 17-29).

After a parenthetical discussion of difficulties suggested by a possible Jewish opponent (iii. 1-8), St. Paul shows that the Jews are not in a worse case than the Gentiles. Both are under the dominion of sin, and Scripture says so. The whole system of Law is a failure. Law does nothing but give a clear knowledge of sin (iii. 9-20).

St. Paul then brings forward his great remedy—the answer of God to the need which is represented by universal human sinfulness. Man has failed to correspond to the suggestions of conscience, he has failed to fulfil the requirements of the written Law, but now he may come into a right relation with God by identifying himself with Jesus Christ. He may be justified (*i.e.* accepted as righteous) by an act of God's grace (*i.e.* by an undeserved act of God's love) on account of the redemption wrought by Christ, whom God has set forth as a propitiation to show His own righteousness. God could no longer allow man to mistake His patience with our sins for slack indifference. Man must no longer seek to be justified before God on the strength of what he himself has done, but on the strength of his faith in Christ, *i.e.* his devoted personal adhesion to Christ (iii. 21-26). St. Paul tells the Romans that this justifying faith excludes glorying, can be realized by Gentile as well as Jew; that by it we establish the Law (iii. 27-31), as the Jewish dispensation, rightly understood, testifies to its necessity. In fact, Abraham himself was justified by faith (iv.) Then St. Paul sets forth in glowing and stately words what are the consequences for us which follow from being so justified. We are at peace with God, and share in His love, and this is the secure ground of Christian hope for life and after death (v. 1-11). The effects of Christ's death are computed by an *argumentum a fortiori* from the results of Adam's fall (v. 12-21).

The apostle now carefully refutes the notion that the doctrine of justification by faith encourages Antinomianism. Liberty does not mean licence. St. Paul was quite alive to the fact that skilful opponents and brainless admirers would misrepresent his doctrine, which was also Christ's. He therefore takes great pains to show that the connection between the righteousness of Christ and the righteousness of a Christian is not arbitrary or fictitious. His argument throughout implies that man actually receives "the righteousness of God," that is, the righteousness which is inherent in God, and is bestowed by God upon man when he unites himself with Christ (vi.-viii.).

Shall I go on sinning that God's mercy may be all the greater in forgiving me? God forbid: for when I went down into the waters of baptism, I shared in the death of Christ; and when I rose from them, I rose as a sharer in His risen life. Because I am united thus to the life of Christ, sin is foreign to my nature (vi. 1-14). I am no longer under law, but under grace: but to be the slave of sin and be occupied with uncleanness, and to gain the wages of death, is inconsistent with being the slave of righteousness, occupied in a course of purification and rewarded with the gift of life (vi. 15-23).

Next, St. Paul asks why it is that we are no longer under the Law? Because we have no connection with that state of sin to which the Law was applicable. Our soul is like a wife whose lawful husband is dead. Or, to put the truth into another form, our old state was killed by our identification with Christ crucified, and we are espoused to Christ risen (vii. 1-6). What, then, shall we think of the Law? Is it sin? No. It reveals the sinfulness of sin, and it irritates dormant sin into activity. A thing cannot be identical with another thing which it exposes and irritates. But why did God permit the Law, which is holy, to prove fatal to my soul (vii. 13)? He did not. The Law was not fatal, though sin was all but fatal. Sin was permitted to do its worst that its real hideousness might be apparent. This is what took place. The Law gave me an ideal, but my better self, which corresponds to the Law, could not keep me from ding wrong or make me do right. I became involved in a terrible conflict. This was the opportunity of Christ. He has delivered me from that state of the body which involved me in sin and death. Without Him, I should still be serving the Law of God with my conscience, and the law of sin with my body (vii. 25).

Where the Law of Moses failed, Christ splendidly succeeds. He not only sets before men an ideal, but also helps them to attain it, and fulfil the righteous claims of the moral Law, by uniting Himself with them by the Spirit (viii. 1-10). Men are now in a new relation to God: they call Him Father, He sees in them His sons. Though with all creation we wait still in fruitful pain for the fulness of redemption, we wait with confident hope. The Spirit is with us to help and to pray, we remember God's high purpose for us, we have known His love in the past, Jesus in infinite exaltation is interceding for us; who, then, shall ever be able to separate us from the love of God (viii. 11-39)?

St. Paul turns now to a parenthetical discussion which necessarily suggests itself here. It has practically happened that God's own people, the children of Abraham, in spite of their privileges, are excluded from this new salvation which comes from acceptance of Christ. This does not mean that God has been unfaithful. St. Paul vindicates His action toward them, and he shows that it has been consistent with His previous action towards the Israelites (ix. 6-13), righteous (ix. 14-21), and merciful (ix. 22-29). God has always shown that He is free to select whom he likes to carry out His purpose in the world.[1] The Jews are rejected because they seek to be justified, on the strength of their own works (ix. 30-33; x. 1-3): now, the method of the Law has been superseded by Christ's, which is an easier method (x. 4-10) and universal (x. 11-13). And the Jews have had every opportunity for hearing of it (x. 14-21). But God has not rejected them entirely or finally (xi. 1-10); and if their fall has led to the preaching of the gospel to the Gentiles, how much more happily fruitful will be their reception into the Church (xi. 11-15)! We may hope for this ultimate acceptance of the gospel by both Jew and Gentile because of the original holiness of the Jewish stock. The Gentiles are grafted into that: just as we may be cut off from it if we sin, so the Jews more easily may be grafted in again if they will (xi. 16-24). St. Paul now shows how the hardening of the Jews and the disobedience of the Gentiles alike have served the purposes of God. Israel as a nation shall be saved by the Messiah. The chapter closes with words of reverent admiration for the wonderful workings of the Divine Providence (xi. 25-36).

After this long doctrinal argument, St. Paul insists upon certain practical duties (xii.-xv. 13). We may notice in xiii. 2 ff. the emphasis which is laid upon the dignity of the civil government, a dignity which was immeasurably degraded ten years later by the wanton persecution of the Roman Christians. And xiii. 13 is a verse ever to be remembered by the Church as the verse by which God brought Augustine from free thinking and licentious living to be numbered among the saints. In xiv. begins some considerate advice about certain Christians "weak in faith." They seem to have formed a party, but not a party which can be identified with any other religious clique mentioned by the apostle. Their vegetarianism and their observance of particular holy days have suggested the theory that they were Christians who followed the ascetic practices of the Jewish sect of Essenes. The theory that they were Gentiles who affected the customs of the Pythagoreans has commended itself to other writers. On the whole, the number of Jews in Rome supports the theory that these were Jewish Christians. St. Paul deals very tenderly with these total abstainers from meat and wine. He evidently does not put them on the same level as the sectaries of Galatia or Colossae.

The Epistle closes with various references to personal matters, including the expression of a desire to visit Spain and Rome (xv. 34).

ANALYSIS

Salutation and introduction (i. 1-15).

(1) DOCTRINAL.—The subject of the Epistle. How is righteousness to be attained? Not by man's work, but by God's gift, through faith, *i.e.* personal attachment to Christ (i. 16, 17).

A. Righteousness as a state of man in the sight of God (Justification): i. 18-v. 21.

a. Righteousness was never attained before Christ came. The Gentiles neglected their conscience until they sank into abominable sins; future judgment will certainly come on all men without respect of persons; the Jews, too, have no right to criticize the Gentiles—they had the Law of Moses, while the Gentiles only had the unwritten law of conscience, yet they failed. The Jewish quibble that there was no good in being a Jew if God condemned him, is refuted. The witness of the Old Testament to the universality of sin is quoted (i. 18-iii. 20).

b. Exposition of the new method of attaining righteousness. It is independent of the Law, is universal, is obtainable through Christ's death which manifests God's righteousness. This method excludes human boasting, and can be experienced by Jew and Gentile alike (iii. 21-31).

c. The relation of this new method to the Old Testament. Abraham, the typical saint of the Old Testament, was not justified because of works, or circumcision, or law. His faith shows that the Old Testament supports the Christian method of salvation (iv.).

d. The blessed state of the justified Christian. He is filled with hope, and this hope is guaranteed by the proved love of God. What a contrast between this blessedness and the effects of Adam's fall! The work of Christ resembles that of Adam, because it passes from one man to all men: it differs greatly, because Adam's fall brought sin, our condemnation, our death. Christ's gift brings grace, our acquittal, our life. The Fall brought sin, Law increased sin; Grace is greater than sin (v.).

B. Righteousness as necessarily involving moral progress (Sanctification); vi.-viii.

a. Refutation of the theory that we may continue to sin in order to give God fresh opportunities of displaying His lovingkindness. Our baptism implies union with the sinless Christ. Refutation of the theory that we may as well sin as not sin because we are no longer under the Law. Our marriage to Christ must be fruitful (vi. 1-vii. 6). The Law is not to be disparaged, though it is impotent to rescue me in the terrible moral conflict under which I should suffer, if it were not for Christ (vii. 6-25).

B. Where the Law of Moses failed, the incarnation of Christ succeeds. The life of Christian righteousness is ruled by the Holy Spirit. It implies filial confidence in God, a glorious inheritance, divine assistance, inviolable security (viii.).

C. The problem raised by the fate of the Jews: ix.-xi.

a. Their rejection from their privileged position a sad contrast to their high destiny; the entire justice of God in forming a new Israel of Jews and Gentiles alike (ix.).

b. The cause of their rejection was that they sought to be justified in their own way and not in God's way, and this in spite of Christian opportunities and prophetic warnings (x.).

c. Consolations which qualify the severity of their fate. Their unbelief is only partial and temporary, and God's purpose is to restore all. Doxology (xi.).

(2) PRACTICAL.—The Christian sacrifice, and the duties of a Christian (xii.). Church and State, the law of love, the approaching judgment (xiii.).

Toleration for weak and eccentric Christians; vegetarians, observers of private holy days and total abstainers, not to be disturbed; we must do nothing that makes a brother stumble. Christ pleased not Himself; He was both a minister of the circumcision and the hope of the Gentiles (xiv. 1-xv. 13).

Personal conclusion (xv. 14-xvi. 27).

[1] The Calvinistic doctrine of predestination, as taught in the writings of Calvin and in the Presbyterian Westminster Confession, is a complete perversion of St. Paul's teaching. Calvin teaches a predestination to heaven or hell; St. Paul here speaks of an appointment to certain duties on earth. The Calvinists asserted that some men "cannot be saved;" St. Paul teaches that God so acted "in order that He might have mercy upon all" (xi. 32).

CHAPTER XIV THE EPISTLE OF PAUL THE APOSTLE TO THE COLOSSIANS—THE EPISTLE OF PAUL TO PHILEMON

THE EPISTLE OF PAUL THE APOSTLE TO THE COLOSSIANS

[Sidenote: The Author.]

There is no good reason for doubting that this beautiful Epistle is the work of St. Paul. It is full of Pauline thought, and is well attested by external evidence. It is apparently quoted in the very ancient work known as the Epistle of Barnabas, and Justin Martyr quotes the title of Christ "the firstborn of all creation" (Col. i. 15). It is included in Marcion's canon and in the *Muratorian Fragment*, as well as in the Old Latin and Peshitta Syriac versions. The notion that it is only a weak reflection of Ephesians seems incredible, for neither of the two Epistles is appreciably inferior to the other, and in each one there are several unique passages which represent as high a level of intellectual and spiritual attainment as the passages which are in some degree common to the two. Moreover, we cannot trace any definite method according to which the one writing has been used for the other, and destructive critics have only destroyed one another's arguments in their attempts to show which of the two Epistles is genuine, or why they both are forged. It is also important to consider the association of this Epistle with that to Philemon: the transparent genuineness of the latter makes it practically certain that Colossians is genuine as well.

Objections to the authenticity of Colossians have been steadily growing fainter. It was denied by Mayerhoff in 1838, and by the whole Tübingen school, in spite of very strong external evidence. (1) The heresy opposed by St. Paul was said to be a form of 2nd-century Gnosticism; but the affinities which it shows with Judaism point rather to the 1st century. (2) There are a large number of words which St. Paul uses nowhere else, thirty-four being found in no other part of the New Testament; but several of these words are called forth by the special error which St. Paul rebukes, and the Epistle does contain eleven Pauline words used by no other New Testament writer. (3) The doctrine has been declared to be not Pauline, but a further development of St. Paul's doctrine of the dignity of Christ. This objection rests entirely on the hypothesis that Jesus Christ was not God, but was gradually deified by successive generations of His followers. The critics who declared that no apostle believed Christ to be more than an ideal or half-divine man, and said that St. John's writings are forgeries of the 2nd century, described the doctrine of Colossians as a transition from the true Pauline doctrine to the doctrine of the Logos contained in the fourth Gospel. But St. Paul states nothing about Christ in this Epistle which is not implied in earlier Epistles. He only makes fresh statements of truth in view of fresh errors.

[Sidenote: To whom written.]

Colossae was the least important town to which any Epistle of St. Paul which now remains was addressed. The place was on the river Lycus in Phrygia, about ten miles from Laodicea and thirteen from Hierapolis, and thus the three towns were the sphere of the missionary work of the Colossian Epaphras (Col. iv. 12, 13). Colossae had been flourishing enough in the time of Herodotus, but now, overshadowed by greater neighbours—Laodicea, Hierapolis, and Chonae—and perhaps shaken by recurring earthquakes, it was sinking fast into decay. Still it derived importance from its situation on the great main road which connected Rome with the eastern provinces, the road by which Xerxes had led his great armament against Greece. And as the people had a special way of their own for producing a rich dye named *Colossinus*, it retained a fair amount of trade. We may account for the presence of Jews at Colossae which is suggested in the Epistle, by remembering its convenient position and its trade speciality. The people were mainly the descendants of Greek settlers and Phrygian natives, and the intellectual atmosphere was the same as that of which we have evidence in other parts of Asia Minor: every one was infected with the Greek keenness for subtle speculation, and the usual Phrygian tendency to superstition and fanaticism. Thirteen miles away, at Hierapolis, was growing into manhood the slave Epictetus, who later on will set out some of the most noble and lofty of pagan thoughts. The persistent love of the people of this neighbourhood for the angel-worship which St. Paul rebukes, is illustrated by the facts that in the 4th century a Church Council at Laodicea condemned the worship of angels, and that, in spite of this, in the 9th and 10th centuries the district was the centre of the worship of St. Michael, who was believed to have opened the chasm of the Lycus, and so saved the people of Chonae from an inundation.

Colossae, being exposed to the raids of the Moslem Saracens, disappeared from history in the 8th century.

The Church at Colossae was not founded by St. Paul, and he was not personally acquainted with it (Col. ii. 1). But we can hardly go so far as to say that he had never seen the town at all.

[Sidenote: Where and when written.]

St. Paul sent this letter, together with that to Philemon and the circular which we call "Ephesians," by Tychicus from Rome, probably in A.D. 60. He alludes to his imprisonment twice incidentally, and again with pathetic simplicity in the postscript added by his own hand, "Remember my bonds."

[Sidenote: Character and Contents.]

Some difficulties are connected with the heresy taught by the religious agitators at Colossae. It is plain that their teaching affected both doctrine and practice. They appealed to visions and a knowledge of the celestial world (ii. 18), and therefore set up a worship of angels which tended to thrust Christ from His true position in the creed of the Church. They treated the body with unsparing severity (ii. 23), they abstained from meat and drink, and paid a punctilious attention to festivals, new moons, and sabbaths (ii. 16). St. Paul calls these practices "material rudiments" (ii. 8), elementary methods now superseded by faith in Christ. Moreover, it is almost certain that literal circumcision was practised (ii. 11). These things point to Judaism. And yet St. Paul does not seem to be rebuking a return to the Judaism of the Old Testament. He could hardly have described a compliance with Old Testament injunctions as an "arbitrary religion" and "doctrines of men" (ii. 1, 22, 23). It might be Pharisaism, but if we look

71

in the direction of Judaism, it is most natural that we should think of a Judaism resembling that of the Essenes. The Essenes were vegetarians, they avoided wine, they kept the sabbath with special scrupulousness, and had some secret teaching about the angels. These resemblances have tempted some commentators to identify the false teachers with the Essenes. But there is nothing to prove that the Essenes worshipped the angels, and St. Paul makes no mention of the Essene veneration for the sun, or their monastic life, or their elaborate process of initiation. Besides this, the principal community of Essenes dwelt by the Dead Sea, and it is very doubtful if any existed in Asia Minor.

It is best to confess our ignorance. All that we can say is that the scruple-mongers at Colossae taught doctrines which had points of contact with Essenism. They employed some affected interpretation of the Old Testament. They also were influenced by heathenism in their conception of half-divine beings intermediate between God and the world. How far they held any definitely dualistic view of matter we cannot tell. But their system was a mischievous theosophy, which they endeavoured to popularize under catchwords like "wisdom" and "philosophy." The fact that there was at this time such a widespread tendency to adopt an exaggerated asceticism and theories about mediatorial spirits, makes it unnecessary to suppose that the Colossian heresy need be affiliated to any particular school of speculation.

The Epistle consists mainly of a more or less indirect argument against the insidious "philosophy" of the heretics, with an exhortation and personal notes.

Perhaps we account most naturally for the broken order and lax coherence of this letter, by the suggestion that, as St. Paul dictated it, there was present with him a sense of almost nervous hesitation. He has exactly a gentleman's reluctance to do an ungracious action: while he knows that it is his duty to warn the Colossians of a serious danger, he knows that unless he does so with much tactful delicacy, they will resent his interference. So he begins by saying what polite things he can about them, and instead of going on at once to talk of the heresy, he first says with plain significance that he perpetually prays for their perfection in knowledge, activity, and constancy. An incidental allusion to God's method for human salvation gives St. Paul an opportunity for making a digression—one of the most important statements in the New Testament—concerning the nature and work of Christ (i. 14-20). He shows the Colossians what views they ought to hold concerning Him. This would keep them from giving to the angels what is due to Christ alone. Christ is the Redeemer. He was born prior to all creation, even the angels, and all creation coheres through union with Him (i. 15-17). He is the Head of the Church in virtue of His resurrection, and as embodying the full number of divine attributes (i. 18, 19). He is the Saviour of angels and men by His death, and in this salvation the Colossians ought to share (i. 20-23).

It seems that now he will deal with the heresy, but again he postpones it. He breaks in with a digression of a pastoral character. He speaks of his commission to preach (i. 24-29), his anxiety even for Churches that he has never visited (ii. 1-5), and he exhorts the Colossians to continue in their original faith (ii. 6, 7).

At last he enters upon the main business of the Epistle and begins dogmatic controversy. After a warning against spurious philosophy, he asserts that Christ is the sole incarnation of Deity, to whom all spirits are subject (ii. 9, 10). This is the true doctrine: God has not divided His attributes among a group of angels; all are to be found in Christ. And the true method of salvation is simply that union with Christ which begins with baptism, the Christian's circumcision. In it we receive that forgiveness which was won for us when Christ died, and both blotted out the Law and triumphed over evil angels (ii. 13-15). The apostle then directly condemns the practices of the false teachers—their anxious and mechanical conduct with regard to food and seasons, their intrusion into celestial secrets and their doctrine of angel-worship, their loose hold on Christ the Head, symptoms of an affected humility which is no real check against the indulgence of the flesh (ii. 16-23).

He then turns to practical exhortation. In the bracing words made familiar to us by the Epistle for Easter Day, St. Paul bids the Colossians leave the gently stimulating exercise of intellectual theorizing and listen to the stern demands made by Christ on life and character. They have risen to a life hid with Christ in God; they must make dead the faculties of sensual action, angry thinking, and evil speaking: this is implied in forsaking heathenism for the universal Christ (iii. 1-11). Live quietly in peace and love, show a gracious life in a gracious worship, consecrate your words and deeds by doing all in the name of the Lord Jesus (iii. 12-17).

Then the special duties of wives and husbands, children and fathers, slaves and masters, are dealt with. Prayer and thanksgiving are enjoined on all alike, and the Christians are bidden to "buy up the opportunity" of furthering the cause of God in their dealings with the outer world, having their speech seasoned with the salt of wholesome wisdom (iii. 18-iv. 6). A few words are said about Tychicus, Onesimus, and other friends, including "Luke, the beloved physician," and the Epistle ends with a farewell which St. Paul wrote with his own hand. Before writing it, the apostle directs that this letter should be read at Laodicea, and that the Colossians should procure another letter which had been left in that city. This was probably the so-called Epistle to the Ephesians.

ANALYSIS

Salutation, thanksgiving, the apostle's prayer for the readers (i. 1-13).

Christ, who redeemed us, is pre-eminent in Person, being the Head of the natural creation, and of the spiritual creation, because the sum of divine attributes dwells in Him (i. 14-19). He is pre-eminent in work, having reconciled us to God (i. 20-23).

St. Paul's own commission and his anxiety (i. 24-ii. 7). Warning against the delusion of a false philosophy. The "fulness" is in Christ, therefore the Colossians must avoid semi-Jewish practices and also avoid the worship of angels (ii. 8-19). The converts have died with Christ to their old life and earthly ordinances (ii. 20-25).

The converts have risen with Christ to a new life and heavenly principles, vices must be made dead, virtues must be put on (iii. 1-17).

Obligations of wives and husbands, children and parents, slaves and masters (iii. 18-iv. 1).

The duty of prayer and thanksgiving, and right behaviour towards the unconverted (iv. 2-6).

Personal conclusion, and a message relating to an Epistle from Laodicea (iv. 7-18).

THE EPISTLE OF PAUL TO PHILEMON

[Sidenote: The Author.]

The genuineness of this winning little letter could never be doubted except by the most dryasdust of pedants. It is no proof of acuteness to detect the artifice of a forger in its earnest simplicity, its thoughtful tact, and affectionate anxiety. There is about it a vivacity and directness which at once and decisively stamp it as genuine. And external evidence shows that it was included in the earliest lists of St. Paul's Epistles. It was accepted by Marcion, included in the *Muratorian Fragment*, and expressly attributed to St. Paul by Origen. It shows a number of coincidences with Colossians, Ephesians, and Philippians, and it is especially connected with Colossians by the proper names which it contains, such as Archippus, Aristarchus, Mark, and Luke. No evidence exists to show that any early Christians denied this Epistle to be by St. Paul. But it does appear that some of them half disliked its inclusion in the Canon, thinking it too trivial to be numbered with the Scriptures. To modern readers it manifests a great treatment of little things, which is one of the surest proofs of inspiration.

[Sidenote: To whom written.]

The Epistle is addressed to Philemon, a substantial citizen of Colossae. He has been converted by St. Paul, who writes with deep appreciation of his faith in Christ, and of the kindness that he has shown to the saints. He gives him the honourable title of "fellow-worker." Religious services and the social gatherings of Christians are held in Philemon's house.

[Sidenote: Where and when written.]

This Epistle was written during St. Paul's first imprisonment in Rome,
A.D. 59-61. In ver. 10 St. Paul alludes to his "bonds."

[Sidenote: Character and Contents.]

Philemon had a Phrygian slave named Onesimus, who first robbed him and then ran away. Onesimus was able without much difficulty to get to Rome, and here he met the apostle, who received him into the Church. The young convert served him with such eager willingness that St. Paul would have been glad to keep him with him, but he decides to send him back to Philemon with this letter to ensure his forgiveness.

We have, therefore, in this letter a picture of St. Paul in a new relation. There is no other letter in the New Testament of such a private nature except 3 John. The great apostle of the Gentiles is taking his pen to provide a dishonest runaway slave with a note that shall shield him from the just anger of his master. He writes both with a strong sense of justice and with his own perfect diplomatic instinct. The letter is at once authoritative, confident, and most gentle. He does not command or insist, yet it is quite clear that Philemon must do just what he asks. There is no violent attack upon slavery as an institution. Any such attack would have been both foolish and criminal. For it would have encouraged slaves to make Christianity a cloak for revolt, and precipitated horrors far worse than those which it could have professed to remove. But St. Paul asserts a principle which will eventually prove fatal to slavery. When he tells Philemon to receive Onesimus "as a brother beloved," he is really saying that our estimate of men must not be based on their social class, but rather on their relation to God.

This letter has been compared with a letter written under similar circumstances by the younger Pliny, one of the best of the pagan gentlemen of Rome. But while the letter of Pliny is more elegant in language, the letter of St. Paul is a finer masterpiece of feeling. A Roman slave was still allowed no rights and no family relationship, and for the smallest offence he might be tortured and killed. In the next century the Emperor Hadrian first took away from masters the power of life and death over their slaves, and it was not until the time of the Emperor Constantine, who established Christianity, that the laws affecting slavery pointed to the future triumph of emancipation. But the ancient conception of slavery was doomed as soon as "slave-girls like Blandina in Gaul, or Felicitas in Africa, having won for themselves the crown of martyrdom, were celebrated in the festivals of the Church with honours denied to the most powerful and noblest born of mankind." [1]

ANALYSIS

Salutation from Paul and Timothy to Philemon and Apphia (? wife), to Archippus and the Church in Philemon's house; thanksgiving for Philemon's faith; a plea for the pardon of Onesimus, St. Paul promises to be responsible for what was stolen; a lodging to be prepared for St. Paul; concluding salutations, benediction.

[1] Lightfoot, *Colossians and Philemon*, p. 325.

CHAPTER XV THE EPISTLE OF PAUL THE APOSTLE TO THE EPHESIANS

[Sidenote: The Author.]

The Pauline authorship of this Epistle is well attested by external evidence. Before 150 we have proof of its wide use among both heretics and Catholics; it is quoted probably by St. Clement and St. Polycarp, and some of its characteristic ideas are to be found in a more developed form in the *Shepherd* of Hermas. There is one clear reference to it in St. Ignatius, and two other possible references. We trace an interesting connection between the thought of this Epistle and that of the Revelation and the Gospel of St. John (*e.g.* ch. xvii.) and the First Epistle of St. Peter. Perhaps we may account for it by accepting Renan's suggestion that St. Peter, St. John, and St. Paul were in Rome together. The strongest argument for the Pauline authorship lies in the undesigned coincidences between Ephesians and Romans. In both we notice the same courtesy of manner and sensitive frankness, the same setting forth of God's method of salvation, the same valuation of the relative position of Jews and Gentiles, and of their union in Jesus Christ; the same thought of God's eternal and unchanging purpose very gradually revealed, and extending in its ultimate operation to all creation. It has been well said that the Epistle to the Ephesians is required to give completeness to the argument of Rom. xv. Though we do not find here the controversial reasoning of the earlier Epistle, we have some of those characteristic passages in which the writer, carried away by emotion, leaves statement for prayer or praise (cf. Rom. xi. 33 and Eph. iii. 20). We have, indeed, in this Epistle evidence which points to a date later than that of some of his Epistles. We miss the expectation of Christ's immediate coming; the Gentiles are now quite secure in the Church; there is proof of the growth of Christian hymns (v. 14, 19). But the names of the ministers of the Church seem very primitive, the words "presbyter" and *episkopos* not being mentioned. And words such as "worlds," "fulness," "generations," which were used in a special sense by the Gnostics of the 2nd century, are here used in an earlier and less technical meaning.

It has been argued that Ephesians is a forged imitation of Colossians, because about half of its verses have parallels in Colossians. This argument has broken down, since it has been shown that it is equally easy to prove that Colossians is based upon Ephesians. And there is nothing strange in the idea that St. Paul wrote two similar letters at the same time to Churches in similar difficulties. The two Epistles resemble one another just as two letters written by one man to two different friends during the same week. The phrase "holy apostles" (iii. 5) is also said to be a formula which St. Paul would not have employed. But the word "holy" is used in his writings almost in the sense of "Christian;" it signifies consecration rather than personal perfection. There would, therefore, be no vanity in the apostle applying such a title to himself. The attempt to make the style furnish an argument against the genuineness of the Epistle has also failed. There are thirty-two words used only in this Epistle, but there are also eighteen which are found in Pauline Epistles and not elsewhere in the New Testament. The assumption of some sceptical writers that an apostle must have been too unintelligent to enrich his vocabulary, scarcely deserves serious examination. No one would think of applying the same rule to a Greek classical writer, and if he attempted to do so, he would find that Xenophon varies his language as much as St. Paul.

The real reason why the authenticity of this Epistle has been attacked is this. Ephesians teaches that the Church is a universal society, visibly united by baptism and the ministry, embracing Jew and Gentile on equal terms. But, according to Baur, this conception of the Church is a product of the 2nd century. He assumed that St. Paul could not include the twelve under the name of the "holy apostles," or teach a Catholic doctrine of the Church.[1] The present school of rationalists is inclining to admit that Ephesians is genuine. But it is hard to see how they will be able to do this without also admitting that the Epistle implies that the other "holy apostles" held, like St. Paul, that Christ is divine.

[Sidenote: To whom written.]

It is almost certainly not primarily a letter to Ephesus, but a circular letter to several Churches in Asia Minor.

In i. 1 we read the words "to the saints which are in Ephesus." But the words "in Ephesus" are omitted in the two great MSS. K and B. Origen also implies that these words were absent in some MSS., and St. Basil definitely says so. And as the Epistle contains no salutation to any individual, it is difficult to imagine that it was specially addressed to Ephesus, where St. Paul's friends were numerous and dear (see Acts xx. 17-38). In some passages St. Paul speaks as if he and those to whom he writes knew each other only through third persons (i. 15; iii. 2). This suggests that the Epistle was written primarily to a Church like that of Colossae which he had never visited.

The probable solution is that it was written to the Christians of Laodicea in the first instance. Tertullian says that Marcion had copies with "Ad Laodicenos" as the title. Now, in this case Marcion had nothing to gain by fraud, and we may therefore suppose that he had honest grounds for using this title. The same title gains some support from Col. ii. 1; iv. 13, 16. The last verse suggests that it was to be passed on from Laodicea. Perhaps several copies of the letter were written at Laodicea, and a blank space left in them for the insertion of the various addresses. No doubt the letter would be forwarded to Ephesus in time.

Laodicea, at present called Eski-Hissar (the "old fortress"), is now utterly deserted. It was probably founded about B.C. 250 by Antiochus II. Theos, and named after his wife Laodike. It was distant eleven miles from Colossae. The population included some Syrians and Jews. It rose to great wealth under the Roman power, and was so rich that when it was destroyed by an earthquake in A.D. 60 it scorned to seek pecuniary aid from the emperor. It was in a central position on the great trade route from the east, and was famous for its banking business, its manufacture of fine garments of black wool, and its "Phrygian powder" for weak eyes. In Rev. iii. 18 there appears to be a veiled allusion to each of these three sources of prosperity. Timothy, Mark, and Epaphras (Col. i. 7) were instrumental in spreading Christianity in this region. Laodicea was the leading bishopric of Phrygia throughout the Christian period.

Ephesus was the capital of the Roman province of Asia. With Antioch in Syria and Alexandria in Egypt, it ranked as one of the greatest cities of the East Mediterranean lands. Planted amid the hills near the mouth of the river Cayster, it was excellently fitted to become a great mart, and was the commercial centre for the whole country on the Roman side of Mount Taurus. The substratum of the population was Asiatic, but the progress and enterprise of the city belonged to the Greeks. There, as in the Florence of the Medici, we find commercial astuteness joined with intense delight in graceful culture. Some of the best work of the greatest Greek sculptors and painters was treasured at Ephesus. A splendid but sensuous worship centred round the gross figure of the goddess Artemis, whose temple was one of the greatest triumphs of ancient art. In the British Museum are preserved some fragments of the old temple built by Croesus, King of Lydia, in B.C. 550. The vast temple which replaced this older structure was built about B.C. 350, with the help of contributions from the whole of Asia. The wealth of the city was increased by the crowds which attended the festivals, and many trades were mainly dependent upon the pilgrims, who required food, victims, images, and shrines. In St. Paul's time the city contained one temple devoted to the worship of a Roman emperor. Ephesus was also a home of magical arts, and was famous for the production of magical formulae known as "Ephesian letters." The actual foundation of the Christian Church in Ephesus may be ascribed to Priscilla and Aquila, whom St. Paul left there on his first visit (Acts xviii. 19), On his return to Ephesus he stayed there for two years (Acts xix. 1, 10), and the opposition of the tradesmen to a creed which affected the vested interests of idolatry was the cause of the riot so vigorously described by St. Luke. Even after the riot the superstitions of the mob were a serious danger to St. Paul (1 Cor. xv. 32; xvi. 9; 2 Cor. i. 8-10). At a later period Ephesus became the residence of St. John.

[Sidenote: Where and when written.]

St. Paul wrote this Epistle during his imprisonment at Rome, which began in A.D. 59 (see iii. 1, 13; iv. 1, vi. 22). Rome is not mentioned in the Epistle, but the connection between Ephesians, Colossians, Philemon, and Philippians points to the high probability that they were all written from the same place. This place is much more likely to have been Rome than Caesarea, the only other possible locality. Ephesians was apparently written later than Colossians, for it shows an emphasis on new points of doctrine—the continuity of the Church, the work of the Holy Spirit, the analogy between family life and the Church, and the simile of the spiritual armour.

[Sidenote: Character and Contents.]

The Epistle is of the nature of a sermon, full of closely interlaced doctrinal arguments on the greatness of that *one* Gospel and that *one* Church by which all distinctions in mankind are bridged over and salvation is made sure. The writer fears that there will be some lack of unity in the Church, and that the moral tone of his converts will sink. He wishes for a Christianity both Catholic and deep. So he presents his readers with the portrait of a Church predestined before all ages, appointed to last through all ages, in which all men will be united in holiness and love. If Galatians and Corinthians are more vivid, Romans more rich, and Philippians more affectionate, Ephesians gives us St. Paul's most mature and complete picture of Christianity.

St. Paul explains how his Gentile readers came to their present position in the Church. They are not to regard it as a matter of chance. They were called to Christ as the result of an eternal counsel of God. God intended from eternity to adopt them in union with His Son. This intention was now made known, to sum up all things again in Christ (i. 10). The apostle prays for his readers that they may receive enlightenment, and grow in knowledge, particularly concerning the power of God shown in the resurrection and ascension of Christ and his consequent relation *to the Church*.[2]

The unity of all things in the Son of God is explained in Colossians as having been involved in His creation of them. In Ephesians St. Paul assumes this relation, and shows that it is largely in abeyance through *sin*. Estrangement has come between man and his God, involving man in death and in the wrath of God (ii. 3-5). A wall of division has also been made between Jew and Gentile (ii. 14). This division was visibly embodied in the Jewish ordinances. But Jew and Gentile alike have now been reconciled to God, and in being reunited with God are reunited with each other. This momentous change was effected by the shedding of Christ's blood on the cross. The readers are to remember that they are being built into God's own habitation, of which Christ is the Corner-Stone (ii. 20).

To the end that they may be filled in their degree with God's attributes, the writer bows his knees (iii. 14) unto the Father. He prays for their strengthening because he has a special charge over the Gentiles. This charge involves the stewardship of a secret (iii. 3), viz. the inclusion of the Gentiles in the promise of God. He, the least of all saints, has been allowed to proclaim this secret, a work which shows to the heavenly powers the wisdom of God corresponding with His eternal purpose (iii. 10, 11). This bounty of God will ever be praised in the Church, which is the monument of that bounty (iii. 21).

Chapters iv.-vi. are largely practical. They set out rules of conduct. But even here doctrine is brought in to enforce practical advice. The readers are to "walk worthily" of their calling. To do this, they must realize unity. The principles of unity are magnificently summed up (iv. 4-6). Then the apostle mentions some means which God has appointed for the maintenance of unity. Christians have various gifts from the ascended Christ (iv. 7-8), and some are specially gifted for ecclesiastical offices (iv. 9-13). These gifts make for the completeness of the Church, of which Christ is the Head and the Life. To "walk worthily" also means that everything connected with heathen habits must be sedulously renounced. The old self must be changed for the new. A basis for social life must be found in truthfulness, uprightness, and kindliness (iv. 25-32). Purity must specially be preserved, impurity being contrasted with love. Light and darkness are then contrasted, and the sober gaiety of the Christian with heathen folly and excess (v. 1-21).

St. Paul passes on to speak of the Christian household—the duties of husband, wife, children, slaves. He seems to pronounce a great benediction over family life as he compares the union of marriage to the association of Christ with His Church. Just as in calling Christ the Head of which the Church is the body, he suggests the entire dependence of the Church upon Christ, so now in describing the Church as the spouse of Christ, he suggests that this dependence must imply a voluntary and conscious submission. The final exhortation vividly describes the Christian's conflict with evil: to fight victoriously he will need to be well armoured with the whole panoply of God (vi. 10-20). There is a short personal conclusion in which St. Paul describes himself as Christ's "ambassador in chains."

ANALYSIS

Salutation (i. 1, 2).

Exposition of God's purpose in adopting the Gentiles as His sons, chosen by the Father, redeemed by the Son, sealed by the Spirit. A prayer for the readers (i.).

Their new state as saved by grace through faith; reconciliation of Jews and Gentiles in Christ (ii.). Paul was made a minister to dispense the grace of God to the Gentiles. He prays for their spiritual progress (iii.).

The unity of Christians in the Church combined with diversity of gifts and offices, a warning against heathen vices, and advice as to duty towards one's neighbour (iv.). Christian love, heathen uncleanness, light and darkness, walking circumspectly, sobriety and song (v. 1-21).

The union of husbands and wives like that of Christ and His Church (v. 22, 23). Duties of children and parents, servants and masters (vi. 1-9).

Wrestling against evil powers with the whole armour of God (vi. 10-18).

Personal conclusion and benediction (vi. 19-24).

[1] See Baur's *Paul*, vol. ii. p. 177 (English translation).

[2] Eph. i. 23. The Church is said to be "the fulness of Him that filleth all in all." The word "fulness" is derived from philosophy, and means that the Church is, or rather is the realization of, the sum of the sacred attributes of Christ, who fills the whole universe with all kinds of gifts. Some commentators translate "fulness" as if it meant the receptacle of Christ's attributes, and others as if it meant the completion of Christ. But the word is used in a philosophical and not in a literal sense. See Lightfoot, *Colossians*, p. 259.

CHAPTER XVI THE EPISTLE OF PAUL THE APOSTLE TO THE PHILIPPIANS

[Sidenote: The Author.]

The genuineness of this Epistle is now admitted by critics of very different schools of thought, including some extreme rationalists. About A.D. 110 St. Polycarp, in his letter to the Philippians, speaks of the letters which they had received from "the blessed and glorious Paul." Although he seems to refer to a number of letters, we may be sure that this letter was among that number. Otherwise it would not have been so universally regarded as genuine during the 2nd century. It is in Marcion's canon, in the *Muratorian Fragment*, the Peshitta Syriac and Old Latin versions. It is also quoted in the letter of the Churches of Lyons and Vienne, in the Epistle of Diognetus, and by Irenaeus and Clement of Alexandria. It was rejected by Baur and others on various grounds. It was urged (1) that the doctrine of Christ's self-surrender or "self-emptying" in Phil. ii. 7 is derived from the Valentinian Gnostics of the 2nd century, who taught that the Spirit "Sophia" fell from the "fulness" of divine spirits in heaven to the "emptiness" of the lower world. This objection is too fantastic to deserve serious refutation. It is, in fact, little more than a play upon words. It was urged (2) that in Phil. ii. 7 the manhood of Christ is said to have come into existence at the incarnation, whereas in 1 Cor. xv. 47-49 it is said to have existed in heaven before the incarnation. This idea rests on a false interpretation; in 1 Cor. xv. Christ is called "of heaven" because His manhood became heavenly at His ascension. It was urged (3) that in Phil. iii. 6 the writer says that he had been, "as touching the righteousness which is in the Law, found blameless," whereas St. Paul in Rom. vii. speaks of his revolt against the Law. But it seems that in Phil. iii. St. Paul is laying stress rather on his external privileges and external conformity, while in Rom. vii. he speaks of what is inward and secret. It was urged (4) that the mention of "bishops" (or rather *episkopoi*) and "deacons" in Phil. i. 1 shows that the Epistle was not written in the apostolic age. But there is nothing to make it impossible that such offices did exist at that period, and there is much evidence in favour of them. Christians who are attached to the historical form of Church government will now note with interest that, since the genuineness of this Epistle has been practically demonstrated, some writers have suggested that these words do not refer to special ecclesiastical offices![1]

[Sidenote: To whom written.]

Philippi was named after Philip, King of Macedon, in the 4th century B.C. It was in Eastern Macedonia, on a steep hill at the edge of a plain; its seaport, Neapolis, was about eight miles distant. It was on the Egnatian road, the great high-road which connected the Aegean and the Adriatic seas, and therefore connected Asia with Europe. It was made into a Roman colony, with the title *Colonia Augusta Julia Philippensium*, after the victory of Antony and Octavian over Brutus and Cassius. Its new name was, therefore, a memorial of the murdered but avenged Julius Caesar. St. Paul brought Christianity to Philippi early in A.D. 50, during his second missionary journey. St. Paul's first visit here is described in Acts xvi. 12-40, and it has a special interest as the story of the apostle's first preaching in a European town. The Jews had no synagogue, only a spot by the river-side in the suburbs, where a few met together on the sabbath. His first convert was Lydia of Thyatira, who was a seller of purple-dyed goods; her house became the centre of the Philippian Church. The imprisonment of St. Paul and St. Silas in consequence of St. Paul's exorcising a heathen slave-girl who professed to be inspired, is one of the most dramatic incidents in Acts. When St. Paul was released he left the town, but returned there, in all probability, in A.D. 55, on his third journey while travelling to Corinth. In A.D. 56 he was there once more, and the last Easter before his imprisonment was spent with these beloved converts (Acts xx. 6).

The Christians of Philippi were pre-eminent in the affections of St. Paul. He calls them, like the Thessalonians, his "joy and crown" (iv. 1), and they alone of his children had the privilege of ministering to his personal necessities.

[Sidenote: Where and when written.]

It may be regarded as almost certain that St. Paul wrote this Epistle in Rome. He was a prisoner, as we see in Phil. i. 7, 13, 14, 17. He sends greeting from those of Caesar's household (iv. 22). The first and last chapters imply that he is in the midst of an active Church, and that he is the centre to which messengers come and from which they go. This accords with the apostle's treatment at Rome. One phrase, however, has been thought to suggest Caesarea rather than Rome. It is "the whole praetorium" (i. 13). This might mean the praetorium or palace of Herod Agrippa II. at Caesarea, but it is possible that it has quite a different meaning. It may either be the imperial guard or the supreme imperial court before which St. Paul had to be judged. The latter interpretation is that suggested by the great historian Mommsen, and seems to be the most satisfactory explanation.

The meaning of the phrase has an important bearing upon the date of the Epistle. If it was not written at Caesarea, it must have been written at Rome between A.D. 59 and A.D. 61. But the critics who are agreed that it was composed at Rome, are divided as to the place which it occupies among the Epistles which St. Paul wrote during his imprisonment. Some place it first, because the vigorous style, and many of the phrases, suggest that it was written not very long after Romans. Others, with greater probability, place it last among the Epistles of the captivity. For even if it was written first among those Epistles, it was written more than three years after Romans. And the Epistle contains several indications of being written late in the captivity. If "praetorium" means the imperial guard, some time would have to elapse before such a large body of men could know much about St. Paul; and if it means the imperial court, the verse implies that he had already appeared before his judges. Phil. ii. 24 shows that he was expecting a speedy decision on his case. Epaphroditus, probably not the Colossian Epaphras who was with St. Paul at Rome (Col. iv. 12), had come as a delegate from the Philippians, bringing their alms to the apostle (ii. 25; iv. 18). After his arrival in Rome he was ill and homesick, and now he is returning to Philippi bearing this letter of thanks. This all seems to imply that Philippians was written a considerable time after the apostle's imprisonment began, and we can therefore reasonably place it after Colossians and Ephesians, and date it early in A.D. 61.

With the exception of 2 Corinthians, this is the most personal and intimate of St. Paul's writings. In both he lays bare his heart. But the tone of the two Epistles is absolutely different. In 2 Corinthians he writes as a man who has been bitterly injured; he asserts his claims to fickle believers whose ears have been charmed by his unscrupulous opponents. In Philippians we chiefly observe a note of frank and loving confidence; buffeted by the world, the apostle finds refreshment in the affection of his friends at Philippi.

After a salutation to all the "saints" at Philippi, including especially the *episkopoi* and deacons, the apostle speaks of the joy which he feels in praying for them, and begs of God that their love may abound, and that they may approve the things that are excellent, being filled with the fruits of righteousness (i. 1-11).

Then St. Paul tells how his captivity has been a means of spreading the gospel in the praetorium and elsewhere. Even the malicious activity of his opponents has been a means of proclaiming Christ, and with true grandeur of soul the apostle rejoices in the fact. So far as he is concerned, death would be a more attractive prospect than life, for death would mean admission into the presence of Christ, but for the sake of the Philippians he is glad to live. With wonderful cheerfulness he says that he is glad if his blood is to be offered like a libation poured over the living sacrifice of the souls and bodies which the Philippians offer to God (ii. 17). Before he speaks of this libation of his blood he makes a tender appeal to his converts to imitate the lowliness of Jesus Christ. He puts into the language of theology the story of the incarnation which his friend St. Luke draws with an artist's pen in the first two chapters of his Gospel. He speaks to them of "the mind" of Christ Jesus, whose life on earth was self-sacrifice in detail. Christ had before the incarnation the "form" or essential attributes of God, but He did not set any store on His equality with God, as though it were a prize,[2] but stripped Himself in self-surrender, and took the "form" or nature of a bond-servant. He looked like men as they actually are, and if men recognized His outward "fashion," they would only have taken Him for a man. And then He made Himself obedient to God up to His very death, and that the death of the cross. This was followed by His exaltation, and worship is now paid to Him in His glorified humanity (ii. 1-11).

In ii. 19 St. Paul returns to personal matters concerning Timothy and Epaphroditus; then he seems on the point of concluding the Epistle (iii. 1). But he suddenly breaks into an abrupt and passionate warning against the Judaizers. The passage almost looks as if it were a page from the Epistle to the Galatians. The Judaizers are called "dogs," and as their circumcision was no longer the sign of a covenant with God, the apostle calls it a mere outward mutilation of the flesh (iii. 2). It is unlikely that Jewish influences were potent at Philippi. The explanation of this passage appears to be that the apostle, before completing his letter, learnt of some new and successful plot of the Judaizers at Rome or elsewhere. Nervously dreading lest they should invade his beloved Philippian Church, he speaks with great severity of these conspirators. The conclusion of the chapter is apparently directed against the licence of certain Gentile converts. These seem to have been "enemies of the cross of Christ" in the looseness of their lives rather than in the corruptness of their creed. It is difficult in this case, as in that of the Judaizers, to know whether these errors already existed at Philippi or not. The passage concludes with an exhortation to steadfastness (iii. 2-iv. 1).

Two women, Euodia and Syntyche, are exhorted to be "of the same mind." A true yokefellow of the apostle, possibly Epaphroditus, and a certain Clement, possibly the Clement who was afterwards Bishop of Rome, are exhorted to try to bring about their reconciliation. All are exhorted to rejoice in the Lord, and are told that the peace of God, which passeth understanding, shall stand sentinel over their hearts and thoughts. Before returning again to personal matters and thanking the Philippians for their gifts, St. Paul urges them to follow whatsoever is true and lovely. His language here seems to consecrate all that was permanently valuable in the sayings of the Greek philosophers. It recalls to us the words of the ancient Church historian, Socrates: "The beautiful, wherever it may be, is the property of truth."

ANALYSIS

Salutation, thanksgiving, prayer (i. 1-11).

The position of affairs at Rome. His imprisonment has stimulated the preaching of the gospel; his own feelings are divided between the desire for death and a willingness to live for their sakes; an exhortation to boldness (i. 12-30).

An exhortation to imitate the humility of Christ, who took the form of man and was willing to die, and was after this abasement exalted above every created being (ii. 1-11).

An exhortation to obedience, quietness, purity, mission and commendation of Timothy and Epaphroditus; farewell (ii. 12-iii. 1).

Strong warning against Judaism, enforced by his own example; against claim to perfection, also enforced by his own example; against Antinomian licence as unworthy of "citizens of heaven", exhortation to steadfastness (iii. 2-iv. 1).

Advice to Euodia, Syntyche, and others; exhortation to think of all things true and lovely (iv. 2-9).

The apostle expresses his joy at the spirit shown by the offerings sent to him from Philippi. Doxology. Salutation (iv. 10-23).

[1] So E. Haupt, *Die Gefangenschaftsbriefe*, p. 3.

[2] The Greek is ordinarily translated as "a prize to be grasped," but it seems quite possible to translate the passage, "He considered not equality with God to involve a process of grasping."

CHAPTER XVII THE PASTORAL EPISTLES

[Sidenote: The Author.]

1 and 2 Timothy and Titus form the fourth and last group of St. Paul's Epistles, and are known as the Pastoral Epistles,[1] because they deal so largely with the duties and qualifications of the men entrusted with the pastoral care of the Church. St. Paul here teaches the teachers.

Their genuineness is more frequently denied than that of any other of St. Paul's Epistles, and this attack upon their genuineness has been mostly based upon the character of their teaching about the office-bearers of the Church. Attempts have sometimes been made to separate some fragments supposed to be genuine from the remaining portions. All such attempts have failed. These Epistles must either be rejected entirely or accepted entirely. Otherwise we become involved in a hopeless tangle of conjectures.

The *external evidence* is excellent. They are found in the Syriac and Old Latin versions, and in the *Muratorian Fragment*. They are all quoted by Irenaeus, and also by Clement of Alexandria and Tertullian. Their authenticity was therefore regarded as a certain fact in the latter part of the 2nd century, and early in the 4th century Eusebius was unaware that any doubts concerning them existed in the Church. Moreover, St. Polycarp, A.D. 110, quotes both 1 and 2 Timothy. The combined evidence of these writers forms a very substantial argument. Against it we sometimes find urged the fact that the heretic Marcion rejected them. Such an objection borders on frivolity. Marcion held a definite doctrinal heresy, and rejected everything which he could not make to coincide with his own belief. The value which is set on the Old Testament (*e.g.* 2 Tim. iii. 16), the assertion of a real incarnation (*e.g.* 1 Tim. ii. 5), and the sustained opposition to a false spiritualism, which these Epistles exhibit, must have been intensely distasteful to Marcion. We have therefore no reason for believing that he would hesitate to reject them, while knowing them to be genuine, any more than he hesitated to reject all the Gospels except Luke.

The *internal evidence* is called in question for the following reasons.

1. *Historical difficulties.*—We cannot place the journey referred to in 1 Tim. i. 3 during the three years' stay at Ephesus mentioned in Acts. The visit to Miletus in 2 Tim. iv. 20 cannot have taken place on the journey to Jerusalem in Acts xx., because Trophimus was with the apostle when he reached that city (Acts xxi. 29). Again, in 2 Tim. iv. 20 Erastus "abode at Corinth." But he had not been to Corinth for a long time before the journey to Rome recorded in Acts. In Tit. i. 5 we see Titus left by St. Paul at Crete; he is to join the apostle in Nicopolis (iii. 12). But Acts allows no room for this, and the reference to Apollos (iii. 13) implies a later period than St. Paul's stay at Corinth (Acts xviii.).

Answer.—All three Epistles may quite well be later than the history related in Acts. There is no reason for denying that St. Paul was set free after his trial at Rome, and arrested again at a later date. Assuming that this liberation did take place, all historical difficulties vanish. There are several points in favour of this liberation. First, the attitude of the Roman government towards Christianity was fairly tolerant until Nero began his persecution in A.D. 64, and the state of the law would have allowed St. Paul's acquittal. Secondly, it was believed in the early Church that St. Paul was set free. The Muratorian Fragment says that he went to Spain, and St. Clement of Rome, writing from Rome about A.D. 95, says that he went "to the boundary of the west," which seems to point to Spain. Thirdly, the chronology implied in the ancient list of the bishops of Rome will not allow us to put St. Paul's martyrdom earlier than A.D. 64. Fourthly, the apostle himself expected to be set free (Phil. ii. 24; Philem. 22). There is therefore no historical reason for denying that St. Paul was set free from the imprisonment in which Acts leaves him.

2. *References to heresies.*—It has been said that these Epistles contain references to heresies later than the apostolic age, such as the Gnosticism of the 2nd century. More especially, it is said that 1 Tim. vi. 20, which speaks of "oppositions of gnosis falsely so called," refers to a work by Marcion called the "Oppositions" (Antitheses), in which he tried to demonstrate that the Old Testament was antagonistic to the New.

Answer.—The heresies here rebuked are not so definitely described that we can determine their precise character. This fact is in favour of the idea that the heresies belong to the 1st century rather than to the 2nd. Stress has been laid upon statements which seem to imply Gnostic heresy, and heresy of a "Docetic" character, *i.e.* teaching a denial of the reality of our Lord's human nature. But there is certainly nothing which suggests that the error here rebuked was as developed as the heresy rebuked by St. Ignatius, or even that denounced by St. John. It is most unlikely that the word "oppositions" can refer to a book bearing that title. The passage 1 Tim. vi. 20 does not suggest this. And if Marcion is really quoted in 1 Tim., how could Polycarp have quoted 1 Tim., as he does, before Marcion's book was written? Something of a Gnostic tendency is betokened by the scorn of material life and the human body shown in 1 Tim. iv. 3, 8 and 2 Tim. ii. 18. But the error is mainly Jewish. The false teachers professed to be "teachers of the Law" (1 Tim. i. 7), which was exactly the title claimed by the Jewish rabbis (see Luke v. 17). The general character of their teaching was "vain talking" (1 Tim. i. 6; cf. Tit. i. 10; iii. 9). It consists of "profane babblings" (1 Tim. vi. 20; 2 Tim. ii. 16). It is further characterized as "foolish questionings, and genealogies, and strifes, and fightings about the law . . . unprofitable and vain" (Tit. iii. 9). It is summed up in the phrases "old wives' fables" (1 Tim. iv. 7), "Jewish fables" (Tit. i. 14). All this shows that the error was not a definite Gnostic heresy with a fundamentally false view of God. It was something intrinsically ridiculous. Therefore the "endless genealogies" (1 Tim. i. 4) can hardly be Gnostic genealogies of the semi-divine beings who took part in the creation. They are Jewish tales about the heroes of the Old Testament. The error is, in fact, primitive, and does not belong to the 2nd century.

3. *Church organization.*—It is said that these Epistles lay down the rules for an organization of the Church which is later than the apostolic age, and resembles the Episcopal system, such as we find it in the 2nd century. Titus and Timothy act as delegates of the apostle, and as the highest officials of the ministry, and they appoint presbyters and deacons. We thus find a threefold ministry which derives its sacred authority through the apostolate. The apostle lays his hands upon his delegate (2 Tim. i. 6), and this delegate lays his hands upon others (1 Tim. v. 22).

Answer.—It is perfectly true that there is a threefold ministry mentioned in these Epistles. But there is no sufficient reason for denying that such a ministry is of apostolic origin. It seems quite certain that at Jerusalem the presbyters and deacons were under the authority of St. James, and after his death under that of Symeon. The same form of government can also be traced back in other places to apostolic times. Moreover, the organization which is mentioned in Acts is fundamentally the same as that in these Epistles. In Acts we find the apostles first appointing deacons and then presbyters. All the additional evidence which has lately been discovered to support the genuineness of Acts therefore favours the genuineness of these Epistles. Finally, we must notice that the titles of the ministry in these Epistles do not correspond with the titles used in the 2nd century. The government is substantially "Episcopal," but the title "episkopos" was in the 2nd century only applied to the chief dignitary who ruled over the "presbyters." But here the title "episkopos" is applied to the presbyters themselves as the overseers of the congregation. We find the same thing in the letter of St. Clement, A.D. 95. St. Clement, although Bishop of Rome, still gives the title of "episkopos" to the presbyters. This inconvenient practice was given up soon after that date, for we find that St. Ignatius, about A.D. 110, applies the title "episkopos" only to the highest ministers of the Church. We conclude, therefore, that while the organization of the Church described in the Pastoral Epistles supports the belief that the threefold ministry, which we now call Episcopal organization, is of apostolic origin, it does not prove that these Epistles are forgeries. And it is natural that St. Paul, knowing that his death must before long come to pass, should devote a large measure of attention to questions of Church government and discipline.

81

The history of the Church in the 2nd and 3rd centuries proves to us that the organization of the Church was almost as important as the inspiration of the Church.

4. *Language.*—This is an important difficulty. There are in these Epistles many words and phrases which do not occur in the other Epistles of St. Paul. We find different Greek words used for "Lord" and for the second "advent," and a fondness for the words "wholesome," "godliness," and "faithful saying." The new element is most prominent in 1 Tim. and Titus.

Answer.—Private letters to individuals and friends in reference to one particular subject are not likely to resemble public letters which were written in reference to other subjects. It would therefore be unreasonable to expect that the style of the Pastoral Epistles should be cast in the same mould as that of the other Epistles of St. Paul. Nevertheless, the objection would have considerable weight, if St. Paul's aptitude for varying his vocabulary could not be shown. But it can be shown; for his other Epistles are marked by an astonishing variation in the Greek. Beneath this diversity there exists a unity. The Pastoral Epistles have many Pauline phrases,[2] many graphic touches, many forcible and original statements, and glow with that personal devotion to Christ combined with a practical capacity for guiding Christians which St. Paul possessed in so singular a degree. If the Pastoral Epistles are spurious, or if they are composite productions written by a forger who inserted some notes of St. Paul in his own effusions, it becomes almost impossible to account for the fact that 2 Tim. differs delicately both in language and subject from 1 Tim. and Titus. In view of this fact we can admire the sagacity of a recent opponent of their authenticity who deprecates "the possibility of extricating the Pauline from the traditional and editorial material"! [3]

THE FIRST EPISTLE OF PAUL THE APOSTLE TO TIMOTHY

[Sidenote: The Author.]

Reasons have already been given for rejecting the arguments which have been alleged against the Pauline authorship of this Epistle. We may add that it is unlikely that a forger would have inserted the word "mercy" (i. 2) in the usual Pauline greeting "grace and peace." The reference to Timothy's "youth" (iv. 12; cf. 2 Tim. ii. 22) has seemed strange to many. But although St. Paul had been acquainted with Timothy for about twelve years, Timothy must have been greatly the junior of St. Paul. Even if Timothy was as old as thirty-five, the word "youth" would be quite natural from the pen of an old man writing to a pupil, whom he had known as a very young man, and whom he was now putting in authority over men old enough to be his own father. We can attribute this Epistle to St. Paul without hesitation.

[Sidenote: To whom written.]

Timothy was one of the apostle's own converts, his "child in faith." We learn from Acts xvi. 1 that he was the son of a Greek-speaking Gentile father and a Jewish mother. He had received a strictly religious Jewish training from his mother Eunice and his grandmother Lois (2 Tim. i. 1-5; iii. 14, 15). He was converted by St. Paul on his first missionary journey, at Lystra or Derbe. On St. Paul's second visit to that district, Timothy was so well reported of that he was thought worthy of being associated with the apostle in his work. Before employing him as a colleague, St. Paul had him circumcised, that he might be able to work among Jews as well as Gentiles (Acts xvi. 3). Some Christian prophets pointed him out as destined for his sacred office (1 Tim. i. 18). He was ordained by the laying on of the hands of St. Paul himself and the presbyters of the Church (1 Tim. iv. 14; 2 Tim. i. 6). He was frequently associated with the apostle in travelling and in the writing of Epistles. His name occurs as sending a salutation in Rom. xvi. 21, and as the fellow-sender of six of the apostle's letters. He was with the apostle during his first imprisonment at Rome (see Phil., Col., and Philemon). From this Epistle we learn that after the apostle's release he was left in charge of the important Church at Ephesus. While he was in this position, the two Epistles which bear his name were written to him.

[Sidenote: Where and when written.]

It is impossible to ascertain the precise direction of St. Paul's journeys after his release, and it is wisest to refrain from mere conjecture. Before writing this letter he had been recently at Ephesus and had been called away to Macedonia (i. 3). He intended to return before long, but had been unexpectedly delayed (iii. 14, 15). This delay rendered it necessary for him to send directions to Timothy. The precise date cannot be exactly fixed. If St. Paul's martyrdom was as early as A.D. 64, and his release as early as A.D. 61, we may reasonably put this letter in A.D. 63.

[Sidenote: Character and Contents.]

The letter is personal, but it is also official. It is intended to guide Timothy in his work of apostolic delegate. In speaking to the presbyters of Ephesus at Miletus (Acts xx. 29, 30), St. Paul had already expressed fears about the future of the Church, and these fears now seem to have been partly realized. Ephesus was a meeting-place of east and west, a place where religious speculations and religious divisions were likely to increase, and where wise supervision of the Christian Church was essential. The contents of the Epistle therefore mainly consist of warnings against Judaism and false knowledge, and directions as to the duties of various classes of Christians, and especially the clergy.

ANALYSIS

The danger of Jewish and Gnostic heresy (i.).

The order of common prayer (ii.).

The qualifications of *episkopoi* (translated "bishops" in the English versions) and deacons (iii.).

Condemnation of Gnostic asceticism and the duty of Timothy towards heresy (iv.).

Counsels as to the treatment of presbyters (translated "elders" in the English versions) and widows (v.).

Warnings against disobedience towards masters, vain disputations, covetousness, and a wrong use of wealth—concluding with a direct appeal to Timothy (vi.).

THE EPISTLE OF PAUL TO TITUS

[Sidenote: The Author.]

This is exactly the kind of letter which we should expect to be written by a writer of strong individuality addressing a disciple entrusted with the duty of ruling a Church threatened by the same troubles as the Church which was under the supervision of Timothy. It is attributed to St. Paul by Irenaeus, and is amply supported by other early writers.

[Sidenote: To whom written.]

"To Titus, my true child after a common faith" (i. 4). Titus was converted by St. Paul (i. 4), and was an uncircumcised Gentile (Gal. ii. 3). He must have been converted at an early period in the apostle's career, for he was with Paul and Barnabas on their visit from Antioch to Jerusalem in A.D. 49. He was therefore present during the great crisis when the freedom of the Gentiles from the ceremonial part of the Jewish law was vindicated. It is suggested by Gal. ii. that Titus was personally known to the Galatians, and possibly he was himself a Galatian. Titus was prominent at another important crisis. When the Church at Corinth was involved in strife, Titus was sent thither. His efforts were attended with success, and he was able to report good news on returning to St. Paul in Macedonia (2 Cor. vii. 6, 7, 13-15). He carried the Second Epistle to the Corinthians to Corinth. We hear no more of him until the period when this Epistle was written. After St. Paul's release from his first imprisonment, Titus was with him in Crete, and was left by the apostle to direct the affairs of the Church in that island (Tit. i. 5). It is plain that the tact and wisdom which he had shown at Corinth had not failed him in the interval, and that St. Paul still regarded him as a worthy delegate and a true evangelist of the gospel of peace.

[Sidenote: Where and when written.]

The similarity to 1 Timothy makes it almost certain that Titus was written about the same time, and before 2 Timothy. The apostle is expecting to winter at Nicopolis, probably the Nicopolis in Epirus. The letter was therefore possibly written from Greece. It seems from iii. 13 that Zenas, a former teacher of the Jewish law, and Apollos, had occasion to travel by Crete, and St. Paul takes the opportunity to send a letter with them to Titus.

[Sidenote: Character and Contents.]

The greeting at the beginning of the Epistle and the character of its general contents show that this letter is official as well as private. Possibly the gospel was first brought to Crete by those Jews or proselytes from Crete who saw the outpouring of the Holy Spirit at Jerusalem on the Day of Pentecost (Acts ii. 11.) Fully thirty years had passed since then, but the Church had not hitherto been sufficiently organized to be independent of the apostle. Now, however, the apostolic delegate will be able to ordain the presbyters required in every city. The manner in which the "episkopoi" are mentioned immediately afterwards (i. 5, 7) strongly favours the idea that the name "episkopos" is here used as a title of the presbyters, as in Acts xx. They form the order under the apostle's delegate. Useless speculations of a Jewish character had invaded the Church (i. 10-14; iii. 9). The teachers of these "fables" were influenced by love of "filthy lucre." St. Paul quotes the saying that the Cretans are "liars, evil beasts, idle gluttons," and attributes it to "one of themselves, a prophet of their own." The saying is by the poet Epimenides, c. B.C. 600. He was a native of Cnossus in Crete, who was regarded as a seer, and his reputation for second-sight is testified by Plato giving him the epithet "divine." St. Paul seems convinced that the Cretan character was as prone to sensuality as in the days of Epimenides, and it is immediately after alluding to their dangers that he utters the memorable words, "unto the pure all things are pure." The apostle's exhortation to "maintain good works" (iii. 8) is one of the verses which have been absurdly alleged to be out of harmony with St. Paul's insistence upon the importance of justification by faith. There is a definite allusion to baptismal regeneration in iii. 5.

ANALYSIS

Titus to ordain elders; the requisite character of "episkopoi",
Judaizing talkers to be checked (i.).

Duties of aged men and women; young women and men; servants; the grace of God and the hope inspired by it (ii.).

Duty towards rulers and all men; the kindness of God; foolish discussions to be avoided; how to deal with a heretic; personal notes (iii.).

THE SECOND EPISTLE OF PAUL THE APOSTLE TO TIMOTHY

[Sidenote: The Author.]

It is generally considered that the authenticity of this Epistle stands or falls with that of the First Epistle. But it bears its own peculiar marks of genuineness. One thoroughly Pauline feature is *thanksgiving* at the beginning, a feature which is found in eight of his other Epistles, but not in the two other Pastoral Epistles. A forger might have had the critical insight which would lead him to compose this thanksgiving. But it is highly improbable that a forger would have put twenty-three proper names into the Epistle without tamely copying names which occur elsewhere, or without betraying any wish to glorify some saint who became popular after the death of the apostle. Neither of these two suspicious tokens can be detected here. For instance, Demas, concerning whom nothing that is discreditable is narrated elsewhere, is here rebuked with a pathetic regret (iv. 10; cf. Col. iv. 14); while Linus, afterwards a famous bishop and martyr of Rome, is mentioned without any honourable distinction at all. Even if the Linus of this Epistle is not the bishop of that name the argument still holds good. For a forger, if he inserted the name of any Linus, would have been almost certain to mention *the* Linus and no other.

[Sidenote: To whom written.]

"To Timothy, my beloved child" (i. 2).

[Sidenote: Where and when written.]

It was written from Rome, where St. Paul is again a prisoner, the reason of his imprisonment being the witness that he has borne to Christ (i. 8, 12, 17). His imprisonment had already lasted some time, for it was known at Ephesus. The apostle had apparently requested two of his friends, Phygellus and Hermogenes, to come to him at Rome, but they had declined. The Ephesian Onesiphorus had acted otherwise, and when in Rome had sought him out. St. Paul anticipates death. His case has already had a first hearing, when no witness appeared in his defence (iv. 16). He is now ready to be offered up. But he does not anticipate an immediate martyrdom, as he urges Timothy to come to Rome before winter. The date is therefore probably some weeks or months before St. Paul's martyrdom. The year is either A.D. 64 or very soon afterwards.

[Sidenote Character and Contents.]

This Epistle is the apostle's farewell pastoral charge. He looks forward to his fate with courage and confidence. He has fought a good fight, and is sure of the crown of righteousness which the Lord will give him. But he sees that a dark future is in store for the Church. Some professing Christians have already deserted him, others have perverted the faith. Among the latter are Hymenseus and Philetus, who assert that the resurrection is past already. It is probable that they were influenced by some Gnostic dislike of the human body, and taught that the only resurrection possible for a Christian was the spiritual resurrection of becoming acquainted with their own Gnostic doctrine. Such a heresy is described by Irenaeus. St. Paul warns Timothy that there are "grievous times" to come (iii. 1). Scripture will be a means of security against the mischief-makers. The various exhortations given to

Timothy are of great force and beauty; he is to endure hardship like a good soldier, and is charged before God to preach and rebuke with long-suffering. The solemnity of these words is equalled by the pungent sarcasm with which the writer alludes to the schismatics who "lead captive silly women" or will "heap to themselves teachers, having itching ears."

We may notice that ii. 11-13 seems to contain part of a Christian hymn, that iii. 8 contains a reference to a Jewish story not found in the Old Testament, and that i. 18 is perhaps a prayer for the dead. The Second Book of Maccabees xii. 44 shows that in the century before the Christian era the Jews were wont to pray for the departed.

ANALYSIS

Exhortation to energy, the failure of friends, the fidelity of Onesiphorus (i.).

Exhortation to endurance as Christ's soldier, profane discussions to be shunned; the error of Hymenseus and Philetus; varieties of character like varieties of vessels; the way to become a vessel of honour (ii.).

Coming corruption, the creeping mischief-makers; Timothy is reminded of St. Paul's manner of life and of the value of Scripture (iii.).

Exhortation to fidelity in ministerial work; the apostle's course drawing to an end, Timothy urged to come; personal notes (iv.).

[1] This title seems to have been first applied to them in 1810 by Wegscheider.

[2] Cf. "according to my gospel" (2 Tim. ii. 8; Rom. ii. 16); "the gospel of the glory" (1 Tim. i. 11; 2 Cor. iv. 4). The Greek phrase for "give occasion to" (1 Tim. v. 14) is found in 2 Cor. v. 12, and nowhere in the New Testament except in St. Paul.

[3] B. W. Bacon, *Introduction to the New Testament*, p. 140.

CHAPTER XVIII THE EPISTLE TO THE HEBREWS

[Sidenote: The Author.]

The question of the authorship of this Epistle is one of the most fascinating problems raised by the criticism of the New Testament. It does not in the least involve any charge of forgery, such as is involved in a consideration of St. John's Gospel or of St. Paul's Epistle to the Ephesians. Nor does it involve the fact of an author absorbing the work of a previous writer, such as we find in the case of St. Luke. The work is one complete and original composition of great finish and perfection, and yet this perfect work contains hardly a hint as to its author. The title which is placed above it in our Bibles deserves serious consideration, as it represents an opinion which was held in many parts of Christendom in the 4th century, and in some parts of Christendom even in the 2nd century. But it by no means represents the universal judgment of the Church, and is contradicted by good evidence, both external and internal. A remarkable divergence of opinion on the subject existed between the Churches of the east and those of the west.

Alexandria appears to have been the first centre of the belief that this Epistle was written by St. Paul. We find that about A.D. 170, Pantaenus, the head of the catechetical school at Alexandria, attributed it to St. Paul. His successor Clement agrees with this, but states that it was written in Hebrew and translated by St. Luke into Greek—a statement which implies that scholars were conscious that the style of Hebrews is not the style ordinarily used by St. Paul. In A.D. 240, Origen, the successor of Clement, defends the Pauline authorship—a defence which shows that the authorship was disputed. In A.D. 245 Origen had learnt to doubt the validity of his former defence, and states that the writer was a disciple of Paul, but "who wrote the Epistle God only knows." In A.D. 269 the famous heretic Paul of Samosata quoted Hebrews as the work of St. Paul in a letter read at the Synod of Antioch which deposed him from his bishopric. Early in the next century Eusebius quotes the Epistle as by St. Paul, but he shows the same perplexity as Clement of Alexandria, for he thinks that it was translated from the Hebrew, possibly by Clement of Rome. After the time of Eusebius the Greek Fathers all ascribe it to St. Paul.

We can therefore sum up the evidence of the Greek Churches by saying that though it mostly favours one theory, it is not so cogent as to remove all our suspicions.

Moreover, the complete absence of references to this Epistle in the extant writings of Irenaeus[1] almost compels us to ask if the Greek Churches of Southern Gaul and Asia Minor regarded this Epistle as Pauline. Irenaeus might naturally omit to quote a short and comparatively unimportant Epistle, but his omission of a long Epistle, well adapted to his arguments, inclines us to place him in a rank opposite to his contemporary, Clement of Alexandria. A Greek writer of the 6th century actually says that Irenaeus, in a passage now lost, denied that St. Paul wrote the Epistle.[2]

The Latin Churches of the west seem to have been for three centuries under the conviction that this Epistle was not by St. Paul. It is quoted by Clement of Rome, A.D. 95, a fact which alone is sufficient to prove its early date and its sacred character. But Clement makes no statement as to its authorship. Caius of Rome, A.D. 200, excludes it from the list of St. Paul's Epistles, and the same hesitation with regard to it existed in the great Latin-speaking Church of Carthage. St. Cyprian, A.D. 250, does not include Hebrews among St. Paul's Epistles. No Latin Father attributes it to St. Paul before Hilary of Poictiers in A.D. 368, and Hilary was in close contact with the East. At the end of the 4th century St. Jerome shows distinct hesitation in attributing it to St. Paul, and it was not commonly attributed to him in the west until the time of St. Augustine, who died in 432.

Internal evidence agrees with the external evidence in making it very difficult for us to believe that St. Paul wrote Hebrews.

(1) The Greek is more elegant than that of St. Paul's Epistles. The styles are widely different. That of St. Paul is abrupt and vehement like a mountain-torrent, that of Hebrews is calm and smooth like a river running through a meadow.

(2) The quotations are very unlike St. Paul's. They are all from the Greek version of the Old Testament, with the exception of that in x. 30, which occurs in the same form in Rom. xii. 19. It had probably taken this shape in popular use. The quotations are introduced by phrases such as "God saith," or "the Holy Spirit saith." But St. Paul often shows a knowledge of the Hebrew when he makes quotations, and he uses such phrases as "it is written," or "the Scripture saith," or "Moses saith."

(3) There is no salutation such as is usual in St. Paul's Epistles.

(4) In Hebrews the incarnate Son is called "Jesus," or "Christ," or "the Lord." In St. Paul's Epistles we find fuller titles employed, such as "our Lord Jesus Christ."

(5) The theological differences are important. The teaching of the author harmonizes with that of St. Paul, but throughout the Epistle we feel that the truths of Christianity are being expounded to us by one whose personal history is different from that of St. Paul. The author starts from the fact of the perfection of Christ's sacrifice, and in his doctrine about the Law he looks at it from that fact. St. Paul, on the other hand, starts from the doctrine of justification by faith, and looks at the Law from the point of that doctrine. Again, the author takes a general view of faith as heroic belief in unseen facts; while St. Paul, though he sometimes does the same, prefers to use the word "faith" in the sense of devoted, personal, adhesion to Christ.

(6) In ii. 3, 4 the author seems to imply that he had not personally seen the Lord.

Many conjectures have been made as to the real author. Few of these conjectures deserve serious consideration. Luther suggested Apollos, and the suggestion has been accepted by many writers. In favour of it are: (1) he was a friend of St. Paul; (2) he was "mighty in the Scriptures," and Hebrews deals with the Old Testament in a masterly way; (3) he was an Alexandrian Jew, and Hebrews was plainly written by a Jew, and apparently by one acquainted with Philo and other Alexandrian authors.[3] Against this theory is the complete absence of traditional support, and the fact that Apollos was taught by Aquila and Priscilla, whereas the author of Hebrews implies that he was taught by a personal disciple of Christ. On the whole, *St. Barnabas* seems to have the best claim. Tertullian not only speaks of it as the work of Barnabas, but also shows by his words that the Church of North Africa regarded it as his work.[4] He is not, therefore, making a conjecture, but assuming a tradition. His evidence is the more valuable, because the Church of North Africa was important and was in close contact with Rome, where the Epistle was venerated at least as early as A.D. 95. In favour of the tradition we can note: (1) St. Barnabas was an influential companion of St. Paul; (2) he was a Levite, and would be interested in Levitical worship; (3) he was a native of Cyprus, which was in close communication with Alexandria; (4) he had been in the regions to which the Epistle was probably addressed.

Against the theory that St. Barnabas was the author, it is said that the author makes surprising errors with regard to the Temple ritual, which St. Barnabas was not likely to do. The so-called "errors" are: (a) the high priest sacrificing *daily* (vii. 27; x. 11)—but the high priest was free to do this; (b) the pot of manna and Aaron's rod placed *in the ark* (ix. 4), though not so described in 1 Kings viii. 9—but in the tabernacle they were at least close to the ark (Exod. xvi. 34; Numb. xvii. 10); (c) the altar of incense is said to belong to the *holiest place* (ix. 4)—but it did belong to it in the sense of sanctifying the approach to it, though it was placed outside it: see 1 Kings vi. 22. No one can reasonably say that these statements are of such a nature as to prove that the Epistle was not written by a Levite.

[Sidenote: To whom written.]

The title says "To the Hebrews." The character of the Epistle suggests this. It was plainly written for Jewish Christians, and apparently for some particular community of them (v. 11, 12; vi. 9, 10; x. 32-34; xiii. 1, 7, 19, 23). Which community, it is difficult to say. The Jewish Christians of Rome have been suggested, and in support of this the reference to Italian Christians (xiii. 24) has been quoted. It is a strange fact that this theory about the destination of the Epistle is favoured by some critics who assign it to a late date. For if it was really written to Rome, the date must be early. It is almost inconceivable that the author should have said, "Ye have not yet resisted unto blood," to the Christians of *Rome* after the persecution of A.D. 64-65. Some town in Syria or Palestine is more likely than Rome, and Antioch seems a probable destination for the Epistle. The community must have been familiar with Greek, and at the same time must have been under strong temptations to relapse into Judaism. They had for the sake of Christ left the warm social life of Judaism. They felt isolated and depressed. The splendour of the temple worship and the zeal of Jewish patriotism were luring them back to their old religion. They felt that they had perhaps deserted a magnificent reality for a shadowy hope. Such circumstances fit with the theory that the community dwelt in Palestine or Syria, and the same theory is supported by the fact that these Christians had been converted long ago (v. 12), and had heard the apostles (ii. 3).

[Sidenote: Where and when written.]

Probably from Italy, as shown by xiii. 24. The date may be put about A.D. 66. A generation of Christians had passed away (xiii. 2). The doom of Jerusalem was approaching (x. 25; viii. 13; xiii. 13). The frequent reference to the Levitical worship, as exerting an attractive force, must imply that the temple was still standing. The Epistle must therefore be earlier than 70.

It is true that the references to the Levitical worship are sometimes more appropriate to the ancient tabernacle than to the temple, and this fact is urged by those who maintain that the temple was already destroyed when the Epistle was written. But this is no answer to the fact that the Jewish worship is throughout assumed to be in existence. The author is not opposing the propaganda of Jewish rabbis or the attractions of synagogues which were connected with the temple by tradition only. He is opposing a great living system with its priesthood and its ritual. And in order to criticize Judaism he deals with the *tabernacle*, concerning which the Old Testament gave definite directions. This was a more effective method than discussing the temple which superseded the tabernacle.

[Sidenote: Character and contents.]

Hebrews is marked by a complete unity of argument. Though the thread of the argument is sometimes dropped for the sake of practical exhortation, it is soon resumed and logically carried on.

Christ as the Son of God is a manifestation of God superior to all other manifestations. He is far above the prophets, and above the angels, who neither created the material world nor have the "world to come" subject unto them. He towers above Moses, who was only a servant and a stone in the house of God, for He is the Son, and built the house. He is above Joshua; for He has won a rest for the people of God, of which the rest of Canaan was a mere type. Neither under Joshua nor under David did the people of God reach the ideal sabbath rest which God has promised (i.-iv. 13).

Christ as High Priest is above the Aaronic priesthood, for He is "after the order of Melchizedek" (Ps. ex. 4) (iv. 14-v. 10). Then the writer, before giving the full interpretation of Christ's high priesthood, makes a digression to urge the need of greater spiritual insight on the part of his readers (v. 11-vi. 12). They can be sure of God's blessing if they have faith and patience (vi. 13-20). The unique position of Melchizedek is then expounded. In Gen. xiv. nothing is said of Melchizedek's descent or of his death. Thus he stands forth in contrast to the Levitical priests whose descent is described, and who die and are succeeded by others. He was also superior to those priests, because Levi, in the person of his father Abraham, paid tithes to Melchizedek. Since Melchizedek's priesthood is superior to that of the Levitical priests, much more is that of Christ, of whom Melchizedek, great as he was, is only a type. Then the author shows that the rise of a new priesthood must imply the birth of a new religious system. Christ "hath His priesthood unchangeable," but needs not to repeat His sacrifice (vii.).

Then the author shows that the new liturgy and the new sanctuary of the Christian Church are superior to the liturgy and the sanctuary of Judaism. Though Christ's blood was shed only once, He retains the character of Priest (viii. 3); He hath "somewhat to offer," viz. Himself in His sacred manhood in heaven. He thus acts as a Mediator of the new covenant promised in the Old Testament (viii. 6-13). The tabernacle was only a temporary parable; Christ acts as High Priest in the holy of holies, the actual presence of God typified by the tabernacle; He has consecrated the new covenant between man and God by His own blood (ix.). The repetition of the Levitical sacrifices proves their impotence. But that of Christ is adequate. It is an offering of inherent value, being the offering of the will of Christ, instead of the offering of unconscious beasts. And we need no other atonement, for His unique offering has a perpetual value (x. 1-18).

The writer then proceeds to insist upon the appropriation and application of the truths which he has expounded. It is our privilege to have full confidence, and our duty to assemble for worship: apostasy is most serious (x. 19-39). The writer next describes the nature of faith, which is a faculty which makes the future as if it were present, and the unseen as if it were visible. It is illustrated by a magnificent roll-call of heroes from Abel to the Incarnation. These heroes, who saw both worlds, and realized how petty the material world is compared with the spiritual, had real insight (xi.). Emulate their example, enduring persecution, knowing that our Mount Zion is superior to Sinai, and our coming to church a reunion with angels and saints (xii.).

The Epistle closes with a practical exhortation concerning brotherly love, hospitality, prisoners, marriage, and contentment. The ministers who had formerly had rule over the readers are to be remembered. We are not to be unsettled by strange teachings. "We have an altar" of which the Jewish priests may not partake. Our sin offering, Jesus, is given to us as food. We must go to Him outside the camp of Judaism. After an injunction to obey the clergy and a request for prayers, the Epistle concludes. Just before the end it is stated that "our brother Timothy hath been set at liberty" (xiii.).

The whole Epistle is peculiarly dignified, eloquent, and persuasive, and its elegant Greek and delicate Alexandrian philosophy make it a literary treasure.

We may conclude with some further remarks on the writer's doctrine of Christ's Person and of the Jewish Law.

Knowing that these Christians were in danger of drifting away from Christ, the writer calls their special attention to His Person, in order that they may carefully consider who He is before deciding to part from Him. The doctrine corresponds most exactly with that which we find in Colossians and in John. It is declared in the most positive manner that Christ is essentially divine. He reflects His Father's glory, is the expression of His essence, and the Sustainer of the universe (i. 3). He is the God whose throne is eternal, and the Lord who made the earth (i. 8, 10). Yet He became "a little lower than the angels" (ii. 9), and, though entirely sinless, He was so truly human as to become the pattern of obedience (x. 7), humility (v. 5), reverent piety (v. 7), and fidelity (iii. 2). By the discipline of suffering He was made perfect for His redeeming work (v. 8, 9). It is made evident that this process of perfection did not consist in the diminution of sin, but in the development of goodness. Nowhere do we find a more profound view of suffering and virtue, or a more pathetic delineation of the character of Jesus.

It has already been hinted that the author regards the Jewish Law differently from St. Paul. The latter had lived under the goad of a Pharisaic interpretation of the Law of Moses, which laid down so many regulations as to what ought to be done, and gave so little assistance towards doing it, that escape from such a system was like an escape from penal servitude. When he speaks of the Law, he regards it primarily as a system of stern moral requirements. But the author of Hebrews regards the Law as primarily a system of worship. He implies that it was in some sense a "good tidings" (iv. 2). He teaches that the Law was a "shadow" of those real "good things" which constitute the world of truth in heaven, while the Gospel is the "image" or adequate representation of those holy realities. The Law is therefore a rough unsubstantial outline of truth, while the Gospel is exact and solid. Both writers regard the Law as divine in origin, and both regard it as insufficient and rudimentary (vii. 16; cf. Gal. iv. 3, 9). But St. Paul thinks of the Law as weak "through the flesh," *unable to overcome* the resistance which it encounters from man's lower instincts, while the author of Hebrews thinks of it as *unable to cleanse and make perfect* the human conscience.

ANALYSIS

The subject of the Epistle: CHRISTIANITY AS THE FINAL RELIGION. The contrast of the Old Revelation and the New in method, time, and messengers; the divine personality and incarnation of the Son (i. 1-4).

A. The superiority of the Son, the Mediator of the New Revelation, to the angels, and to the human founders of the Jewish polity: i. 5-iv. 13.

a. Scripture shows the Son to be above the angels (i. 5-14).

b. The danger of rejecting the Son's revelation (ii. 1-4).

c. The Son of Man through suffering fulfils the high destiny of mankind (ii. 5-18).

d. The dignity of Jesus is far above that of Moses, He is the Maker and Son, Moses represents the house in which he is a servant (iii. 1-6).

e. Faith is necessary if we would enter the promised land of rest (iii. 7-19).

f. Encouragement as well as warning can be based on the failure of the Israelites. Under Joshua they did not reach their rest. The promise of it remains for us (iv. 1-13).

B. The high-priesthood of Christ, superior to that of Aaron's line, universal and royal: iv. 14-vii. 28.

a. Transition to the doctrine of Christ's high priesthood (iv. 14-16).

b. The characteristics of a high priest, human sympathy and divine appointment, fulfilled in Christ (v. 1-10).

c. A digression to urge the readers to advance; the writer's hope for the Hebrews, God's blessing is assured (v. 11-vi. 20).

d. The characteristics of Christ, as perfect and universal High Priest, shadowed forth by Melchizedek (vii.).

C. The liturgy and sanctuary of Christ superior to those of Judaism: viii. i-x. 18.

a. Christ offers sacrifice in heaven (viii. 1-6).

b. Thus He maintains the New Covenant between God and man promised in the Old Testament (viii. 7-13).

c. The sanctuary and priests of the Old Covenant (ix. 1-10).

d. Fuller explanation of the atoning work of Christ under the New Covenant (ix. 11-28).

e. The inadequacy of the old sacrifices, the abiding efficacy of Christ's one sacrifice (x. 1-18).

D. The appropriation and application of the above truths: x. 19-xiii. 25.

a. The privilege of entering the holy place with confidence, the duty of public worship (x. 19-39).

b. The past triumphs of heroes of the faith (xi.).

c. Exhortation to energy, endurance, fidelity to our Mount Zion and its divine utterances (xii.).

d. Detailed instructions (xiii.).

[1] Eusebius, *H. E.* v. 26, says that Irenaeus "mentions the Epistle to the Hebrews and the so-called Wisdom of Solomon, comparing certain expressions from them." Eusebius does not say that Irenaeus attributed it to St. Paul. We can compare words in Heb. i. 1 with Wisd. vii. 22; Heb. i. 3 with Wisd. xvi. 21; Heb. xii. 17 with Wisd. xii. 10; Heb. xiii. 7 with Wisd. ii. 17.

[2] Stephen Gobar, in a passage preserved by Photius, Cod. 232.

[3] The word "effulgence" (Heb. i. 3) is a favourite word with Philo. The interpretation of "King of Salem" as "King of peace" (Heb. vii. 2) occurs in Philo, and Heb. xiii. 5 has a quotation from Josh. i. 5 exactly resembling in form a quotation in Philo, *De conf. ling.*, 33.

[4] *De Pudic*, 20.

CHAPTER XIX THE CATHOLIC EPISTLES

The New Testament contains seven letters known as "Catholic," viz. that of James, 1 and 2 Peter, 1, 2, and 3 John, and that of Jude. These letters were added to the Canon of the New Testament later than the rest of its contents. In ancient manuscripts, versions, and catalogues their position in the New Testament varies, and for a long time they were often placed between Acts and St. Paul's Epistles. 1 Peter and 1 John were the first to be universally received. About A.D. 300 all seven were known and received in the Greek Churches, but nearly as late as A.D. 350 the Syrian Church was unacquainted with any of them except James. After this the Syrian Church adopted 1 Peter and 1 John, and finally the whole seven. This fact with regard to the Syrian Church is of peculiar importance. It shows us that we must take care not to argue that an Epistle is probably a forgery because an important Christian community was unacquainted with it at a comparatively late date. For the evidence for the genuineness of 1 Peter and 1 John is even stronger than the evidence for the genuineness of James. Yet at a time when the best Greek critics were entirely satisfied as to the genuineness of 1 Peter and 1 John, the Syrians did not recognize them. The only reasonable explanation of this is the simplest explanation, namely, that some Epistles were translated at a later date than others. Among Syrian writers we find two distinct tendencies. Writers who were entirely at home with Greek literature, and in communion with the orthodox Greek Church, like St. Ephraim or St. John of Damascus, used the same Catholic Epistles as the Christians of Alexandria or Jerusalem. On the other hand, Christians who were cut off by schism from the main body of Christendom continued for centuries to use exactly the same Canon of Scripture as that which had been employed by their ancestors before the schism. Thus Ebed Jesu, Metropolitan of Nisibis, and the last prelate of the Nestorian sect who wrote important works in Syriac, died in A.D. 1318. But we find that he only uses the three Catholic Epistles contained in the Peshitta Syriac version of the New Testament, probably completed soon after A.D. 400.

If we pass from the extreme east to the extreme west of ancient Christendom, we find ourselves confronted with similar but not identical facts. We find that a superior degree of authority was allowed to belong to 1 Peter and 1 John. There can be no doubt that in all the great centres of Christian life outside Syria these two Epistles were in the Canon by the year 200. The *Muratorian Fragment*, written in Italy about A.D. 180, mentions two Epistles of St. John and that of St. Jude. It contains no mention of 1 Peter, but there are grounds for believing that there was a reference to it in the lost portion which was devoted to Mark. It contains no mention of James, though that Epistle seems to be quoted in the *Shepherd* of Hermas, written at Rome about A.D. 140. It was long before James was universally regarded as part of the Canon. It is quoted as Scripture by Origen of Alexandria early in the 3rd century, but a hundred years later Eusebius says that it was disputed by a minority. It is accepted by Eusebius himself. The very private character of 2 and 3 John accounts for the slowness with which they won acceptance as part of the word of God, yet 2 John is backed by the high authority of Irenaeus, and both Epistles are obviously the work of the same author. The Second Epistle which bears the name of St. Peter is connected with peculiar difficulties, and possesses less evidence in its favour than any of the other Catholic Epistles.

We cannot do better than quote the admirable words in which Dr. Sanday has sketched the adventures of such books. "An Epistle lodged in the archives of a great and cultured Church like the Church of Rome would be one thing, and an Epistle straying about among the smaller communities of Bithynia or Pontus would be another; while an Epistle written to an individual like the Gaius of 3 St. John would have worse chances still. There were busy, careless, neglectful, and unmethodical people in those days as well as now; and we can easily imagine one of these precious rolls found with glad surprise, covered with dust in some forgotten hiding-place, and brought out to the view of a generation which had learnt to be more careful of its treasures. But even then, once off the main roads, circulation was not rapid; an obscure provincial Church might take some time in making its voice heard, and the authorities at headquarters might receive the reported discovery with suspicion. They might, or they might not, as it happened." [1]

But by degrees the customs of the different Churches were levelled. Before the end of the 4th century all the Catholic Epistles were accepted as canonical in Europe, and in a large part of the Christian world which lay beyond Europe. This leads us to inquire why these Epistles bear the name of Catholic. The answer seems to be that the name Catholic or General was given to the more important of the seven, because they were addressed to the Church Universal, or to groups of Churches, and not to individuals or to single Churches. The words Catholic Epistles therefore signify Circular or Encyclical Letters. Origen gives the name of Catholic to 1 Peter, 1 John, and Jude. By the 4th century the name was applied to all the seven. There can be little doubt that 2 and 3 John are not

Catholic in the sense of being Circular or Encyclical. But they were numbered with the others for the sake of convenience, being naturally associated with the first and more important letter by St. John.

The following table gives an idea of the gradual incorporation of the Catholic Epistles into the Canon. An * denotes a direct quotation or the expression of almost no doubt; a ? notes that the writer is aware of decided doubts, a () marks an uncertain reference.

I. COUNCILS—
Laodicea, A.D. 363 . . . . * * * * * * *
Rome, A.D. 382 . . . . * * * * * * *
Carthage, A.D. 397 . . . . * * * * * * *
II. EASTERN LISTS—
(a) *Syria.*
Ephraim, A.D. 370 . . . . . * * * * * * *
Chrysostom, A.D. 400 . . . . * * *
Peshitta version, ? A.D. 410 * * *
Junilius, A.D. 550 . . . . . ? * ? * ? ? ?
John of Damascus, A.D. 750 * * * * * * *
Ebed Jesu, A.D. 1300 . . . . * * *
(b) *Palestine.*
Eusebius, A.D. 330 . . . . . ? * ? * ? ? ?
Cyril, A.D. 348 . . . . . . * * * * * * *
(c) *Alexandria.*
Clement, A.D. 190 . . . . . * * * *
Origen, A.D. 220 . . . . . . * * ? * ? ? *
Athanasius, A.D. 367 . . . . * * * * * * *
(d) *Asia Minor.*
Polycarp, A.D. 110 . . . . . * *
Amphilochius, A.D. 380 . . . * * ? * ? ? ?
Gregory Nazianzen, A.D. 380 * * * * * * *
III. WESTERN LISTS—
(a) *Italy.*
Muratorian, A.D. 180 . . . . * * *
Hippolytus, A.D. 220 . . . . * ( ) *
(b) *Gaul.*
Irenaeus, A.D. 180 . . . . . * * *
(c) *Roman Africa.*
Tertullian, A.D. 200 . . . . * * *
[1] *Inspiration*, p. 368.

CHAPTER XX THE GENERAL EPISTLE OF JAMES

[Sidenote: The Author]

In the 4th century this Epistle was reckoned among the authentic documents of the apostolic period. It does not seem to have been universally known in the Church at an earlier period. It is not in the *Muratorian Fragment*. But it is plainly quoted by Irenaeus, though he does not mention the author's name. The same is true with regard to the *Shepherd* of Hermas, which was written at Rome about A.D. 140. Justin Martyr quotes the words "the devils shudder" (James ii. 19, *Trypho*, 49). Polycarp seems to quote James i. 27, and 1 Peter seems to show traces of its influence. The first writer who both quotes it and mentions the author is Origen.

It opens with the name of "James, a servant of God and of the Lord Jesus Christ." There can be no reasonable doubt that this is James "the Lord's brother." James the son of Zebedee was killed as early as A.D. 44, before which date it is unlikely that the Epistle was written. We have no reason to attribute the Epistle to the Apostle James "the Little." He does not seem to have been of sufficient prominence to write an authoritative letter "to the twelve tribes which are of the Dispersion." But such an action would have been exceedingly natural on the part of a saint who was bishop of "the mother of Churches," Jerusalem itself. It will be convenient to postpone the consideration of such evidence as we possess for the foregoing conclusion until we have discussed the exact relation of St. James to our Lord.

Three important theories must be mentioned as offering a solution of the difficult problem as to this relationship—

(a) That James, Joses, Simon, and Jude, mentioned in the Gospels as the "brethren" of our Lord, were His first cousins on His mother's side.

(b) That they were the children of Joseph and Mary.

(c) That they were the children of Joseph by a former wife.

The theory of St. Jerome (a) may be perhaps discarded without any further comment than that St. Jerome apparently invented it, that he claimed no traditional sanction for it, he did not hold it consistently himself in his later writings, and it is very difficult to reconcile it with Scripture. The theory of Helvidius (b), which called forth St. Jerome's attempted refutation, answers some verbal requirements of the Gospel narrative, and has found some skilful modern advocates. But with the possible exception of Tertullian, no Christian seems to have held it before Helvidius, and the theory that Mary had other children besides Jesus gave a profound shock to Christian sentiment. No argument can be brought against (c), the theory defended, though not originated, by St. Epiphanius, that the brethren of our Lord were children of St. Joseph by a former wife. It is in keeping with the strong tradition which maintained the perpetual virginity of the Blessed Virgin; it helps to explain the attitude of unbelief recorded in the Gospels of Christ's brethren, and at the same time requires no distortion of the literalness of the passages in which they are mentioned. There is hardly sufficient evidence to show that first cousins were ever called "brethren." But it would have been quite natural for those who called St. Joseph "the father of Jesus" to call St. Joseph's sons "the brothers of Jesus." And again, the supposition that the Blessed Virgin had no other son, seems strongly supported by the fact that at the crucifixion our Lord commended her to His beloved disciple, and not to one of St. Joseph's family.

This theory of St. Epiphanius is much older than the 4th century. It is sometimes urged against it that Origen derived it from the Apocryphal Gospels of the 2nd century, and that its popularity in the Church was owing to Origen's influence. But though the Apocryphal Gospels often contained fictions, we cannot argue that everything in them is fictitious. The tradition agrees with the words of Scripture, and gains support from some fragments of Hegesippus, a cultured Palestinian Christian, born about A.D. 100. He states directly that Symeon, the second bishop of Jerusalem, was the *cousin* of our Lord, because son of Clopas who was the brother of Joseph. He also calls James "the brother of the Lord," and in another passage speaks of Jude as "called brother" of the Lord. He therefore plainly distinguishes the cousins from the so-called "brethren." We then get the following genealogy:—

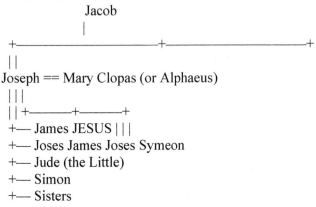

```
                    Jacob
                      |
      +—————————————————+—————————————————+
      ||
Joseph == Mary    Clopas (or Alphaeus)
      |||
      || +———————+———————+
      +— James JESUS |||
      +— Joses  James Joses Symeon
      +— Jude (the Little)
      +— Simon
      +— Sisters
```

We conclude, therefore, that St. James was the son of St. Joseph.

The writer of the Epistle frequently colours his sentences with words from the Old Testament, and assumes a knowledge of it among his readers. He makes no allusion to the Gentiles. He writes in a tone of authority and without any self-advertisement. He briefly uses for illustration certain natural phenomena which would be familiar to the people of Palestine, such as allusions to "the early and latter rain" (v. 7), the effect on vegetation of the burning wind (i. 11), the existence of salt or bitter springs (iii. 11), the cultivation of figs and olives (iii. 12), and the neighbourhood of the sea (i. 6; iii. 4). From such a cursory view of the character of this Epistle, it would seem reasonable to admit that it was written by a Palestinian Jewish Christian for the edification of Christians of the same race and locality.

We get the same impression when we study what is said by the writer about the readers. He speaks as though they had been under a law of bondage, but are now under a law of liberty (i. 25; ii. 12). They are in touch with men who are unbelievers, who blaspheme Christ and persecute Christians (ii. 6, 7). The believers are mostly poor (ii. 5); the few rich who are Christians are in danger of falling away through covetousness and pride (iv. 3-6, 13-16). The rich appear as oppressors, who luxuriously "nourish their hearts in a day of slaughter," and had even "killed the righteous" (v. 5, 6). The Church is ruled by "elders" (v. 14) like the Jewish synagogues, and the Christian "synagogue" is occasionally frequented by rich strangers (ii. 2). All this is well suited to the conditions of Christian life in Palestine. And it is difficult to find any locality equally appropriate. Even as late as the first part of the 2nd century rich Gentiles were reluctant to persecute Christians, and to describe them as blaspheming the name of Christ at any time within or near the apostolic age would be almost impossible. They regarded Christianity with good-natured contempt, not with blasphemous hostility. We have only to read Acts to see that among the Gentiles it was the poor and ignorant rather than the rich who began the persecution of the Christians. On the other hand, if we turn to the Jews, we find that the rich were the leaders of persecution. It was the wealthy Sadducee party in union with the influential Pharisees which harried the Church. The Gospels and Acts give repeated evidence on this point, and the evidence of the Jewish historian Josephus supplies the keystone of that evidence.

Against the Palestinian origin of the Epistle it is urged that the Greek is too correct and rhetorical. The style is vivacious and forcible. It contains many rather unusual Greek words, including six which are neither in the Septuagint version of the Old Testament nor in the rest of the New Testament, a long list of words which are found in the Septuagint and not in the New Testament, and seven rare classical or late Greek words. The whole question of the style of the Epistle requires the most delicate handling. But the style is distinctly unfavourable to the theory that the Epistle was written at a late date in a centre of Gentile Christianity. The Greek is neither the flowing Greek of a Greek, nor the rough provincial Greek which St. Paul spoke and wrote. It is slow and careful, with short sentences linked by repetitions. One epithet is piled effectively on another (*e.g.* iii. 15, 17), and abstract statements are avoided. Galilee was studded with Greek towns, and in Jerusalem Greek was well known. The Epistle might well have been written by a Jew of Palestine who had made a good use of his opportunities. And the introduction of some rare words in the midst of a simple moral exhortation is by no means a proof of complete mastery over Greek. It points, not to a mastery over the language, but to a painstaking familiarity with it.

These facts seem compatible with the few details which we know about St. James. Their full significance can only be appreciated when we know the difficulties which have beset the commentators who assign to the Epistle a date outside his lifetime.

Before considering the question of the date more minutely, we may collect together some points of interest connected with St. James.

St. James, like the other "brethren" of our Lord, watched the development of our Lord's career, but was unconvinced of the truth of His mission. After the Resurrection, our Lord, St. Paul tells us, "was seen of James." Perhaps this was the turning-point of his life, he, like St. Thomas, "saw and believed." The Gospel according to the Hebrews, one of the oldest of the Apocryphal Gospels, says that our Lord, after His Resurrection, "went to James and appeared to him—for James had sworn that he would not eat bread from that hour in which he drank the cup of the Lord, until he saw Him rising from the dead;—and again after a little while. 'Bring hither, saith the Lord, a table and bread.'" . . . "He brought bread, and blessed and brake it, and gave it to James the Just, and said unto him, 'My brother, eat thy bread, for the Son of man hath risen from the dead.'" There are other versions of the story which make the vow to be taken after the death of Christ. In spite of some absurdities in this Apocryphal

Gospel, it is possible that the legend is true, and that the sublime death of the Redeemer began to effect the repentance of His brother. However this may be, before Pentecost, A.D. 29, we find him joined to the Christian community at Jerusalem, where he afterwards attained a foremost position. In Gal. i. we find that St. Paul visited St. James and St. Peter at Jerusalem. In Acts xii. 17 St. Peter, on escaping from prison in A.D. 44, desires that news of his escape should be taken to St. James. In Gal. ii. St. Paul speaks of "James and Cephas and John" as pillars of the Church at Jerusalem. From Acts xv. we find that at this time, A.D. 49, St. James acted as president of the Council which determined how far the Gentile Christians need conform to the customs of the Jews. It is remarkable that the speech of St. James in Acts xv. and the circular despatched from the Council show several coincidences of style with the Epistle. If these coincidences are due to forgery, the forger has certainly used consummate self-restraint and skill.

Again, when St. Paul paid his last visit to Jerusalem, in A.D. 56, and the Jews accused him of advocating the abandonment of the Law of Moses and "the customs," it is St. James and his presbyters who advise him to go up to the Temple and purify himself with four Nazirites, and so reassure the "myriads" of Christian Jews who were zealous for the Law. Once more we cannot help observing how well this anxiety of St. James agrees with the very cautious tone of the Epistle with regard to distinctively Christian doctrine.

The end of St. James is recorded by Hegesippus and by Josephus. Hegesippus represents him living as a strict Nazirite, always frequenting the Temple, with knees as hard as a camel's because of his perpetual prayers.[1] He tells us that St. James was thrown from a pinnacle of the Temple, stoned, and clubbed to death at the order of the scribes and Pharisees for asserting that Jesus was on the right hand of God. From Josephus we learn that his martyrdom took place when a vacancy in the procuratorship caused by the death of Festus (in A.D. 62) gave the Sadducees the opportunity which they desired. He was dragged before the Sanhedrim, condemned and stoned. Josephus also gives us to understand that the more moderate Jews were not in sympathy with such a thoroughly unconstitutional proceeding, and that Agrippa deprived Ananus, the high priest, of his office for invading the rights of the civil power.

[Sidenote: To whom written.]

"The twelve tribes of the Dispersion." We might suppose that the writer had in his mind all the Jews who were dispersed throughout the world, but came to Jerusalem to offer sacrifice when they were able, and who were all bound by the religious obligation to pay the yearly tribute to the temple. There had been several dispersions in the history of the chosen people, to Assyria under Shalmaneser, to Babylon and Egypt in the time of Nebuchadnezzar, and to Rome under Pompeius. But ch. ii. 1 shows that the Epistle was written to men who acknowledged Jesus as Lord. It is therefore natural to think that it was written only to men who were both Christians and of Jewish origin. But there is another interpretation of the phrase "the twelve tribes." Some think that it is merely a symbolical name for the Christian Church composed both of Jews and Gentiles, and forming the new and spiritual Israel. Strong arguments have been brought forward in favour of each of these views, but the former seems to be the sounder. The argument that the Jews at this period could not have been called "twelve" tribes when only two had returned from the captivity, is disproved by the fact that the phrase is unquestionably used in this meaning in Acts xxvi. 7. We must frankly admit that St. Paul speaks of the Gentile Christians as forming part of the new Israel of God, but he never alludes to them as part of twelve tribes. In Rev. vii. the twelve tribes still mean Christian Jews in contrast with the "great multitude" of redeemed Gentiles. Justin Martyr speaks of "your twelve tribes" in addressing Trypho[2] the Jew, and several instances are to be found in early Christian literature where the words are used in this literal sense.

We may therefore rest content with this literal meaning. But we must maintain it with reserve in view of the fact that St. Peter applies the word "dispersion" to the new and ideal Israel. And we must beware of arguing that the word "synagogue" (ii. 2) proves that the readers were necessarily Jews. The word "synagogue" was for a long time occasionally applied to the Gentile Christian congregations, as we find in the *Shepherd* of Hermas[3] (A.D. 140) and Theophilus[4] (A.D. 180).

[Sidenote: When and where written.]

We have already seen that Palestine is the most likely place, and as St. James lived at Jerusalem, the Epistle was probably written there. The date has always been a hopeless problem to those who reject the authenticity of the Epistle. That it was written by a heretic in Palestine about A.D. 70, or by a Catholic at Rome about A.D. 90, or that it represents a "Catholicized Paulinism" of A.D. 140, or that it is a patchwork of homilies written soon after

A.D. 120, are guesses which have been made but not substantiated. The fact that it was written before A.D. 62 is self-evident if we admit that it was written by St. James. But it is also corroborated by the fact that 1 Peter, written about A.D. 64, seems to show a knowledge of this Epistle. Far more complicated is the question as to whether St. James shows any knowledge of St. Paul's Epistles. He insists so pointedly on the need of being justified *by works* that some writers have thought that he is attacking St. Paul's doctrine of justification *by faith.* The idea must be dismissed. Such a masterly writer would not have attacked what an apostle did not really hold. St. James, in attacking a theory of justification by faith, is condemning a faith which means only orthodox intellectual assent. St. Paul, in defending his doctrine of justification by faith, is upholding a faith which implies energetic and loving service. The two doctrines simply supplement one another. When Luther called the Epistle to the Galatians his "wife" and called the Epistle of St. James an "Epistle of straw," he simply showed that he understood neither. St. James is not only not criticizing St. Paul; he is perhaps not even criticizing a popular perversion of St. Paul's doctrine. The question of the justification of Abraham was a favourite subject of discussion among the Jews, and the teaching of our Lord had shown the superiority of a living faith over dead works. There is no difficulty in supposing that some Jewish believers were confused with regard to these great matters before they had read a word of St. Paul's letters. And to such men the Epistle of St. James might be of the highest value.

In spite of this, there often seems to be a verbal connection between this Epistle and those of St. Paul. The connection is admitted by critics of the most different schools. Moreover, some are of opinion that there is a connection between James and the Epistle to the Hebrews, ch. xi. These connections have been exaggerated, but they are hard to deny. Now, if St. James had borrowed from any of these Epistles, it would be very difficult for us to account for the extreme simplicity of his doctrine. On the other hand, there is no difficulty in the fact that they put his words in a more elaborate setting. And as St. Paul's opponents declared that they were backed by St. James, we may be sure that St. Paul would eagerly read anything written by St. James. We may therefore place this Epistle earlier than St. Paul's Epistles to Corinth and Rome, and perhaps earlier than any of his extant Epistles.

It is sometimes objected to this that it is "grotesque" to suppose that St. James would have originated the practice of writing religious Epistles. It is said that the practice must have been begun by an apostle of supreme originality, and one who travelled widely, therefore by St. Paul. But we have no means of deciding the question. And as St. Paul may have written Epistles before he wrote those now extant, we may still hold that St. Paul began the practice, and that this Epistle is nevertheless older than the works of St. Paul which we now possess. We can, therefore, see no good reason for denying that this Epistle is as early as A.D. 50.

[Sidenote: Character and Contents.]

The Epistle is intensely practical, and though it is in no sense anti-doctrinal, it does not discuss doctrine. The evils against which it contends all concern conduct. The good which it recommends is persistent well-doing in accordance with the new moral law of Christianity. The sole validity of the law of love (ii. 8), the gift of a new birth by the word of truth, making us heirs of God (i. 18; ii. 5), the mention of the author's servitude to Christ (i. 1), and the ascription of divine power to His name (v. 14), show conclusively that the writing is not, as some say, of Jewish origin. The tone is austere, and the Epistle contains no word of praise for the readers.

A strong argument in favour of the genuineness of the Epistle is furnished by the numerous parallels which it presents to the Synoptic Gospels. These parallels are not quotations from the Gospels, but they show that the writer was saturated with the kind of teaching which the Gospels record. The connection with the Sermon on the Mount as recorded by St. Matthew is particularly plain. Among the numerous proofs of this connection we must content ourselves with noticing the agreement as to the spiritual view of the Law (Jas. i. 25; ii. 8, 12, 13; Matt. v. 17-44), the blessings of adversity (Jas. i. 2, 13; ii. 5; v. 7, 8; Matt. v. 3-12), the dangers of wealth (Jas. i. 10, 11; ii. 6, 7; iv. 13-16; v. 1-6; Matt. vi. 19-21, 24-34), the true nature of prayer (Jas. i. 5-8; iv. 3; v. 13-18; Matt. vi. 6-13), the necessity of forgiving others (Jas. ii. 13; Matt. vi. 14, 15), the tree known by its fruits (Jas. iii. 11, 12; Matt. vii. 16-20), the prohibition of oaths (Jas. v. 12; Matt. v. 34-37), the Judge before the door (Jas. v. 9; Matt. xxiv. 33). Many other coincidences can be found. The "perfect law" upheld by St. James, a law both "free" and "royal," irresistibly reminds us of the legislation of the Messianic King in our first Gospel.

In v. 14-16 we have a direction given with regard to the anointing of the sick by the presbyters of the Church. This rite, perverted by the Gnostics in the 2nd century, survived that perversion. The first full directions for it in a Catholic document are in the prayers of Bishop Sarapion of Thmuis in Egypt, about A.D. 350. In the Eastern

Church the oil used for this purpose may be consecrated by presbyters, contrary to the usual practice of the West, which requires it to be consecrated by a bishop.

ANALYSIS

Salutation (i. 1).

Human trial and the wisdom which enables us to profit by it, a warning against double-mindedness, Christianity exalts the lowly, riches are transitory, trial brings blessing, trial due to lust is not a trial from God but from self, God is the Source of all our good (i. 2-18).

We must receive the divine word with humility and act upon it, kindness and purity are the best ceremonial (i. 19-27).

Christian behaviour towards rich and poor to be based on the royal law of love; violation of that law is a breach of God's command, which embraces motive as well as action (ii. 1-13).

Intellectual faith is no substitute for godly works, Abraham and Rahab were justified by works (ii. 13-26).

The responsibility of teaching, the difficulty and importance of controlling the tongue (iii. 1-12).

Christian wisdom contrasted with the animal wisdom of faction (iii. 13-18).

The cause of quarrelling is selfish desire, which infects even your prayers, the adultery of a soul which indulges in worldliness and pride, cease from finding fault, worldliness is shown in business plans made without reference to God (iv.).

Luxurious wealth denounced, it is the rich who have persecuted the righteous, patience is commended (v. 1-11).

Swear not, prayer and praise, the anointing of the sick with prayer, mutual confession of sins and prayer, the blessing on those who convert a sinner (v. 12-20).

[1] Quoted by Eusebius, *H. E.* ii. 23.

[2] *Trypho.* 126.

[3] *Mand.* xi. 9.

[4] *Ad Autol.* i. 14.

CHAPTER XXI THE FIRST EPISTLE GENERAL OF PETER

[Sidenote: The Author.]

The author describes himself as "Peter, an apostle of Jesus Christ" (i. 1). Few books of the New Testament are so well attested as this Epistle.

The external evidence for its authenticity is strong, and stronger than that for any other Catholic Epistle except 1 John. It seems to be quoted in *Didaché*, i. 4. The letter of Polycarp written about A.D. 110 shows a complete familiarity with 1 Peter. He evidently regarded it as a letter of the highest authority. His contemporary Papias was acquainted with it, and so far as we can determine from Eusebius, he referred to it directly as the work of St. Peter. The Epistle of Barnabas, the date of which is uncertain, but which is probably as old as A.D. 98 or even older, quotes 1 Pet. ii. 5. Again, it seems certain that the Epistle is quoted, though not by name, in the Epistle of Clement of Rome, A.D. 95. It is quite unnecessary for us to point to important references in writers of the latter part of the 2nd century and onwards. An Epistle which has the triple support of Clement, Polycarp, and Papias is, so far as external evidence is concerned, beyond the reach of any sober criticism.

The apostle was first called "Simon, the son of John" (according to the correct reading in John xxi. 15, 16, 17), and was a fisherman of Bethsaida. He was brought to Jesus by his brother Andrew, and, like him, had been a disciple of John the Baptist. Our Lord at once discerned his capacity, and gave him the surname of Cephas (Aramaic) or Peter (Greek), signifying a rock or stone. Peter was the first disciple to confess the Messiahship of our Lord, and was rewarded by the promise of the keys of the kingdom of heaven (Matt. xvi. 13-19). With John and James he was admitted to a peculiarly close relationship with Jesus (Mark v. 37; Matt. xvii. 1; xxvi. 37; cf. Mark iii. 16, 17). He thrice denied that he was a disciple of Jesus on the night when Jesus was tried and condemned. He bitterly repented, and on the third day after the Crucifixion he, again in the company of John, hastened to the sepulchre and found it empty. He was permitted several times to see the risen Lord, who cancelled his threefold denial by graciously drawing from him a threefold confession of his love, and commanded him to feed His lambs and His sheep. Our Lord also predicted his martyrdom (John xx. and xxi.; Luke xxiv. 33, 34; 1 Cor. xv. 5).

In Acts St. Peter appears as the leader of the Church. At the election of Matthias in place of Judas, at the descent of the Holy Ghost at Pentecost, at the admission of the Gentiles in the person of Cornelius and his family to the privileges of the new covenant, at the emancipation of the Gentile Christians from the Jewish ceremonial law at the Council of Jerusalem, St. Peter is foremost (Acts i. 15-26; ii. 1-42; x.; xv. 6-11). Soon after the Council St. Peter was at Antioch, and weakly "dissembled" by disguising his belief in the truth that the Gentile Christians were on the same spiritual level as the Jewish Christians. He was rebuked by St. Paul (Gal. ii. 11-14).

He does not seem to have laboured in Rome until near the end of his life. The Roman tradition that he was bishop of that city for twenty-five years is almost certainly a legend, based on the fact that twenty-five years elapsed between the year when the apostles were believed to have temporarily left Jerusalem (twelve years after the Crucifixion) and the date of his martyrdom. There is, however, no ground for disputing the fact that he died at Rome during the Neronian persecution. There are several reasons for thinking that he survived St. Paul for a short period, though St. Augustine asserts that he was martyred before St. Paul. He was crucified near the middle of the circus of Nero, on a spot afterwards marked by a "chapel of the crucifixion." He was buried nigh at hand. His tomb, probably in the form of a *cella* or open apse, is mentioned by Caius of Rome about A.D. 200. A huge basilica was built over it by the Emperor Constantine, and remained until it was replaced in the 16th century by the present St. Peter's. In spite of his unique position, St. Peter in 1 Pet. v. 1 speaks of himself as a "presbyter," as St. John does in 2 John 1 and 3 John 1 (compare also 1 Tim. iv. 14, where St. Paul reckons himself as a member of the "presbytery"). At this period, and for many years later, the word "presbyter" was vague enough to be applied to the highest officers of the Church.

The internal evidence afforded by the Epistle is in harmony with St. Peter's experience. (1) The writer claims to have been "a witness of the sufferings of Christ" (v. 1), and contrasts himself and his readers in saying (i. 8), "Whom not having seen ye love." (2) He lays stress upon the pastoral aspect of our Lord's work (ii. 25; v. 2-4), as though writing under a sense of the special pastoral charge given to him by our Lord. (3) His injunction, "all of you gird yourselves with humility"—literally, "put on humility like a slave's apron"—seems to be a reminiscence of the action of our Lord that astonished St. Peter when "He took a towel and girded Himself" at the Last Supper. (4) There are points of resemblance between the Epistle and the speeches delivered by St. Peter in Acts. (5) The appeal to Old Testament predictions of Christ's sufferings (1 Pet. i. 11; Acts iii. 18), the reference to the stone that was rejected by the builders (1 Pet. ii. 7, 8; Acts iv. 11), the description of the cross as the "tree" (1 Pet. ii. 24; Acts v. 30), are coincidences which suggest a common authorship while they seem too small to be designed. (6) The graphic and pictorial style of the Epistle bears resemblance to the style of Mark, which is based on St. Peter's preaching. We may mention the word "put to silence" (ii. 15)—literally, "muzzle"— which St. Mark (i. 25; iv. 39) applies to the subduing of an unclean spirit and the stilling of a rough sea.

Against the authenticity of the Epistle it is sometimes said that it is improbable that St. Peter, whose mission was to the Jews, would address Churches in which St. Paul had laboured, and which were largely composed of Gentiles. But in no case could such action on the part of St. Peter be thought incredible. And if St. Peter survived St. Paul, as he very probably did, it would be particularly fitting for him to write to them after St. Paul's martyrdom. Many critics have been inclined to pronounce the Epistle spurious on the ground that it seems to be so strongly influenced by St. Paul's teaching as to represent St. Paul's own school of thought. We find, as in St. Paul's writings, the phrase "in Christ" (iii. 16; v. 10, 14), and the second advent of Christ called by the name "revelation" (i. 7, 13; iv. 13). Moreover, there are numerous verses which can be compared with verses in St. Paul's Epistles, particularly in Romans and Ephesians.[1] We must not fail to notice in passing, that if this Epistle, which manifestly belongs to the 1st century, does actually quote Ephesians, as some affirm, the authenticity of Ephesians is thereby very strongly corroborated. But in any case the similarity between the Epistle and St. Paul's writings cannot be reasonably urged against its genuineness. The once popular theory that St. Paul held a fundamentally different conception of Christianity from that held by St. Peter has completely broken down. There is not a shred of evidence for believing that the semi-Christian Jews who lived in Palestine in the 2nd century represented St. Peter's type of Christianity, or that the teaching of St. Peter excluded the deep teaching of St. Paul. He was susceptible to external influences, and he may have caught the tone of St. Paul while living in a community which St. Paul had so profoundly influenced. This tone seems to mark 1 Peter.

But a further point must be mentioned in this connection. Modern writers have too readily adopted the habit of labelling certain expressions and doctrines as Pauline and assuming that St. Paul *originated* them. No doubt the apostle of the Gentiles possessed a mind as original as it was fertile. But it is at least reasonable to suppose that a common creed and a common training produced similar habits of thought in many cultivated and eager minds. St. Paul himself frequently writes as if his readers, even those who had not seen his face, were quite familiar with a treasury of words and ideas which he employs. We cannot legitimately argue that he was the first and only coiner of such words and ideas. For instance, the phrase "in Christ," which we have quoted above, is often said to have been directly borrowed from St. Paul. But the idea of abiding in Christ is implied in Matt. and Mark, and expounded in John. It reaches back to the Old Testament idea of abiding "in God" (Ps. lvi. 4; lxii. 7; Isa. xlv. 25). It would be quite natural in any Christian who had adequately realized the truth of the Incarnation. We can therefore repudiate without hesitation the assertion that the writer is more affected "by the teaching of Paul than of Jesus." The imagery employed by the writer is of a distinctive character. It is almost entirely derived from the Old Testament, and is narrower in its range than that of St. Paul. The figures are drawn from birth and family life (i. 3, 14, 17, 22; ii. 2), nomadic life (i. 1, 17; ii. 11), temple and worship (ii. 3; iii. 15), building (ii. 4), fields and pastoral life (i. 4; v. 2, 8), military life (i. 5; ii. 11, iv. 1), painting (ii. 21), working in metals (i. 7; iv. 12). Some of these figures suggest that the author was a Jew by birth, and also that he was not a mere copyist of St. Paul.

Again, we must notice that 1 Peter shows a dependence upon James.[2] While we therefore grant that the author of this Epistle seems to have made use of St. Paul's writings, we must be prepared to grant that he also made use of a document written by one who has been frequently declared by modern critics to have been antagonistic to St. Paul. A tradition found as early as Origen, and in itself extremely probable, represents St. Peter as having organized the Church at Antioch, and St. Peter probably became acquainted with the Epistle of St. James while at Antioch and before his arrival at Rome. In any case, the author shows himself by no means exclusively indebted to St. Paul, and the candid student must therefore admit that it is unreasonable to discredit this Epistle on the ground that it represents St. Peter as preaching "Paulinism."

It is also asserted that the Greek is too flowing to have been written by St. Peter, especially if Papias is right in saying that St. Peter required the services of St. Mark as "interpreter." The style of the Greek is, indeed, good. It contains a considerable number of classical Greek words, though it is also saturated with the language of the Septuagint. It is simple, correct, and impressive. But the large extent to which Greek was spoken in Palestine, and the fact that it was the language of Antioch, make it quite possible that St. Peter obtained a considerable mastery over Greek. We cannot attach a quite definite meaning to the word "interpreter." It need not imply that St. Peter always, or even at any time in his later life, required his Aramaic to be translated into Greek. It is not unusual for a clever modern missionary to lecture and write in correct Chinese after a very few years of practice, and there would be nothing strange if St. Peter soon acquired a comparatively easy language such as Hellenistic Greek. It is therefore quite unnecessary for some half-hearted apologists to suggest that the Epistle was mainly or entirely written for St. Peter by his secretary, Silvanus (1 Pet. v. 12). The expression and connection of the ideas contained in it are far too natural and easy for us to think that two hands were concerned in its composition, and the tone of authority used in v. 1 can only be explained on the theory that St. Peter or a forger wrote the Epistle. The language of ch. v. is most easily explained by the theory that Silvanus, a trusted friend and delegate of St. Peter, carried the letter. The letter was purposely made short (v. 12) because its lessons were to be enforced by Silvanus.

[Sidenote: To whom written.]

"To the elect who are sojourners of the Dispersion in Pontus, Galatia, Cappadocia, Asia, and Bithynia." Considerable difficulty is attached to this address. At first sight it seems to mean those Christians of Asia Minor north of the Taurus mountains who had been converted from Judaism. But there are some verses in the Epistle which seem to imply that the readers had been pagans. These verses are i. 14; ii. 9, 10; iii. 6; iv. 3. They suggest that the readers had led a licentious heathen life, and had been only recently admitted to any covenant with God. The bearing of some of them is a little uncertain. For instance, ii. 10 says that the converts in time past "were no people, but now are the people of God"—the same verse that St. Paul in Rom. ix. 25 applies to the calling of the Gentiles. This verse is thought to furnish a strong argument for those scholars who hold that the Epistle is addressed to Gentiles, and that "sojourners of the Dispersion" must be taken in a figurative sense, meaning Christians who are exiled from the heavenly Canaan. But as the verse is from Hos. i. 10, and is applied by Hosea himself to the Jews, it is certainly *possible* to hold that St. Peter also applies it to Jews. In this case the word "Dispersion" would retain its literal meaning, and the Epistle would be written to converts from Judaism. But the reference to "idolatries" in iv. 3 cannot be applied to Jews. And it would be quite unnatural for St. Peter to speak about the heathen thinking it "strange" that converted *Jews* refused to join in their idolatrous excesses. The word "you" in i. 12 suggests that the readers belonged to a different race from the Hebrew prophets. Finally, the phrase "elect of the Dispersion" must be compared with "in Babylon, elect" (v. 13). Like the name "Babylon" for Rome, the word "Dispersion" is a Jewish phrase taken over by the Christian Church. We agree, then, with St. Jerome and St. Augustine in holding that this Epistle was written to Gentiles.

[Sidenote: Where and when written.]

The Epistle says, "She that is in Babylon, elect together with you, saluteth you" (v. 13). This means the Church in Rome. The name "Babylon" is applied to Rome in the Revelation, and from an early period the Christians would naturally be inclined to give this name to a city which had become, like Babylon of old, the centre of worldliness and oppression. It is practically certain that St. Peter spent his last days in Rome. Moreover, St. Mark was with St. Peter when this Epistle was written (v. 13), and from 2 Tim. iv. 11 we know that St. Mark was invited to Rome about A.D. 64. It is most improbable that "Babylon" signifies either the Babylon near Cairo, or the great city on the Euphrates. Three facts enable us to determine the date: (1) The presence of Mark in Rome. (2) The fact that St. Peter appears never to have been in Rome when Colossians was written in A.D. 60—so that the Epistle cannot be earlier than A.D. 60. (3) The allusion in iv. 13-15 to the fact that Christians are already punished for being named Christians. In the period described in Acts they are not yet punished merely for being Christians, but for specific crimes alleged against them by their opponents. It is often asserted that this Epistle must be later than the time of Nero, on the ground that it was after Nero's time that the name *Christian* ensured the legal condemnation of any one who bore it. But this assertion is not supported by the Roman historians Tacitus and Suetonius. Their words support the contention that the kind of persecution mentioned in this Epistle began under Nero in A.D. 64. When the Epistle was written this persecution had probably begun, but it had not yet assumed its most savage form.[3] (4) St. Peter himself suffered under Nero, not later than A.D. 67. We may therefore confidently date the Epistle about A.D. 64.

It appears from v. 12 that in writing this Epistle St. Peter was assisted by "Silvanus, our faithful brother," as an amanuensis. He is probably the "Silas" (another form of the same name) mentioned in Acts xv. 22, 32, 40, and the Silvanus in 1 Thess. i. 1; 2 Thess. i. 1, 2 Cor. i. 19.

[Sidenote: Character and Contents.]

This Epistle is highly practical, and though it is rich in doctrinal elements, it endeavours to instruct the readers in conduct rather than doctrine. The two key-words of the Epistle are *suffering* and *hope*, and the sufferings of Christ and the glories which crowned them furnish St. Peter with encouragement. Though he writes in plain sympathy with the liberal Christianity of St. Paul, his language throughout bears the impress of the Old Testament. Christ is the "lamb" (i. 19) and the "corner-stone" (ii. 6); Christians are the "elect race" (ii. 9) and the "royal priesthood" (ii. 9). Without discussing the problems raised by God's predestination of the Jews, he says that they were "appointed" unto stumbling, and their stumbling seems to be regarded as the punishment which God attached to their disobedience.

The fact that in i. 2 the names of the Three Persons of the Trinity are given in an order which does not correspond with the order of their revelation in the history of religion, indicates that they are regarded as coequal. We may note that in iv. 19 the Father is called "faithful Creator," a unique expression. The teaching about the work of Christ is full. He is often simply called "Christ" without the name "Jesus." He is called "Lord," and His special divine Sonship is implied (i. 3). The real existence of our Lord before His birth on earth is also implied. It has been said that i. 20 signifies that He was only known to the Father as destined to exist in the future. This interpretation is excluded by i. 11, which shows that His Spirit inspired the prophets before His birth. It is still more definitely excluded by iii. 18, 19. Here it is shown that His personality resided neither in His flesh, nor in His human spirit clothed "in which" He preached to the dead. This spirit was therefore taken by a personality which existed previous to the creation of the spirit. The Atonement is prominent. Christ's death is both an example and a redemption which procured God's grace. He died "for the unrighteous." He carried our sins in His body to the cross (ii. 24). The Resurrection is one of the "glories" which followed His sufferings (i. 11). It is a unique motive to our faith (i. 21), and the cause of the efficacy of our baptism (iii. 21). The Ascension is the fact which guarantees to us the present rule of Christ (iii. 22). In iv. 6 we have an important statement with regard to the dead, which must be studied in relation to iii. 18-20. The purpose of Christ's preaching to those who died before the gospel came was that though judged they yet might live. Blessings which they had not known on earth were offered to them by the dead but living Christ.

The practical side of the Epistle is simple but solemn. It deals with the privileges (i. 3-ii. 10), duties (ii. 11-iv. 11), and trials (iv. 12-v. 11) of the brethren. It seems to be written with the hope that the Christians may perhaps disarm persecution if they abstain from vainly attempting to set every one to rights and are scrupulously loyal to the Government (ii. 14-17).

ANALYSIS

Salutation (i. 1, 2).

The joy of salvation, a joy which springs from faith; this salvation was foretold by the prophets: the fruits of salvation, seriousness, love towards others, growth, the privilege of being built upon Christ: Christians are the true Israel (i. 3-ii. 10).

The Christian brotherhood and its duties, submission to civil magistrates, slaves must obey even unreasonable masters, wives if good and gentle may win their husbands, husbands must reverence their wives: kindness must be the Christian's rule, there must be no return of evil for evil; suffering, if wrongfully endured, has its reward. Christ's sufferings issued in blessing, in His ministerial journey to Hades and His triumphant journey into heaven: Christ our Example, our rule is the will of God: Christian life must be guided in view of the approaching end of all things, each of our gifts is to be used for the good of the whole Church (ii. 11-iv. 11).

The trials of the brethren, trust in God in the midst of suffering, rejoice in your participation in Christ's suffering, bear the reproach that fell on Him, to suffer as a Christian is cause for thanksgiving, suffering to be expected, judgment is beginning: the relation of pastors and people, the presbyters not to act as slaves, hirelings, or tyrants: final counsels to humility and firmness (iv. 12-v. 11).

Commendation of the bearer, and salutations (v. 12-14).

[1] Compare 1 Pet. i. 14 with Rom. xii. 2; 1 Pet. i. 21 with Rom. iv. 24; 1 Pet. ii. 5 with Rom. xii. 1; 1 Pet. ii. 6, 7 with Rom. ix. 33; 1 Pet. ii. 10 with Rom. ix. 25, 26; 1 Pet. ii. 18 with Eph. vi. 5; 1 Pet. iii. 1 with Eph. v. 22; 1 Pet. v. 5 with Eph. v. 21.

[2] Compare 1 Pet. i. 1 with Jas. i. 1; 1 Pet. i. 6 f. with Jas. i. 2 f., 12; 1 Pet. i. 23 with Jas. i. 18; 1 Pet. ii. 1 with Jas. i. 21; 1 Pet. ii. 11 with Jas. iv. 1; 1 Pet. v. 6 with Jas. iv. 7, 10; 1 Pet. v. 9 with Jas. iv. 7; and the quotation in 1 Pet. v. 5 with Jas. iv. 6.

[3] For the persecution and its bearing on the date of this Epistle, see Leighton Pullan, *History of Early Christianity*, p. 105 ff. (Service and Paton, 1898).

CHAPTER XXII THE SECOND EPISTLE GENERAL OF PETER

[Sidenote: The Author.]

The difficulties which are connected with the authorship of this Epistle are greater than those connected with the authorship of any other book of the New Testament. A multitude of objections have been raised against its genuineness, and it has been pronounced spurious by a considerable number even of Christian writers. But while fully admitting that the problem is complicated, we can lawfully simplify it by at once dismissing some of the weaker objections. For instance, the statement that 2 Peter quotes from Josephus, the celebrated Jewish historian, who died c. A.D. 103, is utterly unproved. Again, the often-repeated statement that the doctrine of man being made a partaker of the divine nature (2 Pet. i. 4) is a doctrine which was not taught until after the apostolic age, is unwarrantable, unless we repudiate wholesale many books of the New Testament which we have every reason to regard as apostolic. For the indwelling of the Father in Christ and in the believer through Christ is implied by St. Paul, St. John, St. James, and St. Peter. The writer, in laying stress upon the importance of spiritual knowledge, is once more in agreement with St. Paul and St. John. He plainly does not mean mere intellectual *knowledge*, and the doctrine which he teaches is of a very simple kind. The slight reference made to the Redemption (ii. 1) and the silence manifested as to the Resurrection cannot be considered so crucial as some scholars believe them to be. Readers of the First Epistle could hardly fail to have these facts printed in their very souls. They would not require to have them repeated in a second letter.

The language of the Epistle, especially in the verses which do not depend upon Jude, shows several small coincidences with 1 Peter and with the speeches of St. Peter in Acts. We may compare the phrases in 2 Pet. ii. 15 with Acts i. 18, and 2 Pet. iii. 10 with Acts ii. 19, and

Compare 2 Pet. i. 7 with 1 Pet. i. 22, iii. 8. " " i. 19, 20 " " i. 10-12. " " ii. 1 " " i. 18 " " iii. 6 " " iii. 20. " " iii. 14 " " i. 19.

The writer abstains from copying the designation of the apostle contained in 1 Peter, and does not record the words spoken from heaven at the Transfiguration exactly as they are reported in the Gospels. In both these points a forger would very probably have acted otherwise.

On the whole, the words employed in 2 Peter seem indecisive with regard to the authorship. There is sufficient variation to allow us to believe that it was written or not written by the apostle. One of the most remarkable words in 2 Peter is that employed in i. 16 for an "eye-witness." It is a word used in the Greek heathen mysteries, and some critics think that such a word would not have been used by an orthodox writer until an age when the Church had learnt to borrow Greek religious terms from the Gnostic heretics. It is a sufficient proof of the weakness of this argument that the Greek verb derived from this noun is found in 1 Pet. ii. 12. It is, however, fair to say that the style of 2 Peter is less simple and less closely connected with the Old Testament than that of 1 Peter.

More serious objections are (1) the lack of external evidence in the writers of the 2nd and 3rd centuries; (2) the internal evidence that the Epistle is based upon Jude, and perhaps on the Apocalypse of Peter.

Eusebius is evidently in doubt about it. He says, "We have not indeed received it by tradition to be in the Canon, yet as it appeared useful to many, it was studiously read with the other Scriptures." [1] It is not mentioned by Irenaeus, nor is it in the list given in the *Muratorian Fragment*. But it seems to have been commented on by Clement of Alexandria, though it is not quoted in his extant works. Origen does mention it in his original Greek works, but in a manner which shows that it was disputed in his time. In Rufinus' Latin translation of Origen there are several quotations from 2 Peter, but against this fact it is sometimes urged that Rufinus emended Origen, and that we cannot be absolutely certain that these quotations are genuine. The Epistle seems to have been known to Origen's great contemporary Hippolytus (*Refut.* ix. 7; x. 20 and elsewhere). There are, moreover, passages in still earlier writers which are perhaps based on 2 Peter. These are in Clement of Rome, A.D. 95, Justin Martyr, A.D. 152, and the document which is wrongly called the Second Epistle of Clement, and is really a Roman homily of about A.D. 140. The evidence of these passages is not positive, but if even one of them is quoted from 2 Peter, it becomes quite impossible to assign 2 Peter to A.D. 150-170, which is the date most favoured by those who deny its authenticity. Nor is the omission of any mention of it in Irenaeus and the *Muratorian Fragment* a very destructive fact. The *Muratorian Fragment* is only a fragment, and does not mention 1 Peter, and there is no passage in Irenaeus quoted from James. Yet it is certain that those two Epistles belong to the apostolic age. The fact is that such a very large amount of the literature of the 2nd century has been destroyed, that it is always precarious to argue from omissions in the books which are still extant. Therefore, although the evidence of writers of the 2nd and 3rd centuries is certainly meagre in the case of 2 Peter, we cannot argue that comparative lack of evidence means positively hostile evidence. A notable step towards the determination of the problem will be made if scholars eventually agree to assign a very early date to the two great Egyptian versions of the New Testament. Both these versions contain 2 Peter.

As to the connection between 2 Peter and Jude, it may be regarded as certain that either they both depend on some previous document, or that one of them depends on the other.

Compare Jude 6 with 2 Pet. ii. 4. " " 7 " " ii. 6. " " 8 " " ii. 10. " " 10 " " ii. 12. " " 11 " " ii. 15. " " 12, 13 " " ii. 13, 17. " " 16 " " ii. 18. " " 17, 18 " " iii. 1-3.

An examination of these passages seems to prove that 1 Peter borrows from Jude and not Jude from 2 Peter.[2] In Jude the connection of ideas seems more simple and direct. Various verses in 2 Peter become more intelligible in the light thrown upon them by the corresponding verses in Jude. Thus Jude 10 alludes to the immorality which explains why the heretics are called "animals to be destroyed" in 2 Pet. ii. 12. Jude 13, by calling the heretics "wandering stars," explains why "darkness" is said to be "reserved" for them in 2 Pet. ii. 17. Between 2 Pet. ii. 17 and 18 there is no direct allusion to Enoch as in Jude 14, but some of the material taken from the Book of Enoch still remains.

It will be observed that this connection with Jude is confined to 2 Pet. ii. 1-iii. 7. Now, this passage must have been either inserted in some ancient manuscript of this Epistle, or it was originally part of the Epistle. If it has been inserted, the question of the authenticity of the rest of the Epistle obviously remains untouched. But if it originally formed part of the Epistle, as appears to be the case, can we regard this as a conclusive proof that St. Peter did not write it? Surely not.[3] The fact that St. Luke inserts most of the Gospel of St. Mark is not considered to be any argument against the authenticity of St. Luke's work. Both in the Old Testament and the New we are occasionally confronted by the same phenomenon. Writers repeat what has been said by other writers when their words appear to them to be the best possible words for enforcing a particular lesson.

The question of the authenticity of 2 Peter has lately become still further complicated. There has recently been discovered part of the Apocalypse of Peter mentioned in the *Muratorian Fragment*. This Apocalypse is usually thought to have been forged in Egypt in the first half of the 2nd century. It presents certain points of resemblance with 2 Peter. These points of resemblance affect the first chapter of 2 Peter as well as the second chapter. They therefore furnish an argument against the theory that ch. ii. is a late interpolation into a genuine Epistle, and they suggest that the Epistle is either wholly genuine or wholly forged. But the solution of the problem is not so easy as it seems to many scholars. If we could positively say that the Apocalypse was written in the 2nd century, and positively say that 2 Peter borrows from it, the question would be settled once for all. But this is the very thing which we cannot do with confidence. Some critics of great ability hold it certain that 2 Peter was forged by some one who borrowed from the Apocalypse. Some think that the same writer forged them both. Others think that the Apocalypse is partly derived from 2 Peter. They can strongly support their view by the fact that when Christians were familiar with both writings, it was decided to reject the Apocalypse and keep the Epistle. Lastly, it might be reasonably held that the coincidences in both writings are due to the use of one earlier document or a common stock of ideas and phrases. The popularity of Apocalyptic literature at the beginning of the Christian era makes this theory credible.

We may sum up the evidence for and against 2 Peter as follows:—

1. The external evidence is meagre.

2. The internal evidence is perplexing, and may reasonably be considered adverse.

On the other hand:—

1. The external evidence is not definitely adverse.

2. No convincing reason can be assigned for forging such an Epistle. The critics who believe it to be forged, hold that it was written in Egypt in order to oppose the Gnosticism of c. A.D. 150 or 160. But the Gnosticism rebuked in 2 Peter cannot definitely be assigned to the 2nd century. And it is very difficult to say that the heresy rebuked in 2 Peter belongs to the 2nd century without also maintaining that the heresy rebuked in Jude belongs to the 2nd century.[4] Yet several facts in Jude point so decidedly to the 1st century that some of the ablest writers who deny the authenticity of 2 Peter strongly assert the genuineness of Jude.

We can only conclude by doubting whether we know more about the problem of 2 Peter than the Church of the 3rd and 4th centuries knew. Perhaps we do not know nearly as much. And under these circumstances we cannot effectively criticize the judgment of the Church which decided to admit 2 Peter into the Canon.

[Sidenote: To whom written.]

To the same readers as the First Epistle (iii. 1).

[Sidenote: Where and when written.]

It was probably written in Rome, and some of the earliest references to it are by writers who lived in Rome. Justin Martyr lived in Rome, and if the references in Justin Martyr and other writers before Hippolytus be considered doubtful, Hippolytus is a Roman witness of the first importance.

The date is perhaps between A.D. 63 and 67. If it were later than 70, we might reasonably expect to find a reference to the destruction of Jerusalem after the allusion to God's retribution on the people of Sodom and other malefactors of old times. The errors which are denounced are akin to those which are denounced in 1 and 2

Timothy. The allusion to St. Paul's Epistles in iii. 16 suggests that some collection of these Epistles already existed, and that St. Paul was already dead. It has been urged against the genuineness of the Epistle that it includes the Pauline Epistles in *Scripture* (iii. 16), and that this would have been impossible in the apostolic age. But the statement need not necessarily mean more than that the Epistles were on the margin of a Canon which was in process of formation. There is good reason for believing that the Pauline Epistles occupied this position at a time when men who had known some of the apostles were still living, and perhaps earlier. The manner in which St. Peter has made use of St. Paul's work in his First Epistle, makes it quite possible for us to think that he believed in the peculiar inspiration of his great comrade. And it is an interesting fact that the Syriac *Doctrine of Addai* in speaking of the Epistles of St. Paul, adds, "which Simon Peter sent us from the city of Rome."

[Sidenote: Character and Contents.]

The key-word to the Epistle is not *hope*, as in 1 Peter, but *knowledge* (i. 3, 8; ii. 20). We find, as in 1 Peter, a fondness or the word "glory." But in 1 Peter glory seems to be represented as given to Christ after His sufferings, and promised to Christians in the future after their sufferings (1 Pet. i. 11; iv. 13; v. 1). Here glory is rather spoken of as manifested in all the new dispensation, and especially at the Transfiguration (i. 3, 17). The apostle appeals to the fact that he witnessed the Transfiguration as a guarantee of his prophecy of the second "coming" of Christ. He finds another warrant in the prophecies of the Old Testament, and asserts that prophecy is not a matter for a man's own private unaided interpretation, inasmuch as it was an utterance prompted by the Holy Spirit (i. 19-21).

This description of true religious knowledge is followed by an arraignment of false prophets and speculative heresy. It is possible that the teaching of definitely false doctrine was already combined with previously existing immoral practice. The verse (ii. 1) in which the writer speaks of false *teachers*, refers to the rise of these heretics as future. But in other verses of the chapter the "self-willed" teachers are spoken of as already active. We gather from iii. 16 that the licence which is so sternly rebuked was a system in which St. Paul's doctrine of justification by faith was represented as a justification of vile indulgence. Although this part of the Epistle is a paraphrase of Jude, it is not a mere reproduction. A new feature in 2 Peter is that the heretics were sceptical concerning the second coming of Christ (iii. 4). They argued that since the death of "the fathers," *i.e.* the first followers of Christ, the world continued as before. St. Peter urges that the deluge came, though its coming was doubted, and also that it must be remembered that the Lord does not reckon time as men do. A period which is long to us is not long to Him. The day of the Lord will come suddenly "as a thief in the night," and in view of judgment the readers are exhorted to holiness and patience.

ANALYSIS

Salutation, a list of Christian graces which are to be successively blended with faith, a reminder of the truth of Christianity as testified by the words of God at the Transfiguration, and by the light of prophecy (i.).

Denunciation of the false teachers who are guilty of gross sin and blindly follow their lower instincts (ii.).

Allusion to the former letter, rebuke of those who disbelieve in the last judgment, the coming of the day of the Lord and the destruction of the world, exhortations to holiness, diligence needed, the long-suffering of Christ witnessed to by Paul, growth in grace (iii.).

[1] *H. E.* iii. 3.

[2] The priority of 2 Peter is strongly defended by Spitta, in his *Der Zweite Brief d. Petrus*, 1885.

[3] This is very clearly stated by Dr. G. B. Stevens in his valuable *Theology of the New Testament*, although he decides against the genuineness of 2 Peter.

[4] This is done by Harnack, who places Jude between A.D. 100 and 130.

CHAPTER XXIII THE EPISTLES OF ST. JOHN

THE FIRST EPISTLE GENERAL OF JOHN

[Sidenote: The Author.]

The authenticity of this Epistle is bound up with the authenticity of St. John's Gospel. Like the Gospel, it does not contain any statement as to the name of the author. Like the Gospel, it is attributed by a very ancient tradition to the nearest friend of Jesus Christ. The external evidence is particularly good. We learn from the unimpeachable testimony of Eusebius[1] that it was used by Papias, who was a disciple of St. John. Polycarp, another disciple of St. John, directly quotes 1 John iv. 3 in his still extant letter. It is quoted by Irenaeus, the pupil of Polycarp, and was recognized as genuine in widely distant Churches at the close of the 2nd century.

The internal evidence shows that the writer claims to be an eye-witness and intimate personal friend of Jesus Christ (i. 1-3).[2] And this eye-witness must be St. John, if the fourth Gospel was written by St. John. The style is similar, and the ideas are the same. It is true that Christ is not called our "propitiation" in the Gospel as in this Epistle (ii. 2; iv. 10), that in the Gospel there is no mention of "antichrists" (as in ii. 8), and that the word "Paraclete" is in the Gospel applied to the Holy Ghost, while it is here applied to our Lord (ii. 1). But the idea of propitiation is expressed in the description of our Lord as "the Lamb of God" (John i. 29), the mention of antichrists is uncalled for in the Gospel, and by naming the Holy Ghost "another Paraclete" our Lord gave St. John the best possible reason for calling Christ Himself by the same title. The description of our Lord as "the only begotten Son" (iv. 9) is an important point of contact with John i. 14, 18. The language about "light" and "darkness," "God" and "the world," the "new commandment," the "love" of God, being "born of God," "eternal life," "abiding in Christ," recalls the Gospel at every turn.

The Epistle, however, does contain some phrases and ideas which are not to be found in the Gospel. Such are "love perfected," "a sin unto death," "the lust of the eyes," "to come in the flesh," "to walk in the light," "to do lawlessness," "to be from above." Yet they fit quite naturally with the language and theology of the Gospel. Therefore there does not seem to be any sufficient reason for holding that it was the work of another writer. F. C. Baur and Hilgenfeld thought it to be the work of a second forger of that mysterious band to which they attributed such versatility and success. And several more recent critics who have denied the authenticity of the Gospel, have maintained with Baur that the Epistle is the work of a second forger. But these negations have led to no assured result. They are seen to be fruitless as soon as we realize that these critics have been quite unable to agree whether the Epistle was composed before the Gospel or after it. Some consider that it was a theological balloon sent to try the credulity of Christian readers before the Gospel was despatched. Others consider that there are "overwhelming indications" to prove that the Epistle is only a poor imitation of the Gospel. Renan and Davidson favoured the former view, F. C. Baur and C. Weizsäcker the latter. At the present time the majority of critics, both Christian and non-Christian, believe that it was written by the writer of the fourth Gospel.

[Sidenote: To whom written.]

It seems to be a pastoral letter addressed to all the members of the apostle's flock, intended therefore for the Christians of Asia in and around Ephesus. It is a strange fact that St. Augustine, in quoting iii. 2, describes the passage as "said by John in his Epistle to the *Parthians*." This statement is a riddle which no commentator has been able to answer satisfactorily. As the Eastern Churches had little or no knowledge of this title, we are compelled to regard it as a mistake. It may have arisen from some scribe failing to read a partially illegible manuscript in which St. John may have been given the title of *parthenos* or virgin. But it is most likely that it arose from a confusion with the Second Epistle, which was thought in the time of Clement of Alexandria to be addressed to *parthenoi* or virgins. The absence of quotations from the Old Testament, and the command "guard yourselves from idols" (v. 21), solemnly given at the very end of the Epistle, suggest that the recipients of the letter were converts from heathenism. The Christians of Ephesus, the mother-city of Asiatic idolatry, were peculiarly in need of such an exhortation.

[Sidenote: Where and when written.]

We can hardly doubt that it was written at Ephesus, where the apostle spent his last years. The assertion that St. John did not live at Ephesus is in direct contradiction with the best and earliest traditions. But it has been repeated at intervals during the last sixty years by several critics, who found that they would be compelled to admit the genuineness of the Revelation if they granted that St. John lived at Ephesus, where the Revelation was evidently published.[3] Against such criticism we can confidently marshal the express and independent statements of Apollonius of Ephesus (A.D. 196), Polycrates of Ephesus (A.D. 190), Irenaeus of Lyons (A.D. 185), Clement of Alexandria (A.D. 190), Tertullian of Carthage (A.D. 200), not to mention some valuable indirect evidence of earlier date. If we are to reject such evidence as this, the science of history must be laid in the tomb.

The question as to the exact date is very important for those who believe that the Epistle was not written by the author of the Gospel. They are involved in the most intricate questions about the reproduction of the Gospel in the

Epistle or of the Epistle in the Gospel. For those who do not believe in a diversity of authorship the problem is far less vital. The apostle was evidently advanced in years. He includes all his people under the affectionate name "my little children" (ii. 1). On the whole, it seems probable that it was written rather later than the Gospel. This is suggested by the teaching about the second coming of Christ. Both in the Gospel and in the Epistle we find mentioned or implied a present and a future passing from death to life, and a spiritual presence of Christ now and another hereafter. But in the Epistle it is the future coming of Christ which is more prominent (ii. 28; iii. 2; iv. 17). In the Revelation, A.D. 96, it is still more prominent. The Epistle suggests that St. John's readers were already acquainted with the discourses in his Gospel. The heresy described, and the fact that the heretics are already *outside* the Church, point to a comparatively late date. We can hardly place it before A.D. 85.

[Sidenote: Character and Contents.]

This Epistle contains no reference to any outward dangers. Domitian's persecution had not yet affected the Church, and the controversy with Judaism had closed. There is no trace of any conflict between Jew and Gentile, and St. John, in asserting the truth of the incarnation of the Son of God, is not opposing any heresy resembling that of those semi-Christian Jews of the 2nd century who declared Christ to be *merely* the best of men. He is combating a form of error taught by Cerinthus, who said that Jesus was a man born of Joseph and Mary, and that on this man there descended a divine element named Christ, who left him before the crucifixion. Thus *Christ* never suffered, though the *Jesus* who seemed to be Christ did suffer. In face of these false views St. John asserts the truth. He asserts that One who is both Jesus and Christ came in the flesh (iv. 2), and that He came, that is, was manifested as Christ, both in the water of His baptism and the blood of His cross (v. 6). By this blood He cleanses man from sin (i. 7). We may be sure of His help, for He lives as our Advocate with the Father. To deny that Jesus is the Christ is to deny the Father, to deny God altogether (ii. 22; iv. 3). St. Ignatius and St. Polycarp inveigh in similar language against the Docetists, who flourished between A.D. 110 and 120. It is important to notice that St. John's opponents do not appear to have been Antinomian in conduct. He says, "Every one that doeth sin, doeth also lawlessness; and sin is lawlessness" (iii. 4). If he had been blaming Antinomianism it would have been more natural to say, "Every one that doeth lawlessness, doeth also sin."

The main theme of the Epistle is not controversial. It is to show that in faith and love is the guarantee of our fellowship with God and of our salvation. Since this fellowship implies that He abides in us, it may be recognized by His Spirit being in us (iii. 24). This Spirit is distinguished from the spirit of error by the confession of Christ; so to hear the apostle's teaching about Christ is a sign of the presence of God within us. The moral and the religious life are summed up in the words "God" and "Love," and those who love one another are born of God. Love in action corresponds with a confession of the incarnation in the intellect (iv. 7-12). It is wholly incompatible with sin (iii. 6), and is therefore righteous towards God and man. Every one who, as a child of God, hopes to grow like God, purifies himself as Christ is pure. He cannot love the world, which is a system of selfishness. St. John speaks of the possibility of committing a "sin unto death." This is an old Jewish expression for a sin deserving natural death. But the apostle lifts the phrase to a higher level and slightly alters it. His words literally mean "a sin tending unto death." It is any sin which by its very nature excludes a man from fellowship with Christians. It is a sin which requires chastisement before forgiveness, and St. John does not enjoin, though he does not forbid, prayer for those whose sin makes them unable to share in the privileges of the common life of the Church.

Behind the practical teaching of the Epistle lies that great conception of the Father which the writer had gained from intercourse with the only-begotten Son. God is *Love* (iv. 8, 16), and has given us the greatest of all gifts (iv. 9); God is *Light* (i. 5), and dispels all moral darkness (i. 6); God is *Life* (v. 20), imparting His own existence to man (iii. 9); God is *Father* (ii. 1; iii. 1)—though our relationship with Him is forfeited by sin, perfect and fearless intimacy may be gained through Christ (iv. 15, 18).

ANALYSIS

A promise to impart knowledge of the incarnate Word; God is Light, fellowship with God and forgiveness of sin (i.).

Christ our propitiation, love of our brother a necessary condition of walking in the light, messages to children, fathers, young men, the love of the world, Antichrist and the denial of Christ, abiding in the Son and in the Father (ii.).

The love of God in calling us His children, the manifestation of Christ to take away sin, love of our brother the sign that we are spiritually changed, to believe in Christ and love one another the commandment of God (iii.).

Acknowledgment of the incarnation is the test of spirits, to love one another is to be like God, perfect love loses fear (iv.).

Faith in the incarnation overcomes the world, the three witnesses to the incarnation, eternal life possessed if we have the Son, prayer, freedom from sin, knowledge through Jesus, who is the true God and eternal life (v.).

THE SECOND EPISTLE OF JOHN

[Sidenote: The Author.]

The writer does not insert his name in the Epistle, but simply describes himself as "the elder." Some writers have therefore supposed that it was written by the presbyter named John, who lived at Ephesus about the close of the apostolic age. But Irenaeus, who was not likely to be mistaken in such a matter, certainly regarded it as the work of the apostle, and the *Muratorian Fragment* apparently so regards it. Clement of Alexandria was certainly acquainted with more than one Epistle by St. John, and a Latin translation of his *Hypotyposes* definitely says, "the Second Epistle of John, written to virgins, is very simple." Moreover, the title "elder" or "presbyter" is by no means incompatible with apostolic authorship. St. Peter in 1 Pet. v. 1 expressly describes himself by this title, nor does the title appear to have become confined to the presbyters or priests of the Church until about A.D. 200. The similarity to the First Epistle is strong, seven of the thirteen verses having parallels in the First Epistle. If the Epistle were a forgery, it is probable that the writer would have claimed to be an apostle in unmistakable language. And if the author were not a forger, but the presbyter who was for some years a contemporary of the apostle, it is hardly likely that he would have been content to write this diminutive letter, which does little more than sum up part of the First Epistle. The language of the Second Epistle bears almost the same relation to that of the first as the first bears to that of the Gospel. There is a fundamental likeness combined with a few fresh expressions, such as "walk *according to*," "*coming* in the flesh" instead of "come in the flesh," "to have God."

[Sidenote: To whom written.]

"Unto the elect lady and her children." The interpretation of these words is a notorious difficulty. At first sight the "lady" would be supposed to be a private individual. But if so, why is not the individual's name mentioned, like the name of the recipient of the Third Epistle? Perhaps it is mentioned, for the words translated "the elect lady" may mean "the elect Kyria." The "house" of the lady (ver. 10) also suggests that the lady is an individual. On the other hand, it has been supposed that the lady is a symbolical name for a local *Church*. In favour of this interpretation is the fact that the writer speaks, not only of the children of the lady who are with her, but also of others whom he has met (ver. 4), and in a manner which suggests a large number of persons. The same interpretation can be put upon the "elect sister" mentioned in the last verse of the Epistle. Writers of deserved repute accept this symbolical interpretation. But when a literal meaning and a symbolical meaning are supported by equally good arguments, it seems prudent to accept the simpler, *i.e.* the literal interpretation. It is hard to believe that St. Jerome and Hilgenfeld are right in thinking that it is addressed to the whole Catholic Church. This is surely excluded by the mention of an "elect sister."

[Sidenote: Where and when written.]

Probably from Ephesus, and the contents suggest that it was written later than the first Epistle.

[Sidenote: Character and Contents.]

The letter contains an affectionate expression of happiness due to the steadfast Christianity of the children of the "elect lady." But its main object is to utter a warning against the deceivers who deny that Christ is "come in the flesh." These deceivers were evidently Docetists. In order to appreciate the necessity for such a warning we must remember the extraordinary attraction which many persons who liked a *dilettante* Christianity found in the theory that Christ was a divine Spirit who clothed Himself with flesh in which He did not suffer. At the close of the apostolic age, and for many generations afterwards, orthodox Christianity was often regarded as too materialistic for advanced thinkers. They endeavoured to make Christianity keep pace with the times by infusing into it the decadent Greek or Oriental mysticism which depreciated our human body.

ANALYSIS

Salutation, thanksgiving for certain of the elect lady's children, reminder of the commandments to love and obey, the deceivers who deny the incarnation not to be welcomed; the writer, expecting to visit his correspondents, closes his letter.

THE THIRD EPISTLE OF JOHN

[Sidenote: The Author.]

It is generally admitted, both by those who deny and those who accept the authenticity of the works of St. John, that this Epistle was written by the author of 2 John. It presents several close parallels both with 2 John and with the Gospel. Its obviously private character accounts for the fact that it is seldom quoted in early literature. It is found in the Old Latin version of the New Testament, though not in the *Muratorian Fragment*. It was known to Origen and Dionysius of Alexandria. Eusebius places it among the *Antilegomena* (*H. E.* iii. 25), but it was generally accepted in the 4th century.

[Sidenote: To whom written.]

"Unto Gaius the beloved." The name was a common one, being a form of the Latin "Caius." There is no reason for identifying this Gaius with one of the persons of the same name who are mentioned as living in Corinth, Macedonia, and Derbe respectively, all of whom may have been dead at the late period when this letter was written. The Gaius of this Epistle was evidently a faithful and hospitable Christian. Baur displayed more than even his usual powers of invention by suggesting that Gaius was a Montanist of the latter part of the 2nd century, and "Diotrephes" a symbolical name for one of the Catholic bishops of Rome opposed to Montanism.

[Sidenote: Where and when written.]

Probably at Ephesus; subsequently to the First Epistle, and probably very soon after the Second.

[Sidenote: Character and Contents.]

This little letter gives us a few brief glimpses of the life of the Church near the end of the 1st century. The purpose of the letter is to commend a Christian of good character, named Demetrius, to the hospitable care of Gaius. It appears, therefore, to be one of those "letters of commendation" which are mentioned by St. Paul in 2 Cor. iii. 1, and were common in later times. By the side of this pleasantness there is distress. Connected with the Church to which Gaius belongs there is an ambitious schismatic named Diotrephes, who refuses to admit the authority of the apostle. The fact that he was guilty of casting the friends of the apostle out of the Church (ver. 10), suggests that Diotrephes was at least a presbyter, and perhaps a bishop appointed by the apostle. We are told by Clement of Alexandria that St. John appointed bishops in Asia, and there is no reason for doubting that episcopacy dates back to this period. The apostle evidently intends to punish Diotrephes for his malice when he visits the district again. It is just possible that the letter to the Church (ver. 9) which Diotrephes repudiated is our "Second Epistle" of St. John. This theory will win acceptance with some of those who think that the Second Epistle was not written to an individual, but to a Church.

ANALYSIS

Salutations to Gaius, congratulations that he is walking in the truth, his hospitality to travelling Christians, the tyranny of Diotrephes, recommendation of Demetrius, personal matters.

[1] *H. E.* iii. 39.

[2] It is impossible to accept the recent Rationalist hypothesis that these words were written by a pious Christian who had not seen Jesus, but wished to emphasize the truth that the historical Church was intimately connected with the historical Jesus.

[3] Among these critics must be numbered Lützelberger (1840), Keim (1867), Bousset (1899).

CHAPTER XXIV THE GENERAL EPISTLE OF JUDE

[Sidenote: The Author.]

"Judas, a servant of Jesus Christ, and brother of James." We can be sure that the James here mentioned is the James who acted as the first bishop of the Church at Jerusalem. The author's designation of himself would not be intelligible unless he meant that he was related to a very prominent man of that name. The writer cannot be the Apostle Jude. He does not claim to be an apostle, and he seems indirectly to repudiate the authority of an apostle by describing himself only in relation to his brother and by referring to "the apostles of our Lord Jesus Christ" in a manner which seems to distinguish them for himself. If the Apostle Jude was the *son* of James (as many scholars think), this Jude was clearly another man. If the Apostle was the *brother* of James (as the English Authorised Version holds), then his identification with this Jude is still doubtful.

Jude was a son of St. Joseph. At first he did not believe in our Lord (John vii. 5), but was convinced by the Resurrection (Acts i. 14). He was married (1 Cor. ix. 5). Hegesippus, a writer of the 2nd century, tells us that two of his grandsons were taken before the Emperor Domitian as being of the royal house of David, and therefore dangerous to the empire.[1] He found them to be poor rough-handed men, and dismissed them with good-humoured contempt when they described the kingdom of Christ as heavenly. Philip of Side, about 425, says that Hegesippus gave the names of these two men as Zocer and James.

The Epistle was known to Clement of Alexandria and Tertullian, and is in the *Muratorian Fragment.*

The chief objections to the authenticity of this Epistle fall under three heads. It is said that (a) a late date is indicated by the allusion to the teaching of the apostles in ver. 17. But the allusion seems to correspond exactly with a late date in the apostolic age, for vers. 17 and 18 assume that the readers remember what the apostles had said. It is said that (b) the phrase in ver. 3, "the faith which was once for all delivered unto the saints," indicates that a definite body of doctrine was recognized by the Christians of the period, and that the Christians of the apostolic age did not use the word "faith" in this sense. But it is not difficult to suppose that the word would be soon extended from the act of believing to the facts believed. And in such early passages as Gal. i. 23 and Rom. x. 8 we find the word closely approximating to the latter sense. It is said that (c) the heresy which is described is a heresy of the 2nd century, and implies a definite Gnostic system. But the fact that the Epistle does not describe such a definite system is convincingly shown by the inability of certain critics to determine who the heretics are. The Balaamites of Asia Minor, the Carpocratians of Egypt, and some obscure sects of Syria, are all suggested. There is no evidence to show that the errors here described could not have grown up in apostolic times, and the Epistles of St. Paul contain several passages which point to similar perversions of Christianity. The word "sensual" in ver. 19 was an insulting term applied to ordinary Christians by the Gnostics of the 2nd century, but St. Jude's use of it betrays no consciousness of this later application.

The style of the letter makes it practically certain that it was written by some one who had been a Jew. The Greek is forcible. It shows a considerable knowledge of Greek words, including various poetical and archaic expressions. But the manner is stiff, and the sentences are linked together with difficulty. Several phrases come from the Septuagint, some of them being taken from the Book of Wisdom. It is probable that the author was acquainted with the Hebrew Old Testament, as ver. 12 (from Ezek. xxxiv. 2) and ver. 22 f. (from Zech. iii. 2 f.) suggest this.

[Sidenote: To whom written.]

The Epistle is simply addressed "to them that are called, beloved in God the Father, and kept for Jesus Christ." It seems that these Christians must have been natives of Palestine or Syria. They had been personally instructed by the apostles (ver. 17), which makes this region probable. No place seems more likely than Antioch and its neighbourhood. The libertinism which was endangering the Church would not be likely to arise except in a district where the Christians were in close contact with heathenism. Extreme critics now usually maintain that it was written either in Asia or in Egypt. If written in Asia, it can hardly have been written by the Lord's brother, as we know that his descendants lived in Palestine. If written in Egypt, it can hardly belong to the age of the apostles. These two sceptical theories as to the place where the Epistle was written contradict one another effectively.

[Sidenote: Where and when written.]

The style and contents of the letter show that it was probably written in Palestine and at Jerusalem. The date is probably soon after the martyrdom of St. James in A.D. 62. St. Jude was dead before his grandsons had their interview with Domitian. The Epistle must therefore be before A.D. 81.

[Sidenote: Character and Contents.]

The Epistle is remarkable as containing references to two Jewish books of an apocalyptic character which are not mentioned in the Old Testament. This caused some writers in early days to hesitate to ascribe the Epistle to a brother of St. James, and in recent times the same argument has been revived in a new form. But these quotations seem quite compatible with a belief in the genuineness of the Epistle. The books quoted were in existence in the apostolic age, and would be likely to be valued by a devout Jew. In ver. 9 there is reference to Michael, which Origen says was derived from the *Assumption of Moses*, a Jewish work written at the beginning of the Christian era. In 2 Pet. ii. 11 the allusion to Michael is so modified, that the origin of the reference is no longer obvious. In vers. 4, 6, and 14, there are quotations from the *Book of Enoch*, a Jewish book composed of sections written at various dates, the latest being written in the century before Christ.

The purpose of the Epistle is to warn the Church against certain depravers of God's grace who denied "our only Master and Lord, Jesus Christ" (ver. 4). The author sees fit to remind his readers of ancient examples of unfaithfulness and impurity, and shows that they must be compassionate towards the wavering, and try to save the worst by a desperate effort. It is plain that the false teachers were guilty of gross and unnatural vice, that they were greedy, and destitute of godly fear. They also, like the evil Christians at Corinth, brought discredit upon the Agapé (ver. 12), a social meal which the Christians were first wont to partake of before the Eucharist, and at a later date after the Eucharist. The licence which is rebuked by St. Jude probably arose from a perversion of the doctrine of justification by faith which had been taught by our Lord. Christians who had been taught that they could be saved without observing the Jewish ceremonial law, imagined that they could be saved without any self-discipline or self-restraint. Many parallels to such errors have been found in modern times, the worst example being that afforded by the Anabaptists, who arose in Germany at the time of the Reformation. It is worth noticing that, in spite of the untheological character of this Epistle, the writer shows his belief in the Holy Trinity by the manner in which he refers to the Father and Jesus Christ (ver. 1) and the Holy Ghost (ver. 20). The Epistle gives no encouragement to the theory that the first Jewish Christians were Unitarians.

ANALYSIS

Salutation and charge to maintain "the faith" (1-4). Warnings from the punishment of the Israelites, of the angels, of Sodom and Gomorrha (5-7).

Railing at dignities rebuked (8-10).

Denunciation of those who imitate Cain (murder), Balaam (encouragement of impurity), Korah (schism), and spoil the *Agapé* (11-13).

These sectaries foretold by Enoch (14-16).

And by the apostles (17-19).

Duty of edifying believers, and saving sinners (20-23).

Doxology (24, 25).

[1] Eusebius, *H. E.* iii. 20.

CHAPTER XXV THE REVELATION OF ST. JOHN THE DIVINE

[Sidenote: The Author.]

Like the First Epistle of St. John, the Revelation has particularly strong external evidence in its favour. About A.D. 150 Justin Martyr speaks of it as the work of "John, one of the apostles of Christ," in his dialogue held with Trypho, a Jew, at Ephesus, where St. John had lived. Still earlier, Papias looked upon the book as "inspired," and "bore testimony to its genuineness." Irenaeus, the pupil of Polycarp, the disciple of St. John, quotes it as written by "John, the disciple of the Lord." About A.D. 170 Melito of Sardis, one of the places to which part of the book was specially addressed, wrote a commentary upon it. It was accepted by the Churches of Vienne and Lyons in Gaul in A.D. 177, for they wrote of it as "Scripture" in their letter to the Christians of Asia Minor. Near the same date the *Muratorian Fragment* mentions it twice. It will be observed that this evidence is not only good, but it is also mostly drawn from sources which were most closely connected with St. John. The evidence of the Churches of Vienne and Lyons would be important, even if it stood alone. For these Greek-speaking Churches were allied with the Church of Ephesus, and were not likely to be mistaken about this question. And the evidence of Irenaeus and Melito is still more weighty.

Strange to say, the belief in the authenticity of the Revelation began to waver as time went on. We need pay little heed to the sect known as the Alogi, who attributed both St. John's Gospel and the Revelation to Cerinthus, because they disliked the doctrine of the Logos contained in these two books. They were too ignorant to have been influenced by any real critical knowledge. But it is an important fact that about A.D. 248 Dionysius of Alexandria stated that it was probably written by John the Presbyter, and that the great Eusebius seems at one time to have been inclined to accept the opinion of Dionysius.[1] So far as we can discover, Dionysius founded his opinion solely on the difference of style which can be observed as separating the Revelation from the Gospel. He does not seem to have been in possession of any facts which gave historical support to his theory. Nevertheless, we can legitimately think that there was another reason which induced orthodox Christians to regard the Revelation with less confidence. The Montanist sect, which arose in the latter half of the 2nd century and became powerful in Asia Minor and North Africa, taught an extravagant doctrine about the millennium when Christ would return to reign on earth. This doctrine was partly founded on Rev. xx., and was supported by pretended prophecies. It caused orthodox Christians to be more suspicious about the statements of Christian prophets, and probably made them less anxious to translate and circulate the Revelation. This hesitation was soon overruled, and Eusebius, in spite of his own slight doubts, reckons it as received among the undisputed books of the Canon. This was c. A.D. 320.

In modern times the controversy about the authorship has been revived. About one hundred years ago a school of critics took up the argument of Dionysius. They urged that the Gospel and the Revelation must have been written by two different authors, the Revelation being much more Hebrew in style than the Gospel. The argument was elaborated by F. C. Baur and the Tübingen School. As they were determined to deny the genuineness of the Gospel which so clearly teaches that Jesus is God, they tried to discredit the Gospel by insisting upon the authenticity of the Revelation. The successors of these critics soon found themselves on the horns of a dilemma. A closer examination of the Revelation made it clearer that on many important points the theology of the Revelation is the same as that of the Gospel. If they admit that St. John wrote both the books or one of them, they will be forced to admit that the apostle taught definite orthodox Christian theology.[2] If, on the other hand, they affirm that both the books were written by John the Presbyter, they will shatter the old argument that diversity of style proves diversity of authorship. It will therefore surprise no one to learn that they are now engaged in continuous disputes with regard to the identity of the author, and the materials, Jewish or otherwise, which he is supposed to have used in compiling his book. At the present time the writers who hold the Revelation to have been written by various authors, are divided into no less than four camps, while the rationalists who hold that it was written by one author cannot agree who that author was. It is extremely significant that, in spite of his conviction that the book was not all written at the same date, the critic who is now by far the ablest opponent of orthodox Christianity, holds that the Revelation was (i.) published in the time of Domitian, as the tradition of the Church affirms; (ii.) published by the author of the fourth Gospel, though not by the real St. John.[3]

It must be admitted that the style of the book is more Hebrew and less Greek than that of the Gospel. But some arguments may be reasonably alleged against the theory that this proves the Revelation to be by a different author. The difference in the scope and origin of the two books account in a large measure for the differences of vocabulary and style. No book in the New Testament is so steeped as the Revelation in the imagery of the Old Testament; Daniel, Isaiah, Ezekiel, and Zechariah are constantly used. The thoroughness with which their spirit has been assimilated, and their ideas combined by the writer, would create a Hebrew tendency in his language. Whether St. John made use of the material furnished by non-canonical apocalypses is uncertain. If he did, their style would also influence him in the same way. We must also beware of exaggerating the contrast in style which does exist between the Gospel and the Revelation. The Gospel is not always in correct Greek, and never shows a thorough mastery of that language. But the Revelation is certainly in much rougher Greek. The writer uses the nominative case for the accusative (vii. 9; xiv. 6); similar instances are in iii. 12; xiv. 12. This rugged usage is introduced with magnificent, and perhaps intentional, effect in i. 4, where the author emphasizes the eternity of God by using an entirely ungrammatical construction.[4] Apart from the question of grammar, the language of the Apocalypse shows a remarkable affinity with St. John's Gospel. We may observe the use of such words as "witness," "true," "tabernacle," "have part," "keep the word," and "overcome."

The theology of the two books is in close agreement. This can easily be shown in the case of the doctrine of Christ's Person. He is called the "Lamb" [5] in the Gospel (i. 29, 36) and in the Revelation (v. 6, 8, 12, etc.). He is called the "Word" in the Gospel (i. 1, etc.) and in the Revelation (xix. 13). He is taught to be eternal and divine. He is "the Alpha and the Omega, the first and the last" (xxii. 13; cf. Isa. xliv. 6). He shares the throne of God (xxii. 1, 3); He determines who shall be released from the realm of death (i. 18); He joins in the judgment (vi. 16); He is worshipped by the elders and the angels (v. 8, 11). He is the Bridegroom of the Church (xix. 7; xxi. 2, cf. John iii. 29). The attitude towards Judaism is the same as that in the Gospel. The Jews who oppose Jesus are strongly denounced (iii. 9), and though the Church is a new *Jerusalem*, it is composed of people gathered out of every nation (vii. 9). The necessity of good works is strenuously upheld (ii. 5, 19); but they are not works of rabbinical righteousness, but works of Jesus (ii. 26), and the "righteous acts of the saints" (xix. 8) are based on "the faith of Jesus" (xiv. 12). Salvation is the free gift of Christ (xxi. 6; xxii. 17). The saints who overcome, conquer not by relying upon their own righteousness, but "because of the blood of the Lamb" (xii. 11).

In the Revelation (ii. 17) Jesus promises to believers "the hidden manna;" in the Gospel, referring also to the manna, He promises "the true bread from heaven" (John vi. 32). In the Revelation (xxii. 17) Jesus says, "Let him that is athirst come, and whosoever will, let him take of the water of life freely;" in the Gospel He says, "If any man thirst, let him come unto Me and drink" (John vii. 37). If, then, the Revelation is full of Hebrew expressions, it is essentially and profoundly Christian, and linked with the other Johannine books by the closest kinship. The theology and the style of the Revelation are the same throughout.[6] We can therefore reject without hesitation the recent hypothesis that it is one large Jewish work with numerous Christian interpolations. The difficulty of supposing that the book was ever a purely Jewish Apocalypse can quickly be realized by any one who undertakes to strike out all the Christian allusions in the book.

The author states that he is John, in the strongest fashion both in the beginning and end (i. 4, 9; xxii. 8), and his attitude towards the seven Churches is inexplicable unless the writer held a position of the highest ecclesiastical importance.

[Sidenote: For whom written.]

Plainly for the whole Church, as represented by "the seven Churches which are in Asia" (i. 4).

[Sidenote: Date.]

From i. 9 we learn that the revelation was made to John when he "was in the isle that is called Patmos" (in the Aegean Sea) "for the word of God and the testimony of Jesus." Irenaeus expressly says that the date of this banishment was at the end of the reign of Domitian (Emperor 81-96 A.D.), and therefore he says it was almost within his own generation. On the other hand, some modern writers have assigned part or the whole of the book to the time of Nero (54-68), or a little later. But though some parts of it seem earlier than Domitian, the final form of the book is unquestionably late. A late date is indicated by the corruptions existing in some of the Churches addressed, by the expression "the Lord's day" (i. 10) instead of the older expression "first day of the week," by the strong opposition to Judaism which is called the "synagogue of Satan" (ii. 9; iii. 9), and above all by the attitude of the writer towards Rome. The imperial rule is no longer regarded with the tolerance which we find in Acts and in St. Paul's Epistles. It is no longer the "restraining" and protecting power. It is denounced as cruel and aggressive, and not only is the worship offered to the Roman emperor mentioned as widespread, but also the worship offered to Rome. The city is called the Great Harlot, because in prophetical language idolatry is described as an act of fornication, being a violation of the pure love which should be felt by man towards his Creator. The worship of Rome does not seem to have become common in Asia until late in the 1st century, and it is not even mentioned once in Acts.

The destruction of Jerusalem is definitely mentioned in xi. 2, where the earthly Jerusalem is symbolized as the "court which is without the temple," the temple which the prophet measures being the heavenly temple only (xi. 19). This chapter seems to imply that Jerusalem is already destroyed, and is founded on Ezek. xl., when the prophet measures the ideal city, not the city which had been destroyed previously. We are therefore pointed to a date later than A.D. 70. The same seems to be suggested by xiii. 1 and xvii. 10. For the beast in xiii. 1 is the pagan Roman State as typified by Nero, and so is the number 666 in xiii. 18; for if the words Nero Caesar are written in Hebrew letters, and the numerical values of the letters are added together, the result is 666. In xvii. 8 Nero is described as dead, and in xvii. 10 Vespasian is the sixth emperor, Titus the seventh, and the eighth, in xvii. 11, is Domitian, who plays the Satanic part of Nero. The sixth emperor is described as still living, and we therefore seem compelled to assign part of this passage to Vespasian's reign. Nevertheless, there is abundant internal evidence for thinking that the book was not completed until the time of Domitian. It is worth noting that Domitian exacted a more extravagant worship of his own person than any previous emperor, and that his policy therefore made the publication of the book doubly appropriate.

[Sidenote: Character and Contents.]

There were a number of Jewish books called by the name of Revelation or Apocalypse (*i.e.* revelation or unveiling). In the Old Testament an Apocalypse is to be found in the second part of Daniel, and there is a fine short Apocalypse in Isa. xxiv.-xxvii., where we find striking passages relating to the resurrection and eternal life. The *Book of Enoch* and the *Apocalypse of Baruch* are later examples of this class of literature. These books were generally written with the special purpose of giving encouragement to the servants of God in times of distress and persecution. The Revelation of St. John was written under similar circumstances, but is by far the most sublime of these writings. The interpretation of the Revelation appears to have always been a standing difficulty, in spite of the fact that there has been no age of the Christian Church which has not been able to draw consolation and vigour from its beautiful pages, all illuminated as they are with glowing pictures. The question as to whether different portions of the book were written at different dates, and afterwards edited in one volume by the writer, does not necessarily interfere with the interpretation. For the book is one work, the materials have been fitted into one structure.

The connection between the different parts is organic and internal. Not only is the doctrinal standpoint the same throughout, but the whole book has an immense number of connecting thoughts and words. The letters to the seven Churches contain statements which are taken up in the visions which follow. Among such we may compare ii. 7 with xxii. 2; ii. 11 with xx. 6; ii. 26 with xii. 5, ii. 28 with xxii. 16; iii. 5 with xix. 8; iii. 12 with xxi. 2. The description of the glorified Redeemer in i. 10-18 is reflected in numerous passages, and the strong assertion of the author's personality in i. 9 is again presented in xxii. 8. And the meaning of the book rapidly becomes clearer to the reader if he sees (a) that the notices of contemporary history in each of the seven parts of the book are arranged chronologically in reference to what is contained in that part; (b) that these seven parts are not related to one another in the order of temporal succession: each part is complete in itself, and is a full presentation of one aspect of the whole subject. This is exactly what we find in Isaiah, Amos, and Zechariah.

This leads us to another fact. Some writers have held that the Revelation is to be interpreted simply on *historical* lines, as though it contained a list of events occurring through the whole of history since the time of St. John. Other writers have held that little or no historical meaning can be found in the book, and that it is to be interpreted on *ideal* lines, as teaching certain principles of religion. The truth seems to be that these two methods of interpretation are both partly true. Certain historical facts, such as the Ascension of our Lord, the destruction of Jerusalem, the persecution of the Church, the struggle between the Church and the Roman empire, are taken as a basis. Certain great principles of God's dealings with the world, and of the continued conflict between good and evil, are then illustrated in connection with these facts, and the whole is knit together by the fixed expectation that Christ will come again to vanquish the wicked and rescue the good. While each division of the book thus possesses a real meaning, it seems hardly possible to attach a significance to each detail in the imagery which is employed. Many items and even numbers appear to be introduced in order to make the scenes clear to the mind's eye rather than impart a knowledge of independent events. In after-ages Dante, like St. John, showed this care for minute imagery in the midst of verses of mystic vision. The book is the highest example of Christian imagination led and inspired by the Holy Spirit, and although at is written in prose it is of the nature of a poem.

The book contains seven revelations, which are preceded by a prologue concerning the divine Son of Man and the seven Churches of Asia. Of these seven revelations, the fourth is central both in place and meaning. It represents the kingdom of the world becoming the kingdom of Christ as the result of the coming of the Messiah, born of that glorious mother, the woman whose seed wars against the serpent (Gen. iii. 15), and the maiden who bears Immanuel (Isa. vii. 14), and who also represents the Church banished to the wilderness.

On each side are three revelations, which correspond with one another like the petals of a mystical rose. The *third*, which deals with the divine judgment upon Jerusalem, corresponds with the *fifth*, which contains God's judgment upon Rome. Here we see the triumph of God over corrupt religion and corrupt imperialism. The *second*, which describes the powers of divine judgment kept in check, and the seal of God imprinted on the saints of the new Israel, corresponds with the *sixth*, which describes the war of the Word of God with the Beast, and events which end with the universal judgment. The *first*, which describes the Lamb that was slain and the book of destiny which He alone could open, corresponds with the *seventh*, which describes the Bride of the Lamb, the New Jerusalem in heaven. Thus the final glory of the Church corresponds with the glory which the ascended Jesus already receives in heaven.

The whole closes with a short epilogue.

It will be observed that the book contains seven choric songs. The first revelation contains two such songs, one after each division. The second, third, and fifth revelation, each close with a song. The fourth and central revelation contains two songs; one is sung by the bodyguard of the Lamb before they go to war, the other is sung after the victory is gained. The seventh and last chorus celebrates the fall of Babylon (Rome), and ushers in the marriage of the Lamb. It comes at the end of the fifth revelation. Its form is double, and it sums up the remaining action of the book. Two more facts must be mentioned in this connection. The first is that the words of the song of the bodyguard of the Lamb (xiv. 3) are not told; it can only be learned by the redeemed. It begins with the voice of Christ, the voice "of many waters," and it is taken up by the "thunder" of the cherubim and the harps of the elders. The second is that there is no song between the sixth and seventh revelation. It is simply the voice out of the throne itself, the voice of the cherubim who uphold the throne of God (see iv. 6), which proclaims that the tabernacle of God is now with men, and that He shall wipe away every tear (xxi. 4). The exquisite art of this arrangement of the songs is manifest.

ANALYSIS

Title and description (i. 1-3).

Prologue (i. 4-iii. 22).

The vision of the Son of Man (i. 4-20).

The message to each of the seven Churches of Asia (ii., iii.).

A general idea of conflict is present in this introduction. The Churches of Asia have special temptations against which they must fight, *e.g.* coldness at Ephesus, false prophecy at Thyatira, emperor worship at Pergamum.

I. Revelation of the Book of Destiny: iv.-v.—The throne of God is manifested, surrounded by the elders and by the four living creatures who represent the created universe, *chorus of creation* (iv.). The sealed book which none can open but the Lamb, *chorus of redemption* (v.).

II. Revelation of the Seals: vi.-viii. 1.—The first four seals of the book are opened. Christ appears riding on a white horse, and is followed by four symbolic powers of evil: (a) Apollyon, who rides on a red horse; (b) the Steward, who rides on a black horse, and dispenses corn at a dear price, representing a perverted ministry of the Word, which nevertheless cannot hurt the unction given to the Christian nor the wine of Christ's Passion; (c) Death on a pale horse; and (d) his companion Hell. When the fifth scene is opened, the martyrs who are under the altar which is before the throne cry in expectancy. With the sixth seal there is a warning of prophetic horrors. The day of God's wrath all but comes. But judgment is restrained for a season (vi.). Chastisement is suspended until 144,000 of Israelites are sealed, then a multitude of all nations, *chorus of salvation* (vii.). The seventh seal, which discloses a war against God, can now be opened; silence (viii. 1).

III. Revelation of the Trumpets: viii. 2-xi. 18.—Seven angels receive trumpets, incense offered. With the sounding of each of the first four trumpets a chastisement is sent from above to rouse repentance (viii.). With the fifth, chastisement ascends from the pit; with the sixth, angels and terrific horsemen come from the Euphrates; but men repent not (ix.). Before the seventh trumpet sounds, an angel tells the seer that when it has sounded the mystery of God as declared to the prophets will be finished (x.). Two prophets resembling Elijah and Moses appear as the symbols of Christian prophecy; they are slain in Jerusalem where our Lord was crucified, they ascend like Christ amid the wreck of a tenth of the city. The city confesses God. Then the seventh trumpet proclaims the subject of the next revelation: the kingdoms of the world becoming the kingdoms of Christ, *chorus of God reigning* (xi. 1-18).

IV. Revelation of the Lamb's Redemption: xi. 19-xv. 4.—The ark itself is revealed to show that the coming revelation manifests what is most sacred and most profound. The conflict between Christ and evil is shown first as the conflict of the Child of the Woman against the dragon, then as the conflict of Michael and his angels against the dragon, then as the conflict of the dragon against the woman's seed (xii.). Next come the allies of the dragon, the beast out of the sea, which is imperial pagan Rome; and the beast out of the earth, which is the priesthood of Asia appointed to promote the worship of the emperor (xiii.). Then there is seen on Mount Zion the Lamb with His bodyguard of 144,000, singing *the incommunicable chorus*. An angel proclaims the eternal gospel; another tells that Babylon, *i.e.* pagan Rome, has fallen; another proclaims the eternal punishment of those who worship the beast. Then a voice from heaven announces the blessedness of the dead in Christ. The Son of Man is seen with a sickle; then comes the harvest of the good, and the vintage of those who are to suffer in the winepress of God's wrath (xiv.). Seven angels appear, and the victors over the beast sing *the chorus Of Moses and the Lamb* (xv. 1-4).

V. Revelation of the Bowls: xv. 5-xix. 10.—The heavenly temple opens, and the seven angels come to pour out the seven last punishments from the golden bowls (xv. 6-8). There is a plague, and the turning of the sea, and then of the rivers, into blood, then the sun's heat is intensified, then darkness is poured over Rome. Then, in conformity with Revelation III., we are shown the Euphrates. It is dried up that the kings of the East, probably conceived of as Parthians, may march to destroy Babylon. Other kings come to aid the beast. They muster at Har-Magedon. The seventh bowl is poured on the air. Babylon breaks into three parts. Storms (xvi.). Then an angel shows John Babylon riding triumphantly upon a beast as the mother of harlots, drunken with the blood of the martyrs, and he explains how she shall be destroyed by her subject kings (xvii.). There follows a solemn dirge on Babylon (xviii.). Then comes a *triumphant chorus* for the judgment of the city (xix. 1-8). John is forbidden to worship his angel-guide (xix. 10).

VI. Revelation of the Word of God and the universal Judgment: xix. 11-xx. 15.—It is now shown that judgment is the work of the Word of God Himself. As in Revelation II., He appears upon a white horse. Brief sections display the complete overthrow of the great enemies of Christ, the beast, the false prophet, and the dragon. Then comes the millennium, when the martyrs of Jesus reign with Christ while Satan is bound. Satan is then loosed, and with Gog and Magog, who are leaders of nations hostile to God's people, he is finally vanquished. The final judgment takes place, and Death and Hell are cast into fire.

VII. Revelation of the New Jerusalem: xxi. i-xxii. 5.—From a mountain-top is seen the Church, the holy city, New Jerusalem, the Bride prepared for Jesus. Its luminary and structure are described. It rises on a vast rock of jewels. The throne of God is no longer remote from man, but in the midst of the city. From the throne pours the river of life through the very heart of the city. The river is shaded on both sides by the "tree" or wood of life, with its perpetual variety of fruit. This is in contrast with the one tree and its forbidden fruit which was the means of the Fall.

Epilogue (xxii. 6-21).

The attestation of the angel, the watchword of Jesus, John again forbidden to worship the angel. The book to remain unclosed. The watchword repeated. The attestation of Jesus to Himself and the angel, to His Bride, to the book, to His advent.

The response of John to the Lord Jesus.

Salutation.

[1] *H. E.* iii. 25, 39; vii. 25.

[2] The determination to deny that St. John could have believed in the Divinity of Christ made Zeller maintain that in the Revelation Christ is called the *Word of God* as a mere honorary title. Davidson interpreted it as meaning "the highest creature." Renan tried to extricate himself from the difficulty by saying that St. John did not write the Revelation, but, "having approved of it, saw it circulate under his name without displeasure" (*L'Antichrist*, p. xli.).

[3] Harnack, *Chronologie*, vol. i. pp. 245, 246, 679.

[4] Many of the supposed wrong constructions in the Revelation are capable of justification (Dr. Benson, *The Apocalypse*, p. 131 ff.).

[5] It is true that a different Greek word for Lamb is used in the Revelation from that in the Gospel, but the variation can be accounted for by the author's desire to use a word similar in form to the word used for the Beast, who is contrasted with the Lamb.

[6] The attempt to divide a supposed Judaizing element in the book from a more Catholic element has led to the assertion that vii. 1-8 is inconsistent with vii. 9-17. There is no more incongruity between these two passages than in the statement of St. Paul in Rom. i. 16, that the gospel is a power unto salvation "to the Jew *first*, and also to the Greek."

APPENDIX A

RATIONALIST CRITICISM ON ST. JOHN'S WRITINGS

The following table will illustrate the points of agreement arrived at by the more prominent Rationalist critics of the last sixty years:—

	THE GOSPEL.	1 JOHN.	2 AND 3 JOHN.	REVELATION.
F. C. Baur, 1847.	By a forger, 170 A.D.	By a second forger.	By a third forger.	By St. John.
Th. Keim, 1867.	By the same forger, 100-117 A.D.		——	Not by St. John.
A. Hilgenfeld, 1875.	By a forger, 120-140 A.D.	All by a second forger, 130 A.D.		By St. John.
E. Renan, 1879.	By the Presbyter John and others, who pretended that they were by St. John, 120 A.D.	By ... John, but circulated by him.		Not by St. John.
C. Weizsäcker, 1886.	By a disciple of St. John.	Not by St. John nor by the author of the Gospel.		Not by St. John.
A. Harnack, 1897.	The Gospel and Epistles all probably by the Presbyter John, who did not pretend that they were by St. John, 80-110 A.D.			By the Presbyter John, 96 A.D.
A. C. McGiffert, 1897.	Uncertain.	By the author of the Presbyter Gospel.	Uncertain.	Possibly by the Presbyter John.
B. W. Bacon, 1900.	By an unknown writer, 100-110 A.D.	All by another unknown writer, A.D. 95-100 A.D.		By St. John.
P. W. Schmiedel, 1901.	Not by St. John, nor by the forger.	By a second forger.	By a third Presbyter.	Possibly by the Presbyter John.

APPENDIX B

PAPIAS AND JOHN THE PRESBYTER

Papias, a Phrygian by birth, and Bishop of Hierapolis in Phrygia, wrote in the first half of the 2nd century a book called *Expositions of Oracles of the Lord*. Among the "Elders" whom Irenaeus quotes, Papias and Polycarp alone are called "ancient" (*archaios—Adv. Haer.* v. 33). This helps us to fix the date of Papias. For Polycarp died either in A.D. 155 or 156. He had been a Christian for eighty-six years, and was therefore born in A.D. 70 at the very latest. Papias was therefore probably born about A.D. 70. We know from Irenaeus that Polycarp was a disciple of St. John, and several ancient writers, including Irenaeus, expressly assert that Papias also was a hearer of St. John. Eusebius (*H. E.* iii. 39) says that "in his preface" Papias does not declare that he was an "eye-witness of the holy *apostles*." But Eusebius in his Chronicle (*Syncell*. 655, 14) plainly says that Papias, like Polycarp, was a "hearer" of John the Divine and Apostle. The preface of Papias, which Eusebius transcribes, mentions John the Presbyter. The following is a literal translation of it:—

"But for your advantage I will not hesitate to put side by side with my interpretations everything that in time past I learnt well from the Elders, and remembered well, guaranteeing its truth. For, unlike the many, I did not take pleasure in those who say much, but in those who teach the truth; nor in those who relate alien commandments, but in those who relate such as were given from the Lord to the Faith, and are derived from 'the Truth' itself. And again, on any occasion when a person came who had been a follower of the Elders, I would inquire about the discourses of the Elders—what Andrew or what Peter said, or what Philip or what Thomas or James, or what John or Matthew or any other of the disciples of the Lord, and the things which Aristion and John the Presbyter (Elder), the disciples of the Lord, say. For I did not suppose that the contents of books would profit me so much as the utterances of a living and abiding voice."

The exact meaning of this passage is disputed, but much of it is perfectly clear. It is plain that Papias is referring to his action at a time long past (*pote*), probably about A.D. 100. It is also plain that he had no direct access at that date to the apostles about whose sayings he inquired. They were already dead, their speech was a thing of the past (*eipen*). On the other hand, Aristion and John the Presbyter were then living, their speech was a thing of the present (*legousin*). They survived at the time of his inquiries, and we cannot accept the hypothesis that Papias only meant that he inquired what Aristion and John the Presbyter said in their books. He recorded what they said to his friends, and he quoted them both so freely that Eusebius believed that Papias also wrote down words which Aristion and John the Presbyter said in his own hearing. But whether he heard them or only heard about them, it is evident that he had reached manhood before they were dead. It is also certain that he calls them "disciples of the Lord." He must mean by this that they had been personally in contact with Christ, like the apostles whom he has just mentioned. We therefore can only draw the conclusion that Papias believed that these two men had known the Lord in their boyhood, and the fact that he mentions only two such men favours this interpretation.

With regard to the other Elders, the question at once arises, Did Papias include among those Elders the apostles whom he mentions? If he did *not* include them, he means that he inquired of travellers what they had heard from Elders who had known the apostles. This seems incredible; the information gained would be far inferior to that contained in books, whereas Papias speaks of it as superior. Moreover, it would imply that the knowledge possessed by Papias about those who had known the Lord was less direct than that possessed by Irenaeus! For Irenaeus (1) knew Polycarp (2) and others, who knew St. John and others who had seen the Lord. Whereas, according to this theory, Papias (1) was instructed by travellers (2), who had heard the Elders (3) speak about the apostles. If Papias had no better knowledge than this, Irenaeus would not have referred to Papias with such marked deference. We conclude, therefore, that Papias used the word "Elders" to denote Christians who had actually seen the Lord, including the apostles whom he mentions. This interpretation is supported by the fact that in the New Testament both St. Peter and St. John give themselves this very title.

If the above views are correct, they have an important bearing on the authenticity of St. John's Gospel. The lifetime of Papias, like that of Polycarp, covers the whole period of dates to which modern Rationalists now assign that Gospel. If it was not written by the apostle, it is hard indeed to suppose that Papias did not know the truth, and record it. And it is equally hard to believe that his statements about it would not have been copied by such men as Irenaeus, Dionysius of Alexandria, and Eusebius.

APPENDIX C

THE MURATORIAN FRAGMENT

The *Muratorian Fragment* is part of a Latin list of the books of the New Testament, named after Muratori, the librarian at Milan, who published it in A.D. 1740. The Canon of which the Fragment is a part was probably written about A.D. 180. It begins in the midst of a sentence relating to St. Mark—

[Sidenote: The Gospels.]

". . . at some things, however, he was present, and has thus recorded them."

"The third book of the Gospel according to Luke, Luke compiled in his own name from report, the physician whom Paul took with him after the ascension of Christ, for a companion as devoted to the law: however he did not himself see the Lord in the flesh, and hence begins his account with the birth of John as he was able to trace (matters) up."

[Sidenote: The Epistles of St. John.]

"Of the fourth of the Gospels (the author is) John, one of the disciples. At the instance of his fellow-disciples and bishops he said, 'Fast with me to-day for three days, and whatever shall be revealed to each, let us relate it to one another.' The same night it was revealed to Andrew, one of the apostles, that John should write all in his own name, the rest revising. . . . And therefore, although varying ideas may be taught in the several books of the Evangelists, there is no difference in that which pertains to the faith of believers, since by one Sovereign Spirit in all are declared all things that relate to the nativity (of the Lord), His passion, resurrection, intercourse with His disciples, and concerning His double advent, the first in humble guise, which has taken place, the second splendid with royal power, which is yet to be. . . . What wonder, then, if John in his Epistles also, speaking of his own authorship, so boldly advances each detail, saying, 'What we have seen with our eyes, and have heard with our ears, and our hands have handled, these things we have written unto you.' For thus he professes himself not only an eye-witness, but a hearer, yea, and a writer as well, of all the wonders done by the Lord in their order."

[Sidenote: Acts.]

"But the Acts of all the Apostles are written in a single book, Luke relates them excellently to Theophilus, confining himself to such as fell under his own notice, as he plainly shows by the omission of all reference either to the martyrdom of Peter or the journey of Paul from Rome to Spain. . . ."

[Sidenote: The Epistles of St. Paul.]

"But the letters of Paul themselves make known to those who would know both what they are, and from what place, or what occasion they were sent. At considerable length he wrote to the Corinthians first, forbidding schismatic divisions, then to the Galatians (forbidding) circumcision, and to the Romans (expounding) the general tenor of the Scriptures, showing, however, that Christ is the essence of their teaching; to these (Epistles) we must devote separate discussion; for the blessed Apostle Paul himself, following the example of his predecessor John, wrote by name to seven Churches only in this order: First to the Corinthians, second to the Ephesians, third to the Philippians, fourth to the Colossians, fifth to the Galatians, sixth to the Thessalonians, seventh to the Romans. True, he wrote twice to the Corinthians and Thessalonians for their correction, but he shows thereby[1] the unity of the universal Church; for John also in the Apocalypse, though he writes to seven Churches only, yet speaks to all. He also writes one to Philemon, one to Titus, and two to Timothy, out of personal regard and affection, but these too are hallowed in the respect of the Catholic Church for the arrangement of ecclesiastical discipline. Moreover, there is in circulation an Epistle to the Laodiceans, another to the Alexandrians forged under the name of Paul, looking towards the heresy of Marcion, and several others which cannot be received into the Catholic Church; for gall should not be mixed with honey. However, the Epistle of Jude, and two of John the above named, are received among Catholics. Also the Book of Wisdom written by the friends of Solomon in his honour."

[Sidenote: Apocalypses.]

"We receive, moreover, the Apocalypse of John and Peter only, though some of our body will not have the latter read in the Church. The *Shepherd* indeed was written quite recently in our own times in the city of Rome by Hermas, while his brother Pius occupied the seat of Bishop of the Church of Rome; wherefore the private reading of it is indeed commendable, but it can never be publicly read to the people in the Church whether among the Prophets . . . or among the Apostles."

"We receive nothing whatever of the Arsinoite, or Valentinus, or of Mitias (?) . . . who also were the compilers of the new Book of Psalms (?) for Marcion, together with Basilides. . . ."

[1] As symbolized by the number seven.

APPENDIX D

SOME EARLY WITNESSES TO NEW TESTAMENT WRITINGS[1]

CLEMENT OF ROME. Bishop of Rome.
Epistle to Corinthians . . . . c. A.D. 95

BARNABAS. *Epistle of*, not by the Barnabas who
was St. Paul's companion . . . . c. A.D. 98
DIDACHÉ. "The Teaching of the Twelve
Apostles," a manual of Church regulations . . . . c. A.D. 100
IGNATIUS. Bishop of Antioch and Martyr.
7 Epistles . . . . c. A.D. 110
POLYCARP. Bishop of Smyrna and Martyr.
Epistle to Philippians . . . . c. A.D. 110
PAPIAS. Bishop of Hierapolis. *Expositions of the Oracles of the Lord* (fragments are preserved by Eusebius) . .
. . . . c. A.D. 130
HERMAS. *The Shepherd*, an allegory . . . . c. A.D. 140
MARCION. Heretic from Pontus at Rome . . . . c. A.D. 144
JUSTIN MARTYR. Apologist. *1 and 2 Apologies*
and *Dialogue with Trypho* . . . . A.D. 152-157
EPISTLE TO DIOGNETUS. Anonymous defence
of Christianity . . . . c. A.D. 160
TATIAN. Syrian Apologist, disciple of Justin
Martyr. *Diatessaron*, a harmony of the Gospels A.D. 160-170
THEOPHILUS. Apologist of Antioch. *Ad Autolycum* c. A.D. 180
IRENAEUS. Bishop of Lyons. *Against Heresies* c. A.D. 185
[1] In the case of most of these witnesses the date here given is that of their chief literary activity.

CLEMENT OF ALEXANDRIA. Head of the Catechetical
School. *Paedagogus, Hypotyposes*, etc. . . . . . c. A.D. 190
TERTULLIAN. Of Carthage. Apologist . . . . A.D. 200
HIPPOLYTUS. Presbyter at Rome. *Refutation of
All Heresies* and numerous commentaries . . . . . c. A.D. 220
ORIGEN. Of Alexandria. Successor of Clement,
great philosopher and writer . . . . c. A.D. 230
DIONYSIUS. Bishop of Alexandria . . . . A.D. 248
EUSEBIUS. Bishop of Caesarea. *Ecclesiastical
History*, etc. . . . . A.D. 320
APHRAATES. Syrian writer . . . . A.D. 338
ATHANASIUS. Bishop of Alexandria . . . . A.D. 328-373
EPIPHANIUS. Bishop of Salamis . . . . A.D. 380
JEROME. Author of the revised or "Vulgate"
Latin version of the Bible . . . . A.D. 390

APPENDIX E

BOOKS RECOMMENDED

In this list are included the most useful books written in English or translated into English. An * is placed before those commentaries which contain the whole Greek text of the books indicated, or which comment much on the Greek text.

1. CANON—
Charteris (Prof. A. H.), Canonicity, 18s.
Sanday (Dr. W.), Inspiration, 6s. 6d. (Longmans.)
Westcott (Bishop), History of the Canon, 10s. 6d. (Macmillan.)

2. TEXT—

The Greek Text of the Revised Version, various prices.
  (Oxford University Press.)
Concordance to the Greek Testament, by Moulton (W. F.)
  and Geden (A. S.), 26s. (T. and T. Clark.)

3. TEXTUAL CRITICISM—

Lake (Prof. K.), The Text of the New Testament, 1s. net.
  Oxford Church Text Books. (Rivingtons.)
Nestle (E.), Textual Criticism of the Greek New Testament,
  10s. 6d. (Williams and Norgate.)

4. INTRODUCTION—

Zahn (Prof. Th.), Introduction to the New Testament, 3 vols.,
  English Translation, 36s. (T. and T. Clark.)
Salmon (Prof. G.), Historical Introduction to the Books of
  the New Testament, 9s. (Murray.)
Godet (F.), Introduction to the New Testament. Part I.
  The Epistles of St. Paul, 12s. 6d. (T. and T. Clark.)

5. THE GOSPELS AND THE SYNOPTIC PROBLEM—

Burkitt (Prof. F. C.), The Earliest Sources for the Life of
  Jesus, 1s. net. (Constable.)
Sanday (Dr. W.), Studies in the Synoptic Problem, 12s. 6d.
  (Oxford Clarendon Press.)
Wright (Dr. A.), *A Synopsis of the Gospels in Greek, 10s.
  (Macmillan.)
Campbell (Dr. Colin), *The First Three Gospels in Greek,
  5s. (Williams and Norgate.)

  Hawkins (Sir J. C.), *Horae Synopticae, 7s. 6d.
  (Oxford Clarendon Press.)
Rushbrooke (W. G.), *Synopticon, 35s. (Macmillan.)
Westcott (Bishop), Introduction to the Study of the Gospels,
  10s. 6d. (Macmillan.)
Stanton (Dr. V. H.), The Gospels as Historical Documents,
  Part I. 7s. 6d., Part II. 10s. (Cambridge University Press.)

6. COMMENTARIES—

St. Matthew.—Godet (F.), The Collection of the Four
  Gospels and the Gospel of St. Matthew, 6s. (T. and T. Clark.)
  Allen (Ven. W. C.), *Commentary, 12s. (T. and T. Clark.)
  Plummer (Dr. A.), *Exegetical Commentary on the
  Gospel according to St. Matthew, 12s. (Elliot Stock.)
  Carr (A.), "The Gospel according to St. Matthew, 4s. 6d.
  (Cambridge Greek Testament for Schools and Colleges.)
St. Mark.—Swete (Prof. H. B.), *Greek Text with Notes,
  15s. (Macmillan.)
  Maclear (G. F.), *The Gospel according to St. Mark,
  4s. 6d. (Cambridge Greek Testament for Schools and
  Colleges.)
St. Luke.—Plummer (Dr. A.), *Commentary, 12s.
  (T. and T. Clark.)
St. John.—Godet (F.), Commentary, 3 vols., 31s. 6d.
  (T. and T. Clark.)

Westcott (Bishop), Commentary, 10s. 6d. (Murray.)

Lightfoot (Bishop), Biblical Essays, 12s. (Macmillan.

Sanday (Dr. W.), The Criticism of the Fourth Gospel,
  7s. 6d. (Longmans.)

Acts.—Knowling (Dr. R. J.), in *Expositor's Greek Testament,
  vol. ii., 28s. (Hodder and Stoughton.)

Rackham (R. B.), 12s. 6d. (Methuen.)

Ramsay (Prof. W. M.), The Church in the Roman
  Empire, 12s. (Hodder and Stoughton.)

Ramsay (Prof. W. M.), St. Paul the Traveller and the
  Roman Citizen, 10s. 6d. (Hodder and Stoughton.)

Romans.—Sanday (Dr. W.) and Headlam (A. C.),
*Commentary, 12s. (T. and T. Clark.)

  Liddon (Dr. H. P.), *Analysis, 14s. (Longmans.)

  Gore (Bishop), Exposition, 2 vols., 3s. 6d. each. (Murray.)

1 Corinthians.—Goudge (H. L.), in Westminster
  Commentaries, 6s. (Methuen.)

Findlay (G. G.), in *Expositor's Greek Testament, vol. ii.

2 Corinthians.—Meyer's *Critical Commentary on the New
  Testament, 1 and 2 Cor., in 2 vols., 10s. 6d. each.
  (T. and T. Clark.)

Galatians.—Lightfoot (Bishop), *Text with Introduction,
  12s. (Macmillan.)

Ramsay (Prof. W. M.), Historical Commentary, 12s.
  (Hodder and Stoughton.)

Ephesians.—Abbott (T. K.), *Commentary on Ephesians
  and Colossians, 10s. 6d. (T. and T. Clark.)

Robinson (Dr. J. Armitage), *St. Paul's Epistle to the
  Ephesians, 12s. (Macmillan.)

Westcott (Bishop), *St. Paul's Epistle to the Ephesians,
  10s. 6d. (Macmillan.)

Gore (Bishop), Exposition, 3s. 6d. (Murray.)

Philippians.—Lightfoot (Bishop), Text with Introduction,
  12s. (Macmillan.)

Colossians and Philemon.—Lightfoot (Bishop), *Text with
  Introduction, 12s. (Macmillan.)

1 and 2 Thessalonians.—Milligan (Dr. G.), *Commentary, 12s.
  (Macmillan.)

Ellicott (Bishop), *Commentary, 7s. 6d. (Longmans.)

1 and 2 Timothy, Titus.—Bernard (Dr. J. H.), *Cambridge
  Greek Testament, 3s. 6d. (Cambridge University Press.)

Hebrews.—Westcott (Bishop), *Greek Text with Notes.
  14s. (Macmillan.)

Davidson (Prof. A. B.), Handbook, 2s. 6d.
  (T. and T. Clark.)

St. James.—Mayor (Dr. J. B.), *Greek Text with Notes., 12s.
  (Macmillan.)

Carr (A.), *The General Epistle of St. James, 2s. 6d.
  (Cambridge Greek Testament for Schools and Colleges.)

1 and 2 St. Peter, St. Jude.—Bigg (Dr. C.), *Commentary,
  10s. 6d. (T. and T. Clark.)
Mayor (Dr. J. B.), *The Epistle of St. Jude and the
  Second Epistle of St. Peter, 14s. (Macmillan.)
1, 2, 3 St. John.—Westcott (Bishop), *Greek Text with
  Notes, 12s. 6d. (Macmillan.)

Revelation.—Ramsay (Prof. W. M.), Letters to the Seven
  Churches, 12s. (Hodder and Stoughton.)
Simcox (W. H.), *The Revelation of St. John the
  Divine, 5s. (Cambridge Greek Testament for Schools
  and Colleges.)
Milligan (Prof. W.), Lectures on the Apocalypse, 5s.
  (Macmillan.)
Swete (Prof. H. B.), *The Apocalypse of St. John, 15s.
  (Macmillan.)

CPSIA information can be obtained
at www.ICGtesting.com
Printed in the USA
BVOW07s1056020616

450492BV00019B/140/P

9 781500 100193